ROUTLEDGE LIBRARY EDITIONS: INTERNATIONAL TRADE POLICY

Volume 26

THE TARIFF REFORM MIRAGE

THE TARIFF REFORM MIRAGE

W. E. DOWDING

LONDON AND NEW YORK

First published in 1913 by Methuen & Co. Ltd.

This edition first published in 2018
by Routledge
2 Park Square, Milton Park, Abingdon, Oxon OX14 4RN

and by Routledge
711 Third Avenue, New York, NY 10017

Routledge is an imprint of the Taylor & Francis Group, an informa business

British Library Cataloguing in Publication Data
A catalogue record for this book is available from the British Library

ISBN: 978-1-138-06323-5 (Set)
ISBN: 978-1-315-14339-2 (Set) (ebk)
ISBN: 978-1-138-29805-7 (Volume 26) (hbk)
ISBN: 978-1-138-29807-1 (Volume 26) (pbk)
ISBN: 978-1-315-09885-2 (Volume 26) (ebk)

THE TARIFF REFORM MIRAGE

BY

W. E. DOWDING

WITH AN INTRODUCTION BY

THE RT. HON. SIR JOHN SIMON, K.C., M.P.

METHUEN & CO. LTD.
36 ESSEX STREET W.C.
LONDON

First Published in 1913

INTRODUCTION

BY THE

RIGHT HON. SIR JOHN SIMON, K.C., M.P.

THIS book records the ten years' history of an agitation — the most highly organized, the most lavishly financed, the most loudly advertised, of our time. When the "Missionary of Empire" in 1903 recanted his former fiscal faith, he caused many of his countrymen to examine afresh the foundations of their economic belief, and Free Traders have no reason to regret the revival of the study of the principles upon which British commercial supremacy is based. And since the Unionist Party made "Tariff Reform" the first constructive plank in its platform, the output of printed matter on the subject has been so enormous that it might well have been supposed that the whole field of controversy and criticism was covered. But it is not so. Mr. Dowding, in this book, has added to the library which the Fiscal Question has called forth a volume of a new kind, which should be equally welcomed by both sides. He presents no theoretical arguments; he marshals no elaborate statistics; he merely sets down in due order the story of the Tariff Reform crusade as revealed by the declarations and publications of the crusaders themselves. Every quotation is verified; every extract can be traced. Tariff Reformers can desire no less. Free Traders can want no more. For when this strange and varied record is examined, it becomes obvious why the Tariff Reform League has not thought fit to celebrate its tenth anniversary in the wilderness by itself issuing a connected account of its wanderings. If any fair-minded citizen will read Mr. Dowding's book, he will be enabled to judge, from the statements of Tariff Reformers themselves, how far the policy which is promoted by such methods and involves such contradictions as are there exposed is entitled to call itself business-like and scientific.

JOHN SIMON.

PREFACE

"THE word Mirage," says *Murray*, "is now frequently extended to include other forms of optical illusions produced by atmospheric conditions, *e.g.* the appearance in the sky of a reflected image of a distant object." The *Century Dictionary* adds to its definition that "distorted, displaced, or inverted images are produced" by this optical illusion. A search among other authorities would still further explain why the word was chosen to describe the phantasmal image which still eludes the Tariff Reformers.

The chasing of it began in the "illimitable veldt." It is still being sought in an illimitable political desert. There was a time when the spurious enthusiasm of the wanderers led them to break out into song, mainly at pantomimes, and it is hard in 1913 to appreciate the irritation of the Free Trade theatre-goer who wrote in December 1908 to the *Morning Leader* to complain that his evening's enjoyment was utterly spoiled because "one of the performers, while looking through a telescope, said he saw Tariff Reform coming!"

This book tells the story of the Tariff Reform conspiracy—they chose the word themselves—to produce an optical illusion by atmospheric effect. They have schemed to fill the air with alluring and deceptive shapes, and they have schemed so well that they have overdone it. To-day the country is weary of the long and arid wandering, suspicious of those who have led them by false hopes. The best that Mr. Bonar Law can do when asked to define the vital difference between manufactured articles, which are to be taxed, and raw materials, which are not to be taxed, is to borrow from the oratory of Burke and repeat, "It is difficult to say at what exact moment the daylight merges into darkness, but the difference between night and day is fairly distinct." If the Tariff Reform leader himself is thus doomed to grope in perpetual twilight, how can it be expected that his followers will have a clearer vision?

Protectionist enthusiasm is at a low ebb. There was a publican in the East End of London who proudly told Mr. Chamberlain in 1903 that he had labelled all his bottles "Support Fiscal Reform." "Anything which calls attention to the question is useful at the present time," wrote Mr. Chamberlain to the publican. That was ten years ago. It would be hard to find to-day any publican willing to run the risk of reducing his takings by sticking such a label on the most ardent of his stock in trade.

I take, however, a serious view of the mental confusion that has been created in this persistent atmosphere of deception. Outside our own country there are many in whose minds the dismal chorus of decadence has implanted the idea that Britain is fast sinking into "the fifth *rôle* among nations" which Mr. Chamberlain so patriotically predicted as our future place. Of the distant listeners to the echo of this wail, those who visit the old country quickly learn how deeply deceived they have been. Those who remain away will probably never realize how ill a trick the Tariff Reformers have played on them. Within our own shores, the revival of Protectionism has dealt a wicked blow at the spread of healthy knowledge. The fiscal system of the country was for more than a generation as unchallenged as the Monarchy. Did not Mr. Arnold Forster write in the *Citizen Reader*, of which hundreds of thousands of copies were being read in the elementary schools, that Free Trade was a beneficent thing? Did he not, in the year following Mr. Chamberlain's apostasy, strike out those passages and issue a revised edition which was irreproachable from the Tariff Reform schoolmasters' point of view? Not less could have been expected of him, perhaps, remembering that he was Chairman of the Literature Committee of the Tariff Reform League, which said when he died that one of his titles to fame rested on this same *Citizen Reader* which he mutilated, and that he was "a patriotic citizen" himself.

Indeed, to be "patriotic" in the Tariff Reform sense you are expected to close to your children the history of the Corn Law agitation, to call Cobden a "prince of false prophets," and to denounce Free Traders as desiring to "get rid of the Colonies." There is a chapter in this book on the manner in which the Imperial sentiment has been exploited for Protectionist purposes, and I will stay here only to say that the Tariff Reformers to-day are praying hard that the nation shall soon forget the muddle of the mirage they have been describing all these years, and trying to substitute for it a delusive vision of an Empire that can only be sustained by tariffs of Protective duties. I cut a sharp line between an Imperialist and a Protectionist Imperialist; and I am sure it is only by constantly reminding the country of the great difference that this present gasp of Tariff Reform can be made its last.

If I had asked Mr. Bonar Law to write my Introduction, could he have refused? This book is almost entirely made up of classic Tariff Reform sayings, among which Mr. Bonar's own speeches rank conspicuously beside those of Mr. Joseph Chamberlain. I don't think he could have found fault with them. Every quotation is authenticated. Wherever possible it has been copied from the official journal of the Tariff Reform League. It is a journal I would not recommend to readers with a tendency to vertigo; for almost every issue of it whirls you breathlessly all round the All-Red Route, pelts you with American arguments and German statistics, and sets you down where it took you up, topsy-turvy, as a rule, but glad to get home again.

It is to the Editor of this giddy journal, and to his colleagues who made the leaflets I have found fluttering in the desert, that I owe profusest thanks. Without their wasted industry "The Tariff Reform Mirage" could not have been written. Without the help of Mr. E. G. Brunker, my staunch fellow-traveller in the search for these remains, I could not have brought them all home. He and I have worked together a long time at the joyous task of exposing the mockeries of Tariff Reform, and I ask for no stronger, no abler, comrade. To Mr. G. Bussy, also, I am indebted for a careful revision of the thousand references upon which the whole story relies.

W. E. D.

CONTENTS

IV.—BRITISH TRADE

V.—WORK AND WAGES

"NOTHING is legitimate that cannot be understood. If you cannot explain it properly, then there is something about it that cannot *be* explained at all."

DR. WOODROW WILSON
President of the United States of America
in *The New Freedom*, 1913, p. 125

I.—THE PROTECTIONIST PROPAGANDA

THE ORIGIN OF THE TARIFF REFORM LEAGUE

THE IMPERIAL TARIFF COMMITTEE

THE WORK OF THE LEAGUE

THE "CONFEDERATES"

THE TARIFF COMMISSION

TWO UNOFFICIAL PROGRAMMES

THE DREAD OF DETAILS

WHAT TARIFF REFORM "MEANS"

THE ORIGIN OF THE TARIFF REFORM LEAGUE

THE origin of the Tariff Reform League is not exactly lost in obscurity. Most Tariff Reformers heartily wish it were. It was born of Protectionist parents, and the Tariff Reformers have been trying to hide the fact ever since its birth. The fullest and most authentic record of the event is printed in a Press Directory. Other versions exist, but most of them are ashamed of the parentage and try to slur it over.

No Tariff Reformer has yet been moved to write a complete history of the campaign that Mr. Joseph Chamberlain started in May 1903. And as there is none of its adherents admiring enough to set down its record, so there are not many men anxious to claim the doubtful honour of having been in at the birth of Tariff Reform. When the late President of the Tariff Reform League, the Duke of Sutherland, died in June 1913, an author who spends a lot of his spare time praising Protection panegyrically attributed the origin of the League to a meeting held in the Duke's London house in 1903. Thereupon one of the boldest knights of the cause, Sir Joseph Lawrence, put in a claim for the "pioneer spade work" of others, himself included.[1] * As to that, there were the old Fair Traders, whose names have almost passed out of political memory. They had tried busily to keep the

* References not in the text will be found massed at the end of the book.

Protectionist spirit alive in the United Kingdom; but, as Sir Joseph Lawrence confesses, it was Mr. Joseph Chamberlain's speech at Birmingham on May 15, 1903, that "supplied the driving force." Mr. Austen Chamberlain tells us [2] that the morning after the speech the Duke of Sutherland went to Mr. Chaplin's room with a newspaper in his hand and exclaimed, "Here is something worth fighting for!" It was then, said Mr. Austen Chamberlain, that the movement "leaped into light."

In the speech at Birmingham Mr. Joseph Chamberlain, Secretary for the Colonies, fresh from the solitude of the illimitable veldt, as he called it, said he was still "under the glamour" of the new experience of his visit to South Africa. "My ideas even now run," he said, "more on those questions which are connected with the future of the Empire than upon the smaller controversies upon which depend the fate of bye-elections, and sometimes even the fate of Governments." Therewith he sketched a policy of Preferential Tariffs and a Zollverein—an Imperial Customs Union. The Protectionists, or Fair Traders as they called themselves, descried the signal afar off, and ran to offer Mr. Chamberlain their help. The embrace was mutual. The Protectionists wanted a leader. Mr. Chamberlain wanted followers.

If that Birmingham speech had been sprung upon the political world two days earlier, the Tariff Reform movement might have avoided a very embarrassing association. Protection is a word that has an exceedingly sinister history in the public remembrance. Nevertheless, it was the "Protection League" out of whose loins the Tariff Reform League came, and the Protection League was organized in ignorance of Mr. Chamberlain's intentions just a day before he declared them.

The unfortunate coincidence has led some of the chroniclers of the time to persuade themselves that the Protection League never existed. Thus Sir Joseph Lawrence relates that "before Mr. Chamberlain's memorable speech in May 1903, Mr. E. E. Williams, a well-known journalist who had written largely on the subject of the need of Tariff Revision, and produced a book (*Made in Germany*) with which the late Sir Howard Vincent was greatly taken, had convened a meeting in the House of Commons to organize some movement to improve our Customs Tariff, and meet the dumping and other forms of foreign competition. Mr. Chamberlain's Birmingham speech just delivered supplied the driving force. The late 'Jimmy' Lowther took the chair, and we passed a resolution backing up Mr. Chamberlain's policy, and forming a League, which Mr. Lowther wanted to be called the 'Protection League,' with Lord Masham (Cunliffe Lister) of Bradford as President. I disliked the name of the League, as I was not in favour of 'protection' in its proper economic sense, and in the interval of communicating with Lord Masham we were notified by some other organization we were not entitled to use the name." But it happens that the fullest account of these early days is that written by Mr. Williams himself.[3] He distinctly records that the organization was formally named the "Protection League," and that it met and pursued its work under that name. He writes :—

"In the closing days of March (1903) I was directed by the Editor of the *Financial News* to undertake a vigorous propaganda in that journal on behalf of Protection, and I was requested to supplement that journalistic work by getting together an organization formed for the same end. The direction I obeyed *con amore*; the request I also proceeded to comply with, but with a less enthusiastic belief in the success of the work. I had already been associated with more than one abortive attempt to found a protectionist organization. However, I got to work, and on the invitation of Mr. James Lowther and under his chairmanship, a number of gentlemen assembled in a Committee room of the House of Commons on May 14, for establishing, in the words of their invitation, 'more active co-operation among the opponents of the ruinous fiscal system which has so long hampered our national industries.' The invitations were not sent out broadcast, because only a small preliminary meeting was proposed, and a much larger gathering might have been got together; but Committee Room No. 17 held that afternoon a sufficiently representative number of politicians and business men to indicate that the psychological moment had arrived for making an onslaught upon Cobdenism. The meeting did more than discuss, it formed itself straight away into the Protection League. Not a soul present had an inkling that the very next day Mr. Chamberlain was going to light his torch at Birmingham. On the contrary, we all anticipated a long and possibly a bitter struggle with the Government. Our idea was, while boldly announcing our own entire opposition to the free import principle, to put forward, from time to time, small practical instalments of our principles, such as the concession to the colonies of a rebate of the then existing corn duties, and we proposed to found up and down the country branch organizations, which would put these modest proposals before parliamentary candidates, endeavour to gain their adhesion, and, failing that, to counsel abstention at the polls or, where possible, to run a rival candidate. By this means, which would have resulted in the loss here and there of Conservative seats, we hoped to wake up the official Conservatives to the necessity of making gradual changes in the direction of Protection by throwing sops to us to keep us quiet.

" A week later the Committee of the Protection League, which had been formed at a previous meeting, met again at the House of Commons, and of course proceeded to consider the startling developments which had taken place since the first meeting."

The dates show that Mr. Williams' version is the right one ; and it is confirmed by another record referred to below. The " Protection League " was formed the day before Mr. Chamberlain spoke at Birmingham. It was a close thing. The point is insisted on because, to repeat the distinction, Tariff Reformers have always been anxious not to be known and recognized as Protectionists.

The first test applied to Sir Joseph Lawrence's recollection of the events of 1903, which he wrote down ten years after, shows that his memory is untrustworthy, and it would be misleading to follow him further. Mr. Williams wrote his record within a few months of the events.

In 1908 a third version of the origin of the League was

given to the world by Mr. George Byng,[4] who has been mentioned by both Sir Joseph Lawrence and Mr. Williams as one whose services deserve special recognition. Mr. Byng puts in a claim as being a "Tariff Reformer before Mr. Chamberlain": in 1901 he published a book entitled *Protection!* The chief reason for the following quotation from his story, however, is that it entirely supports Mr. Williams in tracing the genesis of the Tariff Reform League to the Protection League.

"As a manufacturer employing 6000 hands, I have been convinced for many years that if our Free Trade policy was to be continued my own industry and the enterprises of other British manufacturers would be jeopardized. I put my views in a book, entitled *Protection*, and published in 1901. In 1902 I called upon a number of manufacturers to combine with a view to an alteration of our fiscal policy, and in April 1902, twenty-four leading manufacturers assembled in the Princes' Restaurant and gave their support to the formation of a Fiscal Reform Association. Then, with a view to securing the interest of other manufacturers, we issued a manifesto, which is of peculiar interest, inasmuch as it embodies the discontent which was then felt in industrial circles at our Free Trade policy, and shows that the Tariff Reform movement did not spring from the mind of one man, but owed its origin to definite economic conditions. . . . That manifesto was signed by 2500 manufacturers, to whom, in May 1903, I wrote a letter, informing them that a movement was on foot to establish a Protection League. During that agitation in 1902 I was assisted by Mr. Ernest Williams, who did much in these early days for the propaganda of Tariff Reform. He was then on the staff of the *Financial News*, and through him Mr. Harry Marks got informed of the agitation which I had been carrying on and of the success of the manifesto in obtaining so many adherents. Mr. Marks then asked me if he could join me in forwarding the movement. I acquiesced, and both Mr. Marks and myself arranged that meeting on May 14, 1903, at the House of Commons, over which Mr. James Lowther presided. That meeting resulted in the establishment of the Tariff League (changed ultimately into the Imperial Tariff League), and I was appointed treasurer. Now as the founder and treasurer of this League, I knew exactly how much Mr. Marks contributed to its financial support, and the amount of his subscription was exactly the same as mine, £100. . . . In conclusion, I would like to say that the pre-Chamberlain movement was the spontaneous outcome of the feeling among British manufacturers that Free Trade must inevitably kill all producing enterprise, that it was not based on a sordid foundation, but was a legitimate and non-political endeavour to express what manufacturers, who had so many thousands of workers under their care, considered to be the proper fiscal policy for the country to pursue."

Mr. Byng, it may be added, became one of the original members of the Executive Committee of the Tariff Reform League, an undeniable link between Protection so named and Protection otherwise named.

What were "the startling developments" to which Mr. Williams refers, that occurred between the first and the second meeting of the Protection League? They were two. Mr. Ritchie, the Chancellor of the Exchequer, had swept away the shilling corn duty imposed toward meeting the expenses of the South African War; and Mr. Chamberlain had spoken at Birmingham. The speech said enough, to use Mr. Williams' own words, "to indicate that Mr. Chamberlain had taken the field against Mr. Ritchie and the Free Traders." Indeed, "that was the new situation which we had to consider at the first Committee meeting of the Protection League, and we rose to it by altering the title of our League. Prejudice had gathered round the word Protection, and under the new development it was no longer well to use a word, however reasonable, which created prejudice. We realized that under Mr. Chamberlain's leadership a great national movement had begun, and that we had to go out and capture the masses forthwith, and not be content with the suffrages of the chosen few who were already emancipated from prejudice. So our Association became the Tariff League."

It seemed, however, that the Protectionist Tariff Leaguers

were not yet sure of Mr. Chamberlain. "We hardly dared to hope," says Mr. Williams, "that he would break so completely with Free Trade as to make it possible for us to be anything more than an association of Freelances, the independent advance wing of the movement." But on the eve of the Whitsuntide recess, Mr. Chamberlain spoke in the House of Commons, and "we were reassured upon this point." Mr. Williams describes the electrical thrill of that "memorable day. . . . One had the feeling of being present at the birth of big developments." To borrow Mr. Williams' account of the speech, Mr. Chamberlain "repeated the expressions of his views regarding Colonial trade which he had announced at Birmingham, elaborated these views in greater detail, declaring his readiness to go into any mechanic's or labourer's house or to address meetings of workmen, and to carry them with him, even though he proposed to put an import duty on corn. And he went further. He advocated a protective tariff apart from the Colonial preference, by showing how foreign manufacturers were able to sell their goods in this country through the operation of their tariffs, at a lower price than Englishmen could compete with, and yet make a profit." It is a description which accurately reveals the real Protectionist mind of the Tariff Leaguers. They were beside themselves with glee.

"That same evening," says Mr. Williams, "I learned in other ways that Mr. Chamberlain was heartily on the side of a protective tariff, and that our new-born association was no longer to be as a voice crying in the wilderness. We were to work in alliance with England's greatest statesman. I learned also what name for a league to advance his views Mr. Chamberlain would regard as most appropriate. The Imperial Tariff League was the chosen name, and at the next meeting of our committee we changed our title once again, and became the Imperial Tariff League.

"Then we moved into offices in Pall Mall and began our campaign. The work was not easy. The situation was so new and extraordinary. In those early days many who have since thrown in their lot heartily with the movement held aloof, and the usual personal differences which are the bane of political movements hampered our early progress."

Sir Joseph Lawrence supplies one or two details that may be inserted at this point in the story. The Editor of the *Financial News* was Mr. H. H. Marks, and it was he who "offered to provide offices in Pall Mall free of cost for the new League and to contribute £1000 a year to our expenses." The subsequent withdrawal of Mr. Marks, and the absence of his name from all lists of supporters of the Protectionist movement, may throw some light on one of the "personal differences" which hampered the early progress. Sir Joseph Lawrence tells of another. "We had scarcely got to work, having only issued six serial pamphlets," he says, "when we found friction arising from the opposition of the late Sir Howard Vincent, who had a Colonial League of his own. It was at this juncture that it was intimated to some of us that no progress could be made whilst this friction remained, and it was said if we organized the movement on a new and wider basis the Duke of Sutherland and the Duke of Westminster would come into it and help liberally."

The purpose of this chapter having been served by establishing the vital connexion of Tariff Reform with Protection, the "personal differences" with Mr. Marks, and the "friction" with other Protectionists who ran little leagues of their own, may be left for some League chronicler to record. It is more to the point to get down to the final metamorphosis.

The Imperial Tariff League began to issue leaflets, to work at by-elections, and to organize meetings. "A throng of newspaper representatives was daily filled with information regarding our progress," records Mr. Williams. After the Barnard Castle by-election,[5] when "for the first time in English political history an association formed for the express purpose of advocating a protective tariff worked openly and aggressively in a parliamentary election, then came the final development of our organization. It was desirable, and even essential," says Mr. Williams, "that it should expand rapidly, and this expansion was being hindered by the personal differences to which I have referred. I need not particularize these differences, but I may say that they were finally settled by the voluntary retirement from active participation in the work which he had so much at heart of the gentleman who was in reality the founder of, and had been the most generous subscriber to, the League. A Committee of Members of Parliament resolved itself into an organization which came to the Imperial Tariff League and offered amalgamation. The Imperial Tariff League accepted, and handed over its membership, its effects and its goodwill to the new men, and so gave birth to the Tariff Reform League. Our old name, at a later date, was adopted by a similar association which had been formed to work Birmingham and the Midland District."

A few lines lower down in this *Press Directory* article Mr. Williams describes the men who accomplished these things as "the little knot of political and economic conspirators." Conspirators is an accidentally true word. First the Protection League; then, when it was found that Protection "created prejudice," the Tariff League. Presently, Mr. Chamberlain being "heartily on the side of a protective tariff," yet perceiving the danger of calling it so, it was found "appropriate" to rename the organization the Imperial Tariff League; and lastly, because a Protectionist Empire involved food-taxes, it became the plain Tariff Reform League. Sir Joseph Lawrence puts in a good claim to the invention of the final name. He went with Mr. Lowther to see Mr. Chamberlain "and ask his advice generally." "I had suggested the name 'Tariff Reform League,' as I was more impressed with the urgency of the Colonial Preference side of Mr. Chamberlain's policy; but Mr. Lowther would not have the word 'Reform,' as it suggested too much the agitation for the 'Reform' of the Franchise. Mr. Chamberlain smiled at Mr. Lowther's objection, and it was while he and Mr. Lowther were good-humouredly arguing it out that Mr. Parker Smith suggested 'Imperial Tariff League,' which at once satisfied me, and we then left Mr. Chamberlain's room." Afterwards they came back to Sir Joseph Lawrence's suggestion, and nobody is in the least disposed to dispute with him the credit of it. The choice of such a name, suggesting something quite harmless, something indeed almost necessary, is wholly characteristic of Protectionism. It was a suit of sheep's clothing for the wolf, and every Protectionist doubtless thinks it a capital disguise.

In spite of the declaration of Mr. Chamberlain, "I am perfectly certain I am not a Protectionist,"[6] he was at one period very undecided on the subject of names. At Liverpool in 1903 he admitted that Preference involved a "small protection against foreign manufactured goods." Mr. Balfour in 1904 (at Edinburgh, October 3) defined "the object of Protection as "being to encourage home industries. The means by which it attains that object is by the manipulation of a fiscal system to raise home prices. If the home prices are not raised, the industry is not encouraged. If the industry is encouraged, it is by the raising of prices. That is, in a nutshell, protection properly understood." Two days later Mr. Chamberlain admitted that "the policy which I suggest to you is the policy which has been tried and has succeeded on the continent of Europe, in the United States of America, and in our Colonies"; and again, "I invite you to co-operate in a policy which all the world except ourselves have adopted." Yet in 1905 he declared that his proposals were "not Protection on my part" (Birmingham, December 30). A comparison of these utterances might lead one to suppose that he was not ashamed to admit a desire to "protect" manufacturers, but that he felt it unwise to use the same word when talking of the effect of his policy upon the consumers.

It can scarcely be wondered at that some of the strongest journalistic supporters of the Tariff Reform movement have found this tell-tale disguise irksome. In 1908, for example, the *Daily Express*, certainly the most active if not always the most discreet of the friendly newspapers, announced that though "we are entirely opposed to a 'high tariff' of 70 or 80 per cent., we are emphatically in favour of a tariff of 10 or maybe 20 per cent. But we are Protectionists none the less. We stand for the Protection of our own people." And the *Morning Post*, in whose congenial columns appeared the interview with Mr. Byng, the author of "Protection" and the Treasurer of the Protection League that became the

Tariff Reform League, in the same year [7] printed what it described as " the most important statement of Unionist policy that has appeared since the opening of Mr. Chamberlain's campaign in 1903." It was a "statement of constructive policy, drawn up as the outcome of an exchange of views during the past twelve months among some of the most active supporters and influential members of the Unionist Party both in and out of Parliament." In its leading columns the journal said it marked " a decided step in advance " with regard to " the general principles to be followed in framing the new tariff," and added that " there is nothing novel about these principles, which are very generally followed in most of the leading Protectionist countries." Twice in its praise of the document which twelve months' cogitation had produced the *Morning Post* denoted that it was not inconsistent with Protection. In a later page the document itself is reproduced so far as it related to the Tariff Reform movement. Here it is only necessary to say that though it did not use the word Protection, it declared for the principle of " safeguarding home industries." The phrase may be taken as a very glib substitute.

Indeed, it must be admitted that in general the Tariff Reformers have been extremely careful to avoid the word " Protection," though in late years their tongues have tripped more frequently. In its earlier numbers the Tariff Reform League's *Monthly Notes* frequently quoted the *American Protectionist*. It does so no longer, just as it has now deleted from its handbooks and leaflets those tables of other countries' Protective tariffs, which it used to print to emphasize its advocacy of similar tariffs here. In both cases the path of prudence seems to have been chosen as the path to Protection. The substitute proffered by Mr. Marshall Hall, K.C., M.P., who was " not a Protectionist but a Protectivist," [8] did not prove popular. And Mr. Brodrick's (Lord Midleton's) suggestion that " Those who insisted that a man must be either an extreme Protectionist or an unbending Free Trader might almost as well say that a man must be either a bachelor or a Mormon," [9] only served to recall the words of a stout

Australian Protectionist journal that "There can no more be a moderate Protectionist than there can be a man moderately honest or a woman moderately chaste." [10]

The philosophic Secretary of the Birmingham Imperial Tariff Committee, four years after the beginning of the campaign, was still asking [11] "Are Tariff Reformers Protectionists?" His own answer was, "That is a question which many of us have found embarrassing; and it seems desirable that we should agree on the answer. To the serious student of politics any question of labels or nicknames must always appear unimportant; but in popular discussion they cannot be ignored. Labels are useful labour-saving appliances for people to whom the toil of understanding reasons is irksome. In the year 1900 the advantage of the easily-affixed label was with the Unionists, and much trouble was saved by calling a man a Pro-Boer. To-day we are liable to be designated by a name which is still invidious, and we have to make up our minds whether to repudiate the Protectionist label, or to accept and make the best of it."

A good many Tariff Reformers have thought it possible to "make the best of it." Three years ago, for example, the present President of the League (Viscount Ridley) observed that "we could adopt Protection without increasing prices;" [12] and the countries whose fiscal systems we have been asked all along to imitate are those "leading Protectionist countries," referred to by Mr. Chamberlain and the *Morning Post*, the United States of America and Germany. Like Lord Ridley, the Tariff Reform League has been at great pains to prove that the Protective systems of those "vast and prosperous nations," with their "high tariffs against the world," could be adopted without raising prices.[13] At other times the official organ of the League has found it difficult, and sometimes impossible, to allay the disquietude of innocent Tariff Reformers without roundly asserting that Tariff Reform "must not be confounded with the systems of protection in vogue in other countries;" [14] though most of the pages of that same official organ are filled with glowing accounts of the advantages which other countries are said to reap from those same "systems of protection." The persistent struggle to smother the word has not succeeded. The Tariff Reform movement is still regarded throughout the country as the Protectionist movement it really is.

THE IMPERIAL TARIFF COMMITTEE

WHEN the Tariff Reform League changed its pupal form, the discarded skin was taken up by what Mr. Williams described as " a similar association which had been formed to work Birmingham and the Midland District." This was The Imperial Tariff League, originally known as the Birmingham Tariff Committee, which soon afterwards[15] became the Imperial Tariff Committee. Under that title it still exists, though its public duties seem to have been cut down to the sending of wreaths to the funerals of departed Protectionists. Mr. Joseph Chamberlain was its President, and Mr. C. A. Vince still remains its indefatigable secretary. Many references to its publications will be made in the succeeding chapters of this book, so that it may be as well to say here that the Birmingham organization has striven hard to live up to its name. A hundred leaflets and pamphlets the Committee issued bore on their foreheads the inscription " Trade and the Empire," and generally the Committee has conducted itself less noisily than the League.

It was, however, a part of the general " conspiracy." Soon after the May speech of Mr. Chamberlain in 1903, the *Daily Mail* went down to Birmingham to interview Mr. Vince, and came away with the impression that there was a power behind him of which he spoke almost with bated breath.

" Mr. Vince vouchsafed the information that the committee consists of a number of persons, and was formed a month ago. 'Was it elected by the members of the association?' he was asked. 'No. It was not elected,' said Mr. Vince frankly, but he explained that it consisted of certain gentlemen associated with the Liberal Unionist organization who wished to help the 'inquiry' and to assist the country to understand Mr. Chamberlain's views. 'Then who are the members of the Tariff Committee?' was the next question. Mr. Vince looked at a little statuette on the mantelpiece representing Mr. Chamberlain arguing with Mr. Kruger, and looked out of the window at the Chamberlain-square. 'It is a small committee,' he replied. 'The names?' Mr. Vince said that he would not care to publish the names, except that of Mr. Edward Nettlefold, who is treasurer. Mr. Nettlefold is also treasurer of the Liberal Unionist Association, but the funds are separate. 'You see,' he said, 'I take all responsibility for what is done here. I issue the pamphlets and leaflets and circulars, and I may send out things which all the members of the committee have not seen. I should not care to make them responsible for everything I do. The committee does not meet every day and decide what to do. That is not the Birmingham method. It distributes its work, and I am attending to the literary work, while Mr. Jenkins is seeing to the organization.' "[16]

For a short period, when the Tariff Reform League was from some cause out of sorts, the Birmingham Committee published the monthly organ of the movement, *Monthly Notes on Tariff Reform*,[17] and for the first few years of the campaign both organizations were publishing "literature" simultaneously. With Mr. Vince's Committee was associated the "Birmingham and Midlands Women's Imperial Tariff Reform League"—a name that provides a connecting link, though a long one, with the League.

But the Tariff Reform League pushed Mr. Vince right out of the market.

Nothing contrasts more vividly the mild methods of this biographer of John Bright and the methods of the leather-lunged Tariff Reform League, than a sentence from the preface to the Handbook issued by either organization.

For example, in Mr. Vince's *Short Handbook for Speakers and Students of the Policy of Preferential Tariffs* (1st edition, July, 1903), a slim, penny, paper-covered, quietly printed pamphlet of thirty-two pages, the preface states:—

"Brevity has been studied throughout; and *no attempt* has been made to suggest the best method of handling the topics introduced so as to make a favourable impression on a popular audience."

Speakers are advised by Mr. Vince not to cite "exact figures" as given in the statistical section, but to "substitute round numbers as being more readily intelligible." Indeed, "it is hoped that the stress here laid upon statistical proof will not lead any speaker into the error of supplying a popular audience with more calculations than they can digest."

On the other hand, the Tariff Reform League's first *Speaker's Handbook* (October, 1903), though given exactly the same title as Mr. Vince's, is a bold shillingsworth of typography, bound in scarlet cloth, and running to four times the number of pages. It is "not intended as a complete or exhaustive review of the whole subject of our fiscal policy. It has been prepared merely for the use of speakers and debaters who support the demand for Preferential Tariffs within the Empire and Reciprocity with outside nations"—without, one may suppose, knowing much about the matter. But compare this sentence from the preface with the one above :—

"Brevity has been aimed at throughout, and *an attempt has been made,* in the brief chapter on Fiscal Reform, to suggest the best method of handling the numerous topics introduced so as to make a favourable impression on a popular audience."

Mr. Vince's "no" is not a misprint for "an." He timidly persisted in it in later editions, until the Tariff Reform League elbowed him off and took up his business in its own way.

That way must be made familiar to everybody who would know what a terrific and unscrupulous attack the well-proved fiscal system of this country has withstood. The League has called the tune and the Tariff Reform leaders have danced to it. That accounts very largely for the verbal contortions which have been so marked a feature of the performance. The metaphor is not an exaggeration, as he who reads on will find.

THE WORK OF THE LEAGUE

SO great a part of this book is filled with the story the Tariff Reform League has written of its own folly, that there is need in this chapter for no more than an outline of the organization. The leaflets it has scattered over the land will be quoted on many of the succeeding pages. Ever since 1903 the League or the Imperial Tariff Committee has circulated a journal called *Monthly Notes on Tariff Reform.* Numerous booklets have been published; and broadsheets and posters and mottoes of many kinds. Above all this, the League has had the constant advantage of almost unlimited space in the Press; not only of journals that are known throughout the country, but of thousands of obscure local prints, of weekly and monthly publications started especially to advocate Protection, of the many official organs of the Unionist party, and even, here and there, of parish magazines. Besides all this, there have been a vast number of speeches, and an even vaster number of letters to the Press. The League has organized "pub-crawling" and heckling campaigns, cinematograph and magic-lantern displays, and caravan missions. "Never before," as Lord James of Hereford once said,[18] "has a political agitation been carried on by the means which the Tariff Reform League adopt—proceedings so resembling those of Tammany Hall. The originators were a Committee of five men in a back room in Birmingham. They have collected hundreds of thousands of pounds, and during the past eighteen months they have flooded the country with millions of pamphlets, bought up the Press, even subsidized the Pantomimes of the country." Subsidiary organizations, such as the Tariff Reform Scouts, the Women's, and even the Juvenile, Tariff Reform League, and an "Organized Labour Branch," have been numerous; and, as the official organ announced somewhat ambiguously early in the career of the League, at headquarters "an expert staff" was created to supply "any information which sympathizers with the movement may desire, to enable them to meet the arguments of opponents." The Tariff Reform League has never been stuck for want of driving power. It has squandered money splendidly. It has spent all; it has gained nothing. It has shouted through the mouthpiece of a great party, and smashed the mouthpiece.

The League is the epitome of Protectionist methods. The reasons for its failure are written in its own publications. The League has used arguments that have been proved false, and for very shame has been obliged to use them no longer. It has pitched its appeal in every key, and not one of them has syntonized with the voice of the country. It has audaciously appealed in turn to prejudice, to ignorance, to sentiment. The good sense of the nation has rejected every such appeal. The Tariff Reform movement could not have marched so long if this loud-mouthed League had not been yelling at its ear. It is the detailed story of those ten years, now being told, that shows why the movement has failed so far, and how it can be held in check always. The Tariff Reform League has given itself away, and given its "cause" away, so many times that its next blunder can always be foretold with tolerable certainty.

The activities of the League may be said to have commenced simultaneously with Mr. Joseph Chamberlain's autumn campaign of 1903. On September 18 of that year Mr. C. Arthur Pearson, first Chairman of the Executive Committee, wrote to Mr. Chamberlain to say that "Inquiries are coming to the Tariff Reform League from all quarters as to the effect upon its future course of action of the events which have just transpired. The Tariff Reform League was started with the following objects: 'To advocate the examination of the tariff with the view to "its employment to consolidate and develop the resources of the Empire and to defend the industries of the United Kingdom."' It seems to me," said Mr. Pearson, "that the examination of the tariff may be considered sufficiently advanced, and we propose now to use the resources of the League to advocate the employment of the tariff for the objects named. In view of the prominent part which the League must necessarily play in the coming contest, will you be good enough to let me know whether the position outlined above meets with your approval?"

To that very dutiful inquiry Mr. Chamberlain conveniently replied in these words: "I agree with your views. We have sufficient material in the way of facts and figures. We have now to state our conclusions, and to endeavour to get the people to adopt them. As I understand, the Tariff Reform League is prepared to advocate (1) Closer union with the Colonies by means of a Preferential Tariff, and an endeavour to make the Empire self-sufficing as regards food supply. (2) The employment of the tariff as a weapon to secure greater reciprocity with foreign nations, or, failing such an arrangement, to prevent the loss of our home and Imperial markets under the competition of protected countries by retaliating upon them the treatment they mete out to us. On this understanding I wish the Tariff Reform League every success, and trust that it will have the support of every one who desires the union of the Empire and the continued prosperity of our commerce."

That phrase of Mr. Pearson's, "Examination of the tariff," which deceived nobody, presently disappeared from the programme of the League's activities; though a special note should be made of the fact that a few weeks before he started his campaign Mr. Chamberlain had "enough facts and figures." In the literature—the word is used technically to denote the publications of a propagandist body—issued by the League in 1903 [19] it described itself as "The Tariff Reform League for the development and defence of the Industrial Interests of the British Empire"; and its "objects," "To advocate the employment of the Tariff with a view to its use to consolidate and develop the resources of the Empire, and to defend the industries of the United Kingdom." In later publications these high-sounding pretensions also were altogether dropped; nor can they be found in the current literature of the League. The explanation lies, without doubt, in the presence of that awkward word "defend," which means "protect"—much too thin ice for the Tariff Reformers to skate over. Some time afterwards the League issued an official badge. It bore the design of the Union Jack, surrounded by the names of the self-governing Dominions, to which India was afterwards added. But behind the flag still lurks the intention to return to "protection." The Tariff Reform League, the lineal descendant of the Protection League, began its career of duplicity with the avowal to "defend" industry, and gave up the use of even that equivocal term because it was too near the truth. The current "policy" of the League was embodied in a resolution passed at the 1913 annual meeting, originally adopted in 1907, "That our present fiscal system should be reformed, with a view (*a*) of broadening the basis of taxation; (*b*) of safeguarding our great productive industries from unfair competition; (*c*) of strengthening our position for the purpose of negotiation in foreign markets; and (*d*) of establishing preferential commercial arrangements with the Colonies, and securing for British producers and workmen a further advantage over foreign competitors in the Colonial markets." Here the awkward word is changed to "safeguard," perhaps a little less readily associated with "protect," but meaning "protect" all the same.

The League held its first meeting on July 29, with the Duke of Westminster as Chairman of the General Council.

On November 4, 1903, it issued its first public appeal for funds, signed by the Duke of Sutherland and Mr. Chamberlain. They hoped to find "at least 100 sympathisers who will each contribute £1000 in four annual equal sums of £250." Twenty supporters had already subscribed £1000 under these conditions. In a covering letter Mr. Pearson stated "it is not proposed to publish a list of subscriptions," —a rule to which the League, in accordance with the general rule of political organizations, has kept ever since, though it is somewhat unusual to find a public invitation to subscribe to such an organization safeguarded by such an announcement of secrecy. It was apparently necessary to emphasize it.

Assuredly the League did not expect ten years of fruitless labour. "I suppose that we may look forward to two or three years of the same kind of work as that which we have already undertaken," Mr. Chamberlain observed about eighteen months after its formation.[20] At the first annual meeting of the League [21] he had thought they were "more fortunate than Mr. Cobden," for "we have the support of 200 members of the House of Commons, we have the aid of the most influential portion of the Press, and we have the enthusiastic approval of the vast majority of the Unionist party." At its fifth annual meeting Lord Ridley enthusiastically reminded the League that "they had 2942 vice-presidents, including 345 members of the House of Commons and prospective candidates, and 184 peers, while the others were gentlemen representative of every district in the country and of every trade and interest. He did not believe it would be possible to get together a more representative body, and the Committee were thankful to them for the work they had done. They helped the cause in their own districts, and they were the living embodiment of the truth that the League was not representative of one section, one person, or one party, but was representative of the best brains of the country." [22]

That boast of the noble lord's bears a moment's examination. There is no need to doubt its figures. The "184 peers" may be taken for granted. Indeed, it was a peer (Lord Hardinge) who told the Kent Branch of the League at its first annual meeting that "in his opinion, according to experience in his own neighbourhood, the only way to get hold of the working-man was to hold entertainments in public-houses." [23] Kindred advice, coming from what Lord Ridley called the "best brains of the country," has been acted on with exemplary diligence by the Tariff Reform League. Let this instance of its methods from South Herefordshire, during a bye-election, be enough.[24] "A miserable specimen of humanity makes his appearance at a public-house. Apparently he is a tramp, and a miserable object at that, of doleful visage, and clad in a grimy, greasy, ragged attire. He addresses a pathetic plea for food, or for any help the kind gentlemen in the kitchen may be pleased to bestow. He tells a pitiful story of prosperous days clouded by unemployment brought about through the importation of foreign goods. To the baneful practice of dumping he attributes the wretched condition in which he is obliged to present himself. Then, naturally enough, under the stimulating influence of the drink offered by sympathetic yokels, a discussion on the great remedy, Tariff Reform, is started. The stranger waxes eloquent on the need of broadening the basis of taxation, the utter harmlessness of little duties, the skill with which the changes upon food taxes are to be rung, the joy of fleecing the foreigner, and the like, until his hearers might well imagine that they were entertaining a Tariff Reform lecturer unawares. If there is a suspicious one present, he notices that the visitor wears sound, water-tight boots, and that through the external shabbiness meet for the character of a tramp are signs of sound, warm under-clothing. In fact, he is really a Protectionist emissary playing a part."

All kinds of men have been scooped into the movement. Mr. S. L. Hughes, M.P., has recorded [25] that a correspondent sent him the card of a gentleman describing himself as "Professor of the Euphonium and Bombardon and any Military Instrument, and Lecturer on Tariff Reform," which may serve as a reminder that the unconsciously humorous inclusion of a Tariff Reform speech and a conjuring entertainment in the same programme of a political occasion is not unusual.[26] But the choicest specimen of all these products of the "best brains" was found in a Tariff Reform newspaper circulating in the neighbourhood of the Houses of Parliament, the *Westminster Express* of November 24, 1911, which printed the following characteristically cogent Protectionist appeal:—

"Tariff Reform is the socialism you should emblazon on your banner. It is the ornament for your mantel-boards, in the full glare of the mirror in which you look, gaze, and reflect; and you will, if you gaze long enough, see Free Trade dissolving into dew and gradually fading from view, while the glorious attributes of Tariff Reform will give shape make, and character to your new-born existence by planting the pith and marrow of porsperity (*sic*) to the embodiment of the times. Go, then, brave fellows, and adjust your demands to the circumstances confronting you, and reappear the new men that Tariff Reform is sure to make you. Give up dull sloth and idle dreaming, and pay no heed to pessimists or cranks and feather-brained faddists, but be guided by that good old pilot, Tariff Reform."

A good deal of writing and even more speaking of that kind has been generated by the Tariff Reform movement. The specimens are not presented as typical, any more than Lord Ridley's parade of "184 peers" is typical. They are put at the end of this sketch of the most virulent propagandist body the world has ever seen in order to show how wide the Protectionist net has drifted. The "most influential newspapers," the "best brains of the country," peers, pub-crawlers, and the *Westminster Express*, have all become involved in it.

"THE CONFEDERATES."

Mr. Williams described the League as a "little knot of political and economic conspirators." Mr. Chamberlain called it "a political association which is not a party association," and "independent of the considerations which move these people"; [27] and in this record it is not proposed to describe the purely political mischief that has been wrought by it. The pursuit of a Protectionist propaganda has, however, touched the heart of our public life and debased its standard; so that no account of its methods would be complete that did not mention the most noxious of their results.

The League being a tongue-in-the-cheek, non-political body, only ready to "give cordial support to Members of Parliament and Candidates who are in favour of Tariff Reform," left the "mere party considerations" which Mr. Chamberlain spurned to a secret body that came into being after the General Election of 1906 and adopted the name "The Confederates." Several accounts of this organization are extant.[28] Each is written by a member of the "Confederacy." At the head of an article by "One of Them," the *Daily Mail* wrote: "Much curiosity has been aroused as to the identity of the members of this body, each of whom, while at liberty to avow his own adhesion, stands under an obligation not to reveal the names of his colleagues." This anonymous writer declared that the Confederacy had come into existence because "we feel there is an urgent need of an active and effective agency to counteract the work of the Unionist Free Trade Club," which of course was pledged to active and energetic opposition to Tariff Reform. The "Confederates" proposed to treat these Unionist Free Traders with "their own medicine." An extra association like this was necessary because "The Tariff Reform League numbers its tens of thousands, and it is not a very convenient body to carry out the objects we have in view. When serious work of detail is to be done a small body works best."

And what, if you please, was this "serious work of detail"? Its main purpose was to turn out Free Trade Unionists in possession of Conservative seats—in other words, to hound a Conservative who opposed Protection out of political life. "With few exceptions, the Confederates are men of considerable political influence, and several of them are of national reputation. More than twenty are Peers, thirty are members of the House of Commons, and another thirty may safely be reckoned amongst members of the next House of Commons. They are very serious, and quite equal to the task they have undertaken."

It is not a little amusing to note this recurring emphasis on the presence of Peers in the Protectionist movement. Note, also, that to the "best brains" are here added the "most money." "Money, and sufficient, for its wants the Confederacy can safely rely upon. . . . The Confederacy comprises many men whose pockets are as deep as their political convictions, and just as full." "As to our financial resources—well, they are limitless. We can draw exactly what we want upon occasion. We have only to ask, and we receive. There are in our membership those who willingly pass over a blank cheque on occasion that the cause may prosper."

When these accounts appeared, the Confederates had already threatened to bring out and finance Tariff Reform Unionists to oppose Free Trade Unionists in nine constituencies, and had found the money required among themselves. In other constituencies, they held that their threatenings had brought candidates "into line." Finally, "While the chief aim of the Confederacy is to render Conservative seats safe from any attack, open or covert, by the Unionist opponents of Tariff Reform, it is not intended to restrict its operations to electioneering work. It is to be a permanent organization which, in view of the lack of definite leadership in the past, will take all possible measures to ensure that there shall be no hesitation or procrastination in the future. It will help the forces marching under the flag of Tariff Reform to reach the citadel, and will see to it that they do their duty when they get there."

This is the secret body, boasting that "its efforts are recognized by many in influential quarters," supplied by limitless funds, and led by more than a score of Peers, that has done its utmost to hound the "best brains" of the party out of public life. Its influence has been exercised more or less effectively. It was "prepared to go to all necessary lengths for what we regard as the supreme cause." Often it went them. In 1912, when by-election candidates showed a disposition to put Tariff Reform and food-taxes aside as an electioneering hindrance, the Confederates published broadcast a warning in these terms :[29] "We are requested to state that the members of the 'Confederacy,' an organization about which little has lately been heard, have been carefully considering the tendency shown by several Unionist candidates at recent by-elections to place Tariff Reform in the background of their programme, or even to repudiate Imperial Preference altogether. The Confederates, who have ample means at their disposal, have fully determined that in the event of any Unionist candidate adopting a similar policy at any future election they will put forward a candidate of their own who will subscribe to the full policy of the Unionist party."

With the threat of political ruin dangled over their heads

many of the candidates have bowed ignominiously. This little confederacy of traitors to the country's welfare has helped to make history in the United Kingdom. It has served to emphasize the well-founded suspicion that Protection is a plot against the people ; and it has destroyed all pretence that Tariff Reform is a non-political movement. To a large extent its methods have been copied by the Tariff Reform League, which at its last annual meeting, on March 14, 1913, declined to bind itself to the change in the party programme involving a postponement of the food-taxing proposals and passed the following resolution : "That the rank and file of the Tariff Reform League adhere to the full policy of Tariff Reform as advocated by their leaders since 1903, and would regard any departure from it as equally disastrous to the cause of Tariff Reform as to the interests of the Unionist Party." So far from being a non-party body, the Tariff Reform League now clearly insists upon associating its cause with the fortunes of the Unionists.

THE TARIFF COMMISSION

TOWERING above all mean and devious ways of foolish Protectionist plotters, with their pockets full of money, stands the broken monument to the crooked diligence of the Tariff Commission. Some people, who took Mr. Chamberlain seriously, gravely suggested soon after his first speeches that a Royal Commission should be appointed to inquire into the conditions of commerce. The Government wisely refrained from giving such a testimonial to the sincerity of the arch-plotter; and presently Mr. Chamberlain formed a "Tariff Commission" of his own, adopting even this clumsy device from a German precedent.

It will be recalled that the Tariff Reform League itself was originally endowed with the duty of "examining the tariff," and that it got through the little pretence quite easily. The Commission was given a much wider reference. "What would happen if Mr. Chamberlain's policy were adopted," wrote his secretary, "would be that an expert committee would be appointed to collect evidence from all the manufacturers before fixing the tariff, and to take into consideration the special circumstances of each trade and the part played in its success by the different articles used in the production. This is the scientific spirit in which the Germans work, and Mr. Chamberlain would desire to imitate."[30]

In December Mr. Chamberlain, who had said in September that "we have sufficient material in the way of facts and figures," thus described the work which his Commission would undertake:[31]—"We are going to form, we have gone a long way in the direction of forming, a commission, not a political commission, but a non-political commission of experts to consider the conditions of our trade and the remedies which are to be found for it. This commission will comprise leading representatives of every principal industry and of every group of industries representative of the trade of India, the Crown colonies, and the great self-governing colonies. It will invite before it witnesses from every trade, and it will endeavour, after hearing all that can be said, not merely in regard to the special interests of any particular trade, but also in regard to the interests of all the other trades which may be in any sense related to it—it is going after that to frame a model tariff. You know the principle I laid down at Glasgow was that we should have a tariff averaging 10 per cent. on manufactures, and that that tariff should be arranged so as to put the highest rate of duty on the imports which have most labour in them, as compared with partly manufactured goods, the importation of which does not deprive us of so much employment. . . . Now, whenever the country is ready to give us the mandate for which we ask, and a Government is in power which is prepared to accept our principles, we will have ready all the information, or at all events, a great part of the information, that it will desire, and it will have before it, at all events, a tariff which has been presented to the country, and upon which they have had every opportunity of expressing their opinion."

" It is true," he said, " we are told that we cannot make a scientific tariff, that we cannot distinguish between the raw material and manufactures, that we cannot be fair all round, that if, for instance, we stop the dumping of iron below cost we shall ruin the tinplate trade, that if we stop the excessive importation of cheap foreign labour we shall destroy the boot and shoe trade, that if we are to stop the importation of woollen yarns there will be an end of the clothing industry." But " why should we suppose that our scientific economists, that our manufacturers cannot do what every other country has been able to do . . . without finding their way into those exaggerated difficulties ? Now we are going to try to do it."

A month later, on January 15, 1904, the Commission was " opened." Mr. W. A. S. Hewins, a former lecturer on Political Economy in the University of London, and now

M.P. for Hereford, was appointed Secretary, with Mr. Percy A. Hurd to assist him. Five years later Mr. Hewins was conspicuously nominated by a grateful enthusiast President of the Board of Trade in the first Tariff Reform Ministry.[32] As to that, the country has yet to see. There were sixty members of the Commission, and the Tariff Reform League, in issuing the list of their names, added that " the members of many trades will, it is feared, be disappointed that one of themselves is not included in the Commission. It was, however, plainly impossible that a place could be found for a representative of every one of the hundreds of trades in the country. The fullest opportunity will be given to members of every trade to state their views before the Commission both verbally and in writing. The question of agriculture is so large and so diverse that it has been felt impossible to represent it adequately upon the Commission without unduly increasing the membership. The position of the agriculturist needs most careful consideration, and the conditions under which farming is pursued differ so much in various parts of the British Isles that no representation could be considered complete unless it included representatives from every district in the kingdom. It is intended, therefore, to form a sub-committee of agricultural experts which will investigate in detail the many complicated agricultural issues and will submit the conclusions arrived at to the Commission."

Behind this treatment of Agriculture there lurked a good deal of ill feeling. Obviously, the Commission did not wish to be too deeply involved in food-taxing proposals, and farmed the job out to a " sub-committee," whose work could be repudiated if necessary. Lord Heneage, who describes himself as " one of the original movers in fiscal reform agitation," has told us so late as in 1913 (in the *Morning Post* and other journals of August 7) that " I do not ever recollect approving the unauthorized tariff reform of an irresponsible private commission, as I am entirely opposed to it, although I considered, and do now consider, that our present one-sided Free Trade requires to be revised and greater freedom given to our Foreign Secretaries in making commercial treaties with other nations who have Protectionist tariffs. I was one of the original movers in fiscal reform agitation, but I resigned my connexion with them when the agitation got into the hands of unpractical Protectionists and the agricultural interests were refused a practical representation of the agricultural and farming industry on the Commission, as Mr. Chamberlain and I desired." It will be seen that this was not the only time when the headstrong Mr. Chamberlain and the cold-blooded Mr. Hewins disagreed. Mr. Hewins probably knew more about the difficulties of tariffs than Mr. Chamberlain did.

The "Commission" did not include the name of any working man, or of any tenant farmer,—to note only the most glaring of the many omissions. Mr. Chamberlain said in his opening speech :[33]—"Another great complaint has been made, that labour as such is not represented on the Commission. I think this is partly due to a misapprehension. On this Commission trades are represented but not classes ; and, as I have pointed out, I deny absolutely any distinction between classes in reference to the interests of trade. The interests of trade are really identical for the employers and the employed ; in my opinion it would be absolutely impossible to prepare a tariff which would develop trade and industry, and thereby add to the profits of the employers without at the same time benefiting the employed, both by increase of employment and increase of wages. Anybody who supposes in the existing conditions, which differ absolutely from those when the doctrine of Free Trade was first established—anybody who supposes that under existing conditions it would be possible for any class in the country to keep the whole advantage of a fiscal change in their own pockets, must be entirely ignorant of the actualities of the case. And, of course, although that would not be a reason for excluding working men, it must be evident to all that if we were to seek the advice of working men as such we must take men who are at work—in other words, the men who have at the present time practical knowledge of and acquaintance with the conditions under which their class is employed are precisely the men who could not give the time to attend to the work of a Commission of this sort."

A wistful attempt was made to exalt the importance of the Commission. It met at the palatial Hotel Cecil to inaugurate itself. "We are here," said Mr. Chamberlain, "to find a method of reform which will involve the slightest disturbance to our great trade, which will conduce to the prosperity of all classes; and that being our object, that being the basis upon which we proceed, then I say unhesitatingly that I defy any impartial man to deny the authority which this Commission possesses." It was an "absolutely unparalleled," or, as he called it later at Liverpool, "the most remarkable representation of British trade and industry that has ever been put together."

Two days after Mr. Chamberlain's eulogium at Leeds a Unionist Free Trade newspaper, the *Standard* (which less than a year afterwards passed to the control of the first Chairman of the Tariff Reform League Executive Committee, Mr. Pearson), provided the country with what still remains the shrewdest summing-up of the Tariff Commission:[34] "There will be no necessity for the Cabinet to elaborate a policy, or for the Chancellor of the Exchequer to devise a tariff," said the *Standard*. "The task will have been performed in advance by Mr. Chamberlain's Committee of Public Safety. The victory, if it is won, will be claimed by this section; the 'Commission's' report will be put forward as the party 'ticket,' and it will only remain for the majority in Parliament to ratify it. There is no exaggeration in saying that this involves a complete change in our Constitutional methods, and something like a defiance of the authority, alike of the Crown, the Cabinet, and the Legislature. It is a sort of bastard Referendum worked by a caucus, for which no parallel exists. . . . We are quite willing to believe that all these gentlemen are capable and honest, and some, at least, we know to have attained success in their own trades and professions. But there is hardly one of them who would have any claim to a seat on a really strong Royal Commission, or Departmental Committee, appointed to inquire into the conditions of British trade and industry; and there is, so far as we can see, not one who can be said to represent the great middle-class community, the consuming masses, or the millions of the working population. Where are the bankers, the retail traders, the co-operative societies, the professional classes, and the labour unions? The 'Commission' seems to be a group of plutocratic manufacturers and exporters, mitigated by nonentities; and all its members, big and little, are Protectionists *pur sang*. And this is the 'independent inquiry,' whose conclusions we are to accept in preference to the tables and figures of the Board of Trade Memorandum!"

The authority of these "sixty wise men" of "unbiassed minds," as Lord Ridley ingenuously called them,[35] was questioned by many politicians on the same side. In March, in the House of Lords,[36] the Earl of Wemyss moved an address to the King praying for the appointment of a small commission to inquire into the condition and prospects of trade, and whether any change of method was needed; but Lord Lansdowne said "they had already obtained sufficient information for their fiscal policy, and they did not think a Royal Commission was necessary to justify the limited policy they had submitted." At this time, it should be said, Lord Lansdowne was not so fully committed to Tariff Reform as he is to-day, and he probably meant to show how little he thought of the Tariff Commission which Mr. Chamberlain had devised to do "a great service to our law-givers." Yet it is amusing to reflect how from different angles Mr. Chamberlain was ready to state his conclusions without further evidence, and Lord Lansdowne thought the information already accumulated "sufficient for their fiscal policy," while the Tariff Commission was solemnly preparing to collect the evidence and accumulate the information. The result showed that both men were justified in their confidence; for the Commission has not dared to trespass over the limits of Mr. Chamberlain's outline; and as to Lord Lansdowne, has he not within the last few months set the whole business at naught by refusing to move even within the limits Mr. Chamberlain sketched out?

How seriously Mr. Hewins accepted the responsibility

thrust upon him may be gathered from a correspondence that took place between himself and Mr. Herbert (now Lord) Gladstone in 1904.[37] Mr. Gladstone had criticized the methods of the Commission, and pointed out that Mr. Chamberlain had repeatedly declared his case "proved" without any inquiry at all. To this Mr. Hewins replied that "many detailed schemes might be made which, without consulting the interests involved, would seem to satisfy the conditions laid down by Mr. Chamberlain in his general plan." "Mr. Chamberlain," he added, "has sketched the general features of his proposals. They unquestionably involve the construction of a 'scientific tariff,' but what detailed recommendations should be made it is quite impossible to say on the evidence available in existing official records. If I may be allowed to criticize your letter," he said to Mr. Gladstone, "I do not think you appreciate the method by which alone such a tariff can be constructed. It is quite impossible without a rigorously fair and impartial analysis of existing conditions. To make that analysis as thorough and complete as possible is the present work of Mr. Chamberlain's Tariff Commission." From this it may be gathered that Mr. Hewins had already begun to doubt the possibility of carrying out the instructions given to him in front of the whole country. He felt it necessary to select another task as "the present work" of the Commission. Indeed, speaking at Middlesborough about the same time,[38] he rebuked his master's unscientific enthusiasm still more plainly by observing that a scientific tariff, "if it came, would come at a later stage." In other words, the only man considered capable enough to draw up a scientific tariff, considered his task an impossibility. And the bald fact is that after more than nine years' labour, and though there have been three general elections meanwhile, the Commission has not fulfilled a single part of the duty it was established to fulfil. The tariff is not only incomplete, but such small portions of it as have been published have been so hacked about as to be now almost unrecognizable. Mr. Hewins himself succeeded in minimizing the usefulness of the Commission as a Protectionist weapon when he said [39] that "it was free to report in favour of Free Trade if it thought fit to do so." That is characteristic of him. Mr. Hewins has all the time been trying to invest his Commission with a reputation for the dumb wisdom of an owl.

The Commission began its work ardently enough. A few weeks after its appointment it announced that eleven meetings had been held with an average attendance of forty. Early in 1904 it published its first report, which dealt with the Iron and Steel Industries. Then followed the Report on the Cotton industry, and in 1906 the Report of the Committee on Agriculture. Each of these reports contained a record of evidence given by numerous witnesses, many pages of recommendations by the Commission itself, and a "provisional scale of duties." To the first of these three Reports this note was appended: "Although, in making this report on iron and steel, we have had before us sufficient evidence, relating to other industries, to justify the provisional conclusions we have reached, our final recommendations must necessarily be delayed until we have completed our inquiry into all the trades—including agriculture—which may be directly or indirectly affected." [40] In the last of them a similar note indicated that the "provisional scale" was "only an indication of the nature of the scheme which may hereafter be recommended" when the Commission's inquiry into other "trades and interests" had been completed and the final report of the Commission had been prepared. The three "provisional scales" are reprinted at the end of this book for the use of the curious in such matters; [41] and in the succeeding section on Agriculture some extracts from the Report on that subject are given. It will be noticed how the more or less specific recommendations in regard to duties on agricultural products and on manufactures of iron and steel compare with a ludicrously bald "tariff" in regard to cotton. The Cotton Report, it is worth observing, is now labelled "out of print" in the list of the Commission's publications.

And that is all the Commission has done towards publishing a "model," a "scientific" tariff in the "German spirit." It has issued reports of evidence on Pottery, Glass, Sugar and Confectionery, Wool, Hosiery, Lace, Carpet, Silk, Flax, Jute and Hemp, and several memoranda on various subjects, from unemployment to the financial clauses of the Home Rule Bill; but not one of these documents approaches the other three in fullness or in candour, and not one of them recommends any scale of duties, provisional or otherwise.

The stillborn summaries of the evidence on those minor industries, like their predecessors, were characterized by notable omissions. Lord Eversley has pointed out [42] that "in all these cases the witnesses, with rare exceptions, were all of one mind—favourable to protective duties, more or less. It was not stated by whom the inquiries were held or who was responsible for the summaries. It does not appear that in any one of them there was any sifting of evidence or any cross-examination. The witnesses gave their opinion as to the expediency of levying import duties on imported products in competition with them. No question appears to have been put to them as to the effect on their industries of import duties on other articles used by them in their manufactures. Not a single working-man employed in these trades was examined as to the effect, on their class, of duties on food and other articles of necessity, though the general effect of the evidence was that such duties would raise the prices of articles thus taxed. It was also the almost universal testimony of witnesses that wages of working-men in other countries in Europe, and especially in Germany, were lower than in England and the hours of work were longer; and this was a main ground for their employers asking for import duties, with the object, no doubt, of raising prices." It is not only that the Commission has failed to carry out its undertaking to present a tariff of any kind for the consideration of the country, but the march of events has utterly nullified whatever use the published reports may have had for them. Ten years is a long time in the history of commerce; and in that period the Tariff Reformers have learned that the only way to get a tariff through is to smuggle it through secretly. There are to be no more details published.

Yet do these ponderous volumes already published supply

plenty of effective evidence against Protection, directly and indirectly. Among the witnesses were many actual opponents of Tariff Reform and many doubters. Even more thickly are the pages of the evidence sprinkled with frank admissions of manufacturers desiring higher prices and loudly complaining that Mr. Chamberlain's proposed ten per cent. average duty would be insufficient to raise prices high enough for them. They grumble continuously at the competition of foreign manufacturers who pay their workmen low wages and work them long hours; who are not hampered by factory legislation; can freely employ women and children; and who "get more work out of their men than we do because they are more under control. In cases of strikes the military are immediately made use of." Throughout the evidence there is a note of opposition to the British trades unions, which all the time were being held up by the Tariff Reform League as examples of Protectionism among workmen, and as proof that the British workman was acting illogically and unjustly in thus securing Protection for himself and voting against the Protection of his employer! In succeeding chapters many extracts will be given from these Reports. Here it is only necessary to add that while summing up the evidence the Tariff Reformers have as far as possible suppressed all reference to the points mentioned above. The Commission has published "Popular and Abridged Editions" of the Reports, and in the act of abridgement in order to popularize them the editors have cut out the adverse evidence. The Commission's Report on the Iron and Steel Trades provides one instance of this. Among the evidence printed therein were such items as these:—

Firm 350: "It cannot be too strongly pointed out that a tax on foreign imported blooms would seriously hamper our manufactures in competing with the foreigner in the markets of the world, whilst at the same time, through the closing of our market to him, it would make that competition more strenuous than hitherto."

Firm 768: "Should a duty be put upon the partly manufactured articles a higher duty would, we presume, be applied to the finished article. If, however, we were asked for a suggestion, we would certainly think that a duty of 25 per cent. *ad valorem* might advantageously be imposed."

Firm 1178 also required 25 per cent.; Firm 1379, 33⅓ per cent.

Firm 350: "It would lead to an immense reliance on the tariff. Germany and America have given ample evidence of the conditions under which alone a strongly protected country can do an export trade. They keep up high prices at home and dump abroad, viz., bleed their home consumer to give the foreigner cheap material."

The "abridged popular edition" omitted all this evidence, calculated to tell against the tariff proposals; yet it found room for numerous coloured diagrams that were expected to have an opposite effect. If the abridged edition had been issued by the "Tariff Reform League" no complaint could be made—for the methods of the League have a suppressive peculiarity of their own—but the fact that this so-called "Commission" should have distorted its own previous publications and ignored the evidence of so many representative firms, is sufficient to show its one-sided character and deprive it of all claim to serious consideration.

Nor has the Commission made any attempt to balance the advantages of its proposals against the disadvantages to any given industry. Promises have been made of a "Final Report" which should solve these vital problems, but that Final Report has not yet appeared, and is not likely to appear, although it was promised to appear before the general election of 1906. The Tariff Commission was called into being by Mr. Chamberlain as a device to lead the country to believe that the return to Protection would be along well-considered ways. It was a piece of deceit so ill-considered that the Commission in ten years has not achieved a hundredth part of the work it was set to do.

TWO UNOFFICIAL PROGRAMMES

TWICE has an attempt been made to fill the gap left yawning by the futile Commission. In 1908 the *Morning Post,* the most consistent of all the British Protectionist journals, tried its 'prentice hand; and a year later the *Birmingham Post* tried again. The latter—an eve-of-the-election attempt—was taken also to indicate the mind of the Chamberlain faction at that time. Neither of them went into details. They shirked the responsibility the Commission shirked.

The London journal's scheme,[43] "drawn up as the outcome of an exchange of views during the past twelve months among some of the most active supporters and influential members of the Unionist party both in and out of Parliament," was described by the paper itself as "a decided step in advance" in the statement of "the general principles to be followed in framing the new tariff."

"Though there is nothing which conflicts in any way with the principles officially formulated at Birmingham a year ago, the revision now made has evidently been framed to meet some of the verbal objections which the Free Traders are fond of exploiting. The undertaking to admit raw material free of duty has given rise to two such objections. The first is that it is impossible to define raw material. Secondly, Tariff Reformers who advocate a duty on imported hops, the non-manufactured raw material of beer, are charged with inconsistency. The new pronouncement re-states the theory of the tariff in such a way as to show the futility of these supposed dilemmas. According to the revised proposals the free list will, include such imported articles as could not be taxed without handicapping English manufacturers in oversea markets, and also articles which it is not worth while to tax either for revenue or for protection of home industry. It is suggested, however, that in some cases the expedient of allowing a rebate on the export of manufactured articles, in respect of material which had already paid duty, might be adopted as an alternative to placing that material on the free list. There is nothing novel about these principles, which are very generally followed in most of the leading Protectionist countries, and have enabled those countries to surmount all the difficulties which the Free Traders have declared to be insuperable."

Some of the passages from the statement itself may be quoted :—

"The basis of a reformed tariff should be the principle of placing moderate duties, both for purposes of revenue and for safeguarding home industries, upon all imports excepting those as regards which it may be shown either—

"(*a*) That the difficulty or inconvenience of levying a duty would out-weigh the advantage sought, or

"(*b*) That the duty would restrict production or handicap the competition of important industries in oversea markets. In certain cases the expedient of allowing a drawback of the duty on re-exportation might be considered as a possible alternative to exemption from import duty.

"In all cases the products or manufactures of any part of the Empire should be admitted at a lower rate of duty than competing foreign goods.

"At the same time the Government of the day should have discretion to reduce the rates of the general tariff in favour of foreign countries offering reciprocal concessions, provided always that the lower rates still left a preference in favour of Imperial products. Generally speaking, the amount of the import duty should vary with the value, in the article imported, of the labour which might have been employed upon it in this country."

"The Unionist party is already committed, through the pledges given by so many of its representatives, to a general intention of remitting a substantial portion of the present excessive taxation on articles of universal consumption, such as tea, sugar, tobacco, etc. Beyond this point it is highly inexpedient to anticipate the allocation of future revenue, recent developments at home and abroad having created a situation of serious complexity in national finance. . . ."

Under the sub-title "Agrarian Reform," the journal stated that "a thorough-going reform of local taxation, transferring certain charges to the National Exchequer, must also form part of any serious attempt to improve and expand agricultural production. Duties on imported foodstuffs, even if too small to affect prices, would nevertheless, by producing national revenue mainly at the expense of the farmer's foreign competitors, and in relief of his own taxation, tend to mitigate the severity of foreign competition. But in special cases, as, for instance, in the case of hops, which are the raw material of a luxury already subject to special taxation, the recognized objections to an import duty large enough to raise the price are not necessarily conclusive."

This was vague enough; and the programme is printed here only to emphasize that vagueness.

The Birmingham journal [44] went a little more into detail, though it confessed it was only printing "the broad outlines of the scheme which we believe will be adopted by the Cabinet should the Unionist party be returned to power next month." Some portions of that scheme are copied here:—

"It is proposed to establish a general tariff placing duties on practically all goods which are not deemed to be raw material, with the object, first, of raising revenue; secondly, of giving the turn of the market to the home producer when in competition with a foreign rival; thirdly, of making preferential agreements with the Colonies; fourthly, of securing better terms of entry into foreign countries which now exclude us by prohibitive duties; and finally, of giving such encouragement to home producers that the evils of unemployment will be substantially mitigated."

"The tariff is to be of the simplest possible form, and is not to be 'protective' in the sense in which that word is understood in Germany or the United States. There is no intention, we believe, of having multifarious rates which throw open the door for Parliamentary intrigue or lobbying.

There will be three rates of duty only, giving an average of about 10 per cent."

"The plan which we believe to be at present favoured is to allow raw materials to come in free, to place a duty of 5 per cent. on goods on which little labour has been spent, 10 per cent. on goods more nearly approaching the finished state, and 15 per cent. on completely manufactured articles. There will be no variations from this scale, unless some very exceptional case can be proved. Thus the work of classification will be greatly simplified."

It was not going to be difficult to decide what were raw materials and what were not, for "each article will almost naturally fall into its proper class, and even when there is doubt no great difficulty can arise." Going a step farther into the bog, the journal added that, "just as there are to be three rates of duty, so there will be three scales in each rate. To take an example by way of illustration: If an article is deemed to come under the 10 per cent. rate, that will be the standard duty applicable to foreigners who are commercially 'friendly.' But there will be a lower duty—possibly 7½ per cent.—to be charged on Colonial produce, and a higher duty—possibly 12½ or 15 per cent.—to be charged on the produce of countries which seek unduly to penalize British goods. The figures we give are intended only to be illustrative. They may be varied in the actual working out of the tariff."

This plan, with a duty on foreign-grown corn and a higher duty on flour, was calculated to produce a revenue of from 16 to 20 millions. But most interesting of all was the Birmingham journal's confident announcement that the long-expected Tariff Reform performance was just a-going to begin. "An immense amount of work," it said, "has already been done with a view to producing a Tariff Reform Budget at comparatively short notice, and if the Unionist party are returned to power next January every possible effort will be made to embody the new duties in the Budget of 1910. If this is found to be impracticable we may expect to see a 'beginning,' which will take the form of giving tangible proof of the intention to give Colonial Preference worth having to the Colonies and of placing duties on certain articles which can conveniently be selected. In this event the full Tariff Reform Budget would make its appearance in 1911, with this exception, that the maximum duty would remain in abeyance for two years so as to give time for the friendly negotiations of commerical agreements with foreign powers."

What these unofficial programmes make clear is that all the official promises of a definitely drawn, scientific tariff on the German model, to be produced *before* an election, were six years afterwards entirely withdrawn, and in their place was substituted a shadowy scheme that might or might not be put in operation *after* an election, supposing the Tariff Reformers to be returned. That remains the deceptive attitude of the Tariff Reformers toward their first duty to-day.

THE DREAD OF DETAILS

IT is easy to see why the Protectionists dread the too previous publication of details. If schedules were issued every man would begin to calculate how the tariff would affect him personally. The promises of Protection would be checked off by the proposed performances. The incessant clamour for details all through the ten years' controversy is itself the best indication of how apprehensive of loss the country has been. The consistent denial of details, in face of the repeated promises to produce them, shows that the makers of the tariff know it would cause that loss. At first people were inclined to believe the promises and to trust in the Tariff Reform League and the Imperial Tariff Committee, whose " function " Mr. Chamberlain said it was to supply " statistics and details." [44a] But early in 1904 the denials began, and when one of Mr. Chamberlain's first lieutenants, Mr. C. A. Vince, was speaking to the furniture makers at Barnstaple [45] he was asked, " Having regard to the fact that most of us are interested in furniture manufacture, how will Mr. Chamberlain's scheme benefit us, seeing our chief competitors are Canadians ? " To this Mr. Vince somewhat petulantly answered, " For about an hour I have tried to show how Mr. Chamberlain's scheme will benefit the country at large. I am not qualified to go into the details of the trade with which you are all very well acquainted, and of which unfortunately I know very little. But I have given you reasons for believing that Mr. Chamberlain's scheme will benefit the country of which you are all members, and I can only hope that you will all get a fair share."

How little this kind of thing satisfied the " country at large " was indicated in the following January by Mr. Joseph Chamberlain himself.[46] He, who had made up his own mind without their aid, could now only counsel the country to wait for the reports of the Tariff Commission. "I have never pretended, although a man of business, that I knew enough about other men's business to say what would be good for them," he said. "When I was challenged about this, I asked the most representative men in every industry to join in a Tariff Commission which would examine into the circumstances of our trade and make recommendations after that examination was concluded; and therefore I say to these gentlemen, some of whom I think have already been examined by the Commission, Wait for their report; see what the men who know most about it recommend, and whether they consider that any of these things should be treated either as raw material or as manufactured goods."

Within the doors of the Commission the difficulties of fair dealing were already beginning to be made apparent. In March of this same year Mr. Henry Chaplin declared [47] that "the construction of a tariff was one of the most difficult things in the world," and that "changes had to be made afterwards." In July, Mr. J. Chamberlain [48] retorted that "we cannot afford to be obscure." "We have a definite and a constructive policy," he said, "let no man join us who does not agree with the whole of it. It is our desire to put that policy before our people so that it shall be understanded of them all. We have no object to gain in concealing anything." In this speech he repeated that "it must be a scientific tariff." In the same year he "assured the Leicester manufacturers that all the difficulties in the way of drawing up a tariff equally satisfactory to the maker of leather and the maker of boots and shoes would be satisfactorily adjusted by a Committee of experts on the German model." [49]

Still the tariff remained obstinately "obscure," and even after the publication of the few details the Tariff Commission vouchsafed to the country a Tariff Reform candidate [50] declared that "no one out of a lunatic asylum would suppose that they were going to publish the proposals the next Unionist Government would lay down in the matter of Tariff Reform." A year afterwards, when Mr. Wyndham, "speaking for himself only," [51] said: "I think we should be very foolish if we did not put a small tax on wood with a small preference to our colonies,"—wood being a raw material that no other Tariff Reformer had undertaken to tax—Mr. Basil E. Peto, then a Tariff Reform candidate in Wiltshire, answered that " he did not care a damn for what Mr. Wyndham said ! " [52]

At the end of 1909 Mr. Hewins,[53] who had persistently declined to do anything to fulfil Mr. Chamberlain's undertaking to the country, found it possible to say that " no policy had been more carefully defined than that of Tariff Reform." " Everybody," he said, " knew perfectly well the general nature of what would be undertaken ; they knew also that there was not the slightest chance of a large German or American tariff scheme being introduced into this country. Mr. Balfour believed all that was required was the simple application of a simple principle." Then, avoiding what Mr. Chamberlain had said, Mr. Hewins went on, " Looking at it in that way he did not know that anybody required more to decide this attitude towards Tariff Reform. Another reason why more details should not be disclosed was that they had not yet got rid of the present Government, and they did not know what mess of international affairs they might make. A further reason why Mr. Balfour should not give other details was because a Tariff scheme which might be suitable for November 1909, might be blown to smithereens by the folly and short-sightedness of the Radical Government."

That was merely a hastily conceived catalogue of excuses, necessary for the platform. In more reflective language, the official organ of the Tariff Reform League [54] replied to an anxious correspondent that " no alteration has been so far proposed by any Tariff Reformer in Mr. Chamberlain's proposal to remit part of the existing duties on tea, sugar, etc., in the detailed tariff scheme which will ultimately be adopted. The extent to which it will be possible to reduce such duties must, however, obviously and necessarily depend very largely upon the revenue necessities of the country when Tariff Reform comes into operation, and Tariff Reformers will do wisely to refrain from in any way pledging themselves or their party in advance to any specific plan in regard to such reduction of duties. You will remember that Mr. Chamberlain himself, in putting forward his original proposals, was careful to point out that he asked no one to pledge himself in any way on points of detail." So he did, but he also pledged himself that these very essential "points of detail" should be published.

Mr. Bonar Law, the successor to Mr. Chamberlain in the leadership of the Tariff Reformers, has also great hope of the "scientific tariff" that never appears. "With a scientific tariff," he said, "at least everyone in the trade itself is put in a position of exact equality, and there is room for complete freedom and complete competition." [55]

In 1910, the year of the two general elections, the more penetrating writers on the Protectionist side perceived the danger of refusing any longer to be frank with the country. "What is wanted is not a declaration that if you preach Tariff Reform you will win, but an outline of the future tariff," said the *Morning Post*,[56] which had apparently found the "outline" it published of its own accord two years earlier insufficient. And another Protectionist paper, *The World*,[57] still more anxious, declared that "in the matter of Tariff Reform, the time has come for Mr. Balfour to state the general character of the proposed tariff on manufactured goods. Is it to contain three rates—minimum, intermediate, and penal—and, if so, what is the average level of those rates to be? Again, are Colonial manufactures to come in free, or are they to share the minimum tariff with the products of foreign States giving us especially favourable terms? Above all, what about foodstuffs? What articles are to be included? What is to be the amount of the duty on foreign wheat? Is there to be a smaller duty on Colonial wheat, too, by way of helping British agriculture? Are the duties on wheat to be balanced by remissions on tea and sugar?" Then the *Daily Mail* came along and tried to save the reputation of the Tariff Reformers for faithfulness to their promises. Mr. W. Chrimes, of Warrington, had written to the President of the Warrington branch of the Tariff Reform League to say he had tried many times to learn from the highest sources what taxation was proposed in order to protect his own trade. "To these inquiries the only reply I can get is that such details will be settled by experts when a Tariff Reform Government comes into power." But he had grown tired of hearing and making this excuse for seven weary years; and, satisfied at last that "the people of England will never take a leap in the dark," he had resigned his membership of the League. "What indications are there," he asked, "that the leaders and manufacturers generally have any settled convictions, and are in real earnest about it? . . . For instance, one wire manufacturer in Warrington suggests a tax on cheap German steel, which is a raw material for wire manufacturing; and another wire manufacturer, equally experienced, suggests that it should still come in free. Both of them are leaders of the Tariff Reform Party." The *Daily Mail* told Mr. Chrimes that he had forgotten "the principle of democratic government," which was this: "The general principles of legislation are submitted to the electorate, and the details, when once the general principles have been confirmed, are worked out by the Administration." So that now, on the brink of another downfall at the polls, the responsibility for not carrying out pre-election pledges was cast upon the democracy itself!

In the election that followed the Tariff Reformers acquitted themselves no more creditably. The air was full of "general principles" and particular promises, but the details were still stubbornly lacking. Mr. Hewins himself went down to Manchester to address a meeting of business men on "the Tariff as it affects agents for foreign goods." [60] He was asked, "Will Swiss embroideries be on your free list?"

"No," he replied, "they will not."

"You have not read the whole of my question," said his interrogator.

Mr. Hewins answered: "The rest is simply a comment. It is this: 'If not, it will be bad for Lancashire, as all the cloth is made here.'"

"Yes," retorted the questioner, "and if they are not on the free list it means that we shall be paying taxes on our own goods."

Whereupon Mr. Hewins closed the discussion by saying,

"I have already declined to discuss the taxation of particular articles."

A month or so later, in the less critical atmosphere of a Tariff Reform League "Speakers' Class," he returned to the safe ground of generalities. "When they had a tariff," he promised the fledglings, "they would have a complete tariff."[61] And being only fledglings, the Speakers' Class probably thought that was a satisfyingly eloquent way of putting it.

Mr. Hewins' last pronouncement on what must seem to him this indecent demand to show up the nakedness of Protection was in February of 1913, when he said[62] that "what I feel about the whole Tariff Reform movement and the whole Empire movement is this. If we frankly state our convictions, and you must have convictions, and persuade the people of the United Kingdom that we have a policy which we believe in, and which we will certainly carry into effect, I believe Englishmen have far too much practical sagacity to worry their heads perpetually about details; they will return us to power at the proper time and they will make us carry out our policy, trusting our statesmen they will leave it to them to adjust the measures and the details as the need arises. Do not bother your politicians too much about mere details."

It would be wearisome to go on piling up evidence of the way in which the Tariff Reformers have struggled, for a decade, and with a considerable amount of success, to shake off the shackles of veracity. Room must be found, however, for a reference to the classic problem of leather, which in tannery constituencies, where leather is a finished product, Tariff reformers argue should be taxed; but which in boot-making constituencies, where it is a raw material, they argue should not be taxed. Right down to the present day that conflict of profit and loss has not been solved. The last official pronouncements on the subject were made in 1912, when Mr. Richard T. Golding, of Liverpool, wrote to the Secretary of the Tariff Reform League to ask (March 20): "Whether under the present Tariff Reform proposals a duty is to be imposed upon imports of raw material, such duty varying with the amount of work done to the material, and, if this is so, upon which of our imports it is considered that no work has been done ?" The Literary Secretary of the Tariff Reform League replied that "the practical question, as to what shall be treated for tariff purposes as 'raw material' and therefore non-dutiable, can only be authoritatively determined by the Government responsible for the tariff." It will be observed that the wary League did not encourage the exact definition of raw material. It is to be raw material only when they treat it "for tariff purposes" as raw material. Then Mr. Golding reminded the League about leather, and the Literary Secretary replied (April 11) that "leather is a manufactured article, and is classed as such by our Board of Trade and by the tariffs of all civilized countries." But "manures" also are so classed by our Board of Trade, said Mr. Golding; yet the Tariff Reform League's own publications declare that "feeding stuffs and manures" are to be admitted free of duty. The Literary Secretary seems to have become rather uncomfortable when this contradiction was newly revealed to him. He wrote (April 16): "I cannot accept your suggestion that I have said that imports of leather 'are to be taxed,' having no authority to say anything of the kind. I have merely stated the fact, now admitted by you, that leather is a manufactured article. But under Tariff Reform an import will not necessarily be dutiable merely because it is a manufactured article. Whether it will be found desirable to impose a small duty on such imports of leather as compete with British production remains to be seen. Personally, I think it more than likely, being convinced that the case for such a duty is unanswerable, and this is not from the point of view of the tanning trade alone, but of all users of leather in this country. In any event, it will no doubt be found expedient to place on the Free List any class, or classes, of leather which cannot advantageously be produced in this country."

And as with leather, everything else "remains to be seen." The cautious attitude of the officers of the Tariff Reform League has been imitated all over the country by Tariff Reform candidates, and by none so faithfully as by the successful Tariff Reform candidate in one of the 1911 by-elections.[63]

"Are you in favour of Tariff Reform?" he was asked.

"I am certainly in favour of Tariff Reform," he replied.

"Then are you in favour of putting on a 10 per cent. duty according to the Unionist policy?"

The candidate smelled a rat. "There is no Unionist policy that I know of at the present time," he said, "but I will not vote for anything that will increase the cost of living."

But his questioner persisted: "I ask you if you are prepared to support a 10 per cent. duty on manufactured articles coming into this country?"

At this alarm the poor candidate took fright utterly: "Nothing has been settled yet at all that I know of," he declared. "I have seen no proposals at all about Tariff Reform."

Lest it be thought, however, that the work of preparing this "scientific tariff" has been entirely dropped, there must be recorded some evidence of industry outside the cobwebbed doors of the Tariff Commission. In 1911 there appeared in several provincial newspapers[64] an article brightly entitled "Eye-Openers for Working-Men." No. 15 of these "eye-openers" sparkled under the sub-title of "Free Trade Hottuns," and at the end of this particular "Hottun" was the following "Special Request": "I want to compile a list of foreign articles which may be recommended for taxation when imported into this country, together with suggested rates of taxation according to value. For example: Motor cars, 50 per cent.; pianos, 50 per cent.; gold watches, 50 per cent.; precious stones, 50 per cent., etc. Will my readers kindly assist? Please arrange in alphabetical order, and address to Peter Gray, *News* Office, Stroud, Glos. When complete the list will be forwarded to the Secretary, Tariff Reform League."

What has the Secretary of the Tariff Reform League done with these helpful recommendations?

WHAT TARIFF REFORM "MEANS"

IF details of the proposed taxes have been lacking, the space has been bounteously filled with promises. Every industry in turn has been offered something out of the pockets of the others. Tariff Reform candidates seeking the suffrages of the electorate have been prolific in the invention of advantages; and the leaflets of the League abound with vague sketches of an industrial millennium. Its leaflet No. 186, for example, indicates that Tariff Reform "will help to" (*in small type*) "Increase Production, Improve Trade, Increase Employment, Raise Wages, Lower the Poor Rate, Lighten Taxation" (*these in big type*); and gives a list of the people who will be "helped." They include 'bus drivers and barristers; solicitors and museum employees; warders and clergymen; bankers and publicans; hairdressers and chimney sweeps; nurses and policemen; shopkeepers and park-keepers; typists and journalists, and so on, each being told that "Tariff Reform will help *YOU*!"

Fortunately, the task of collecting evidence of these foolish promises has been saved us by the patient ingenuity of the *Daily Express*, which for nearly three years published at the head of its news columns a text announcing that "Tariff Reform means"—something or other. The *Express* has been throughout the most reckless of all the Protectionist journals, and for a long while it was under the control of Mr. C. A. Pearson, the first Chairman of the Executive Committee of the Tariff Reform League. It began the regular publication of the text on May 26, 1908, and ended in June 1911. Sometimes Tariff Reform meant a by-election victory, or a change in the weather, or some purely topical event whose significance was ephemeral. Weeding these transient meanings out of the list, there remained assurances that "Tariff Reform means": More Work and Fewer

Workhouses; Real Pensions for Old Age; Pensions at 65; Higher Wages; Protection for Home Industries (the *Express* did not avoid the danger-word); Protection for British Workmen; Fewer Trade Disputes; An Adequate Navy; Lower Poor Rates; Work and Food for the Poor; Protection (the word recurs many times); A Check to Socialism; Protecting our Workers as Other Countries protect theirs; Naval Supremacy in 1915; Higher Standard of Living; Wealth; Less Emigration; A Tax on Foreign Hops; Making Your Way in the World; High Wages; Christmas Presents made at Home; Home Bred Christmas Dinners; Peace and Plenty; British Toys for British Boys (this series of four ended on December 24); More Money to buy Warm Clothing (when the weather was cold); What Mr. Chamberlain says in Another Column; Making Goods, not Merely Handling Them; Fewer Burglaries; Imperial Salvation (these two were on consecutive days); More and Higher Wages; Money for Dreadnoughts; England Expects the Foreigner to pay its Duties; The Dumper Dished; The Dawn of a Golden Era; Rule Britannia; Higher Pay, More Savings; Plenty of Money for the Navy; Money for the Holidays (this came at Eastertide); Decent Wages; A Tax on Gowns Made in Paris; Home Grown Wheat; Better Clothes; Money in Your Pocket; Regeneration; Equality of Chance for All; British Trade out of Handcuffs; Protection for our Vanishing Industries; More Tanneries for Bermondsey; More Wages in Bermondsey (there was a by-election going on in Bermondsey); Everything to the Working Man; Pauperism Banished; Less Money for German Dreadnoughts; No Wrangling to Find Taxes (this would be quite true, though the *Express* meant it as a sarcastic comment on the Budget); Fewer Officials and More Workmen; No Necessity to Emigrate; Prosperity by Protection; Commercial Sunshine; Protecting the Weak; Benefit to All; Gold for the Nation; More Wages for Ironstone Miners (another by-election); Defence not Defiance; The Right to Bargain; Employment and Happiness; No Politics in Trade; Real Land Reform; Fewer Bankruptcies; Fewer Tramps in England; Labour Leaders working for a Living;

No Oppressive Home Taxation; The Noble Art of Self-Defence; No Yellow Perils like Form IV.; Reversing the Fiscal Policy; Protection for Those Who should be Protected; National Credit Restored; An Impregnable Armament; Work and its Reward; Business before Party Politics; Development Not Degeneration; A Real Mandate; Revenue From Abroad; The Compliments of the Season (it was Christmas Eve again); Invincibility; Reciprocate or We Retaliate; Minting Gold; Keeping, not losing, Our Colonies; The Five Senses of a Nation; Trade Reform of the World; Less Work in the Workhouse; Joy for Workers; The Magic of Prosperity; The Best Possible Budget; A Check to Stupidity (an accidentally appropriate end to the selections).

In short, as *Punch* put it when the exhausting series was yet young, "Tariff Reform means Diamond Tiaras for Workmen's Wives; Tariff Reform means Motor Cars and Monte Carlo for the Artisan; Tariff Reform means any Blessed Thing you may be hankering for at the Moment."

II.—AGRICULTURE

THE STORM CENTRE OF THE TARIFF REFORM MOVEMENT

" THE SALVATION OF ERIN "

THE WELBECK SPEECH

THE TARIFF COMMISSION'S BARREN REPORT

" THE WHOLE POLICY " OF SUBSTITUTES

THE STORM CENTRE OF THE TARIFF REFORM MOVEMENT

AGRICULTURE is the storm-centre of the Tariff Reform movement because it is a food-producing industry. Imperial Preference, food prices, wages, employment, taxes on manufactures—all the conflicting elements of the unsolvable problem converge on the distracted head of the agriculturist. He has been the innocent sport of those elements all through. From the day in 1903, very early in the Protectionist revival, when Mr. Joseph Chamberlain made his mouth water by observing that a Preference to the Colonies must involve "a tax on food," right down to the present moment, when he is countering the proposal to put a tax on manufactures and not on food, Tariff Reform has tried to befool the farmer. No man knows it better than he. He is quite alive to the pit his claims have digged for the Tariff Reformer. He is prepared to dig it deeper rather than agree to any distribution of the "benefits of Protection" that leaves him in the lurch.

The kind of Tariff Reform the agriculturist wants is the kind the other Protectionists want, but it cannot be promised to him in any other but plain terms of food-taxes. "If you think it worth while agitating in favour of the [corn] tax on the ground that is it a boon to the British farmer," said Mr. Balfour on May 1, 1903, a few days before Mr. Chamberlain's Protectionist campaign opened, "you are condemned to the proposition that it must be injurious to the British consumer. There is absolutely no escape from that dilemma." Mr. Balfour was more guileless than he knew. He had, in 1903, seen nothing of the Tariff Reform League's work. How was he to foresee that the Tariff Reformer would find an escape from the dilemma by means of a lie, the biggest of all the big lies this ten years' campaign of duplicity has seen? For, ever since 1903, the farmer has been promised higher prices, definitely and repeatedly, and the farm-labourer has been promised more wages out of the higher prices; while the forty million consumers of the food they produce have been assured, every day for a decade past, that nothing taken to fill the pockets of the cultivators of the soil shall come out of the pockets of the people who eat the produce of the soil.

It is a shameful thing that almost all Tariff Reformers have silently acquiesced in this deception; all the more shameful because the whole country has been aware of it and marvelling at their silence. Yet have Tariff Reformers holding high positions in public life acquiesced in it because to acknowledge it openly would have been to pull down the whole of their pretty pagoda of cards.

The tardy confession of the deception to-day only makes it the more shameful. It was confessed indirectly by the party decision, early in 1913, to postpone the food-tax issue to a second General Election. This incident will be described in its proper place in the course of this review. Here is placed on record, as the keynote to all that follows, the candid public confession of at least one Protectionist, and he a prominent man in the movement from the first, a member of the Executive of the Tariff Reform League, Sir Thomas Wrightson, who said in a letter to *The Times* on March 26, 1913: "Look at the presentation of the case as now put forward. The Radical Party point out with effect that the emissaries of Tariff Reform are sent into the towns to preach that food-taxes will not raise the price of food. The next day they are found preaching to the country people that food-taxes will raise the price of food. The two statements are incompatible, and will never serve as a basis for political education. The appeal to selfish motive will have to be dropped if we want to educate plain-spoken and plain-thinking men. Why not trust to an appeal for justice and fair play?"

Ten years of the appeal to selfishness, and now a proposal to appeal for justice! "When the devil was ill, the devil a saint would be," etc.

Mr. Joseph Chamberlain was always uncomfortably aware of this incompatibility which Sir Thomas Wrightson discovered ten years later. During the first few months of his campaign, and in all the important speeches with which he opened it, Mr. Chamberlain failed to satisfy the natural expectancy of the agriculturist. He hinted that this great industry would profit along with the rest under his hazy scheme. His vague language was both flattering and promissory. "Agriculture, the greatest of all trades and industries of this country," he said at Greenock in October 1903, "has been practically destroyed." And Mr. Henry Chaplin, then representing the wholly agricultural constituency of Sleaford in Parliament, and regarded as the champion of the farmers' cause, told how a leading agriculturist had said to him, "If the present state of things continues, and if we go on in the agricultural world as we are going now, in four or five years at the latest you will see one-third of the whole of this great country gone out of cultivation altogether." [1] * Mr. Chaplin gave it out as his own deliberate opinion that in the circumstances foreshadowed such a disaster was far from being impossible. Yet could Mr. Chamberlain find no bolder thing to say than that the man who had kept one pig under Free Trade should keep two under Protection, and that we should return to the grinding of corn between revolving stones driven by wind or water-power.

"I propose," said Mr. Chamberlain in his Glasgow speech,[2] "I propose to put a low duty on foreign corn, no duty at all on the corn coming from our British possessions. But I propose to put a low duty on foreign corn, not exceeding two shillings a quarter. I propose to put no tax whatever on maize, partly because maize is a food of some of the very poorest of the people, and partly also because it is a raw material for the farmers, who feed their stock with it. I propose that the corresponding tax which will have to be put on flour should give a substantial preference to the miller. I do that in order to re-establish one of our most ancient

* References not in the text will be found massed at the end of the book.

industries in this country, believing that if that is done, not only will more work be found in agricultural districts with some tendency, perhaps, operating against the constant migration from the country into the towns, and also because by re-establishing the milling industry in this country, the offals as they are called—the refuse of the wheat—will remain in the country and will give to the farmers or the agricultural population a food for their stock and their pigs at very much lower rates.

"That will benefit not merely the farmer," he went on, "but it will benefit the little man, the small owner of the plot, or even the allotment owner who keeps a single pig. I am told by a high agricultural authority that, if this were done, so great an effect would be produced on the price of the food of the animal, that where an agricultural labourer keeps one pig now, he might keep two in future. I propose to put a small tax of about 5 per cent. on foreign meat and dairy produce. I propose to exclude bacon, because, once more, bacon is a popular food with some of the poorest of the population."

The taxes he enumerated Mr. Chamberlain described as "additions to your present burden," thus admitting that prices would be higher; and he proposed to balance them by "some great remissions," thus admitting that the additions to the existing taxation would be great also. The new food duties were to raise the prices of wheat and meat and dairy produce; and the "great remissions" were to lower the prices of tea and sugar and cocoa and coffee. Putting duties on would raise prices; taking duties off would lower prices. Nothing can be clearer than that Mr. Chamberlain knew the British agriculturist would expect to get higher prices for British produce through Protection. It was the second promise of gain to the industry. The record of the succeeding years will show how the promise was builded on, how it was diminished, and how in the end it was razed to the ground and is now become an irredeemable mortgage on the party's reputation.

There were some adverse criticisms, even thus early, from people entitled to voice the mind of the agriculturist.

The late Earl Percy "frankly confessed that he did not think Mr. Chamberlain's corn taxation proposals would benefit the agricultural industry at home." [3] He believed in them, he said, and he believed it would be to the advantage of the country to adopt them, and "the agricultural industry would tend to be rather better off, if anything," for them; "but they would not save the agricultural industry." Mr. J. W. Lowther, a Conservative member, raised an even more pronounced difficulty in a speech at Carlisle.[4] When he asked his audience whether the free admission of Colonial produce was "a proposal which would induce farmers to lay more land under corn, or to invest more capital in the production of meat," he was answered by protesting cries of "No, no." It was not in that way the farmer had thought of making more money. Mr. Lowther, however, stuck to his point, and insisted on the farmer giving the question deep consideration.

"He confessed that those farmers he had had an opportunity of speaking to in Norfolk and Suffolk, where most of the corn was grown in this country, scouted the idea of laying down a single acre more because of a duty of 2s. upon foreign corn. They had pooh-poohed the idea of 2s. being sufficient, and had said nothing under 7s. 6d. or 10s. would be of the slightest use to them; but, of course, a 7s. 6d. or 10s. duty upon foreign corn would raise the price of corn in England to a very considerable extent, and they would remember that Mr. Chamberlain had pledged himself that under no circumstances whatever should the cost of food be increased to the working-classes of this country. (*"That is where his difficulty comes in."*) That was the first question for consideration: Should they be satisfied with 2s. on corn? Should not they be asking for 10s. or 7s. 6d.? Should they be satisfied with a 5 per cent. duty on foreign meat, or should they be asking for 15 to 20 per cent. to do them any good?

"Another point was"—Mr. Lowther went on—"supposing this scheme was successful, how would the British agriculturists benefit? The scheme, as he understood it, was to develop the Colonies at the expense of foreign countries, the idea being to unite the Colonies to this country in closer fiscal bonds with ourselves. They were to shut out the products of foreign countries to develop the resources of the Colonies; they were to substitute colonial corn and meat for foreign. Supposing they did that, and it was successful, how were the agriculturists of this country to benefit? They would have to compete with colonial corn instead of foreign corn, with Australian beef, New Zealand mutton, and Canadian beef and mutton, instead of, as now, competing with Argentine or American."

Those are two examples of the cautious criticisms of the few people who took Mr. Chamberlain seriously. The Protectionist crowd entered glibly into the game of promise and prophecy, and elaborated Mr. Chamberlain's halting utterance into an inexhaustible treasury of blessings for everybody. The *Rural World*, the organ of the Rural Labourers' League, did not stop at the doubling of the pig population. Feeding at a cheaper rate (assuming, that is, that offals would become cheaper), "the man who had one cow would go in for two cows," and "the larger farmers would benefit in a corresponding degree."[5] Twice as many pigs; twice as many cows! That was not all; more live stock meant more stockmen, "and stockmen invariably get a little more per week in the way of wages than the general run of agricultural labourers."

Mr. Chamberlain's own Imperial Tariff Committee at Birmingham, under Mr. C. A. Vince, published several leaflets embellishing the speech. *The Times* said the leaflets were issued with "high official approval," meaning that what Mr. Chamberlain did not care to say on a public platform, he allowed to be published anonymously in a printed pamphlet. No. 3 of these leaflets was a good example of them all. It set forth that "a small tax on wheat" would encourage emigration to Canada and Australia, and at the same time bring back to cultivation "thousands of acres of derelict land" in Britain. It would "encourage British farming"—which it could only do by gaining higher prices for farm produce—and at the same time it would reduce the price of food. To-day, after more than ten years of similar stuff, there is nothing strange in these astounding contradictions; but as one of the earliest examples of the kind of thing upon which the Tariff Reform case is founded, let some extracts from this particular leaflet be printed here to confirm the contradictory conclusions summarized above:—

"A small duty on wheat will give a great stimulus to Colonial farming. It will, therefore, provide occupation for thousands of Englishmen, Scotchmen, and Irishmen thrown out of work by the decay of British agriculture, who will emigrate to Canada and Australia, instead of flocking to the towns, overcrowding the slums, and overstocking the urban labour market."

"By encouraging British farming it will bring back to cultivation thousands of acres of derelict land."

"But it is certain that a 2s. duty does not mean a 2s. rise in price. . . . It is sometimes laid down by old-fashioned and ill-instructed economists that 'import duties on food are paid wholly by the consumer.' This is taken for granted by many critics of the new policy. But it is not true. The statement is contradicted by common sense. The duty will encourage the production of wheat at home and in the Colonies. It will, therefore, increase the amount of wheat in the world; and an increase of supply must mean a falling of price."

If the author dared not make it explicitly clear in this leaflet that he expected Tariff Reform to raise the prices of home-grown food, he repaired the emphasis in a subsequent leaflet, No. 37, which promised that not only would production be cheaper, but that both prices and wages would be better. "Tariff Reform will do at least something," said the leaflet, "to alter this deplorable state of affairs; (1) by encouraging farmers to grow more corn, meat, etc., at a cheaper rate than now, and with the certainty of securing better prices; (2) by attracting the labourers to the soil and securing both better wages than now, and an improved prospect for them of sharing (as cultivators on their own account) in the benefits accruing to the larger farmers."

Yet all the while Mr. Vince knew what was in the back of the farmer's mind; and in one of his frequent fits of candour the advocate who was responsible for the leaflets quoted above fairly admitted the poverty of the promise to agriculture, when you get down to the bones of it. In his book, *Mr. Chamberlain's Proposals*, he wrote: "Even though the British farmer is not benefited, as wheat grower, by an import duty on wheat, he may reap great advantage, as cattle and pig feeder, from such an import duty on flour as will restore British milling, and therewith the old abundance and cheapness of flour-offals."

In one statement this authoritative exponent of Mr. Chamberlain's opinions promised the certainty of better prices for corn, and in the next doubted the possibility of any such benefit. Corn and meat, be it observed, are here mentioned specifically.

The boisterous rival of the Birmingham Imperial Tariff Committee, the Tariff Reform League, tackled the nettle with more heedless grip. The League concocted a leaflet that damned the "demon of cheapness," and appealed to the "Imperial minds" of the "dwellers in the cities" to exorcise it. The leaflet did not say in so many words that the 2s. duty would raise prices to the dwellers in the cities; the inference was that cheapness is an evil, and that if townsmen cultivated the Imperial mind they would bear the sacrifice of higher prices heroically. It is a fine specimen of the early twentieth-century style of Protectionist literature.[6]

THE "DEMON OF CHEAPNESS"

NATURE'S REVENGE

"To-day we try to solve the problem of hooliganism, we look aghast at the growth of pauperism, we are perturbed at the physical degeneration of the dwellers in the cities. Why? Are not these things the natural outcome of a short-sighted suicidal policy—the lack of recognition of the fact that we owe everything to the land, that we are dependent on the land for everything we eat, drink, or wear? We may defy nature for a time, but nature takes her revenge, and when she does so, when we shout for the cheap loaf, we find that the motive of our actions has been the demon of cheapness.

THE IMPORTANCE OF "THE PRODUCER"

"Mr. Chamberlain has truly said, 'It is not only the consumer you have got to consider, the producer is of still more importance; and to buy in the cheapest market is not the sole duty of man, and it is not in the best interest of the working-classes.' A bold statement, truly! A far-seeing statement made by a far-seeing statesman, the man who has begged us 'to learn to think Imperially.' Will not the dwellers in the cities learn to look on the agricultural industry with wider and more Imperial minds? Is not the existence, the prosperity of this industry, necessary to their own existence? Should not even the selfishness of self-preservation force them to appreciate the importance of supporting within their own domains the industry which should give them the food necessary for their existence?"

Having sought to prepare the mind of the "dwellers in the cities" who would pay the higher prices, the League turned to the cultivators of the soil and told them to open their mouths as wide as they could to receive the promised "benefits." In a series of leaflets [7] the League drew attention to the "millions of pounds' worth" of "competitive foreign fruit," onions, tomatoes, potatoes, dairy produce, poultry, eggs, meat, and bacon, "that are allowed into this country every year free of duty," and asked, what use were small holdings so long as the duty-free imports continue? One of these leaflets reminded the agricultural labourer that Tariff Reform would "increase his employment and wages," while another bade him "Remember that wages are paid out of profits, and low profits must mean low wages," adding that the "remedy" was "called Tariff Reform." It may be thought that even an agricultural labourer would discern the absurdity of such reasoning about the relation of wages to profits; but this record cannot stay to demolish all the Tariff Reform absurdities. The leaflets are quoted to show that, having swelled the expectancy of the home producer, the League, a few days later, informed the city clerk, the telegraphist, the nurse, the typist, the clergy, museum employees, and others, that "the moderate duties which Tariff Reformers propose to place upon foreign corn, meat, and dairy produce, would tend to lower prices rather than to raise them, because they would undoubtedly lead to largely increased home and Colonial supplies. Will Tariff Reform raise prices ?" asked this batch of leaflets. The answer, in the biggest type every time, was a loud "No !" In its anxiety to placate the food-consumers, the League even quoted Lord Rosebery as having said that the 2s. duty "would only stimulate an illimitable area of competition."

"THE SALVATION OF ERIN"

IN Ireland, the Tariff Reform League evidently realized that such blarney would not bear the attractiveness of novelty. When Ireland was first thought of in this amazing propaganda, Mr. Joseph Chamberlain was asked how she would be affected by the new fiscal proposals. His Secretary wrote in reply [8] to say that the Protectionist leader was "so much occupied that it is impossible for him to comply with your request, and that, in his opinion, the effect of our present tariff or proposed modification should be considered by a purely Irish association." Apparently Mr. Chamberlain sent the inquiry on to the Tariff Reform League, bidding them do their best with it; for about this time the League issued a leaflet entitled "The Salvation of Erin." Ireland was to be saved, in so many words, by an extra profit of six shillings on the food grown on each acre of her land. That was definite enough, surely. The leaflet is No. 22. After a reference to depopulation, it proceeded in words whose original slap-dash of capital letters is here retained:—

"*MR. CHAMBERLAIN'S PLAN.*—Mr. Chamberlain now proposes to give a moderate protection to the staple articles which Ireland produces—corn, meat, and dairy produce, while at the same time reducing the duty on tea, sugar, and perhaps tobacco, which are all articles of large consumption in Ireland. So that Ireland will reap a double harvest of advantage. She will secure both a higher price for all she sells in the English market by being protected from the competition of America, Denmark, and France, and she will pay less for what she purchases, the duties having been largely reduced.

"*BENEFIT TO THE IRISH FARMER.*—Let us make a rough budget of the profit of the new fiscal departure for the Irish farmer, who, under the new Land Act, is the proprietor of forty acres of average land. An acre of such land, if devoted to wheat, would produce about three quarters; as the proposed duty on foreign wheat is 2s., THE PROFIT REPRESENTED BY THE ADVANCE IN

THE PRICE OF WHEAT IN THE ENGLISH MARKET WILL BE SIX SHILLINGS PER ACRE. It would not be possible to state with exactness the profit per acre from the increased prices of dairy produce and meat, because of the imposition of a duty on these foreign products which compete with Irish, but it is safe to reckon it also at quite six shillings per acre. Now the so-called 'second term' rents on such a farm as this are about fourteen shillings per acre, or £28 a year; these rents under the 'zone' system of purchase in the new Land Act will be reduced on an average quite fifteen per cent., or to twelve shillings per acre; so that MR. CHAMBERLAIN'S PROPOSAL WILL, IN EFFECT, REDUCE THE ANNUAL INSTALMENTS ON THIS LAND FROM TWELVE SHILLINGS PER ACRE TO SIX SHILLINGS, A FURTHER RENT REDUCTION OF NO LESS THAN FIFTY PER CENT.!

"*BENEFIT TO THE IRISH CONSUMER.*—Such is the profit which will accrue to the Irishman as a PRODUCER; now let us consider Ireland's profit from the standpoint of her *consumers*. The Royal Commission on Financial Relations reckoned that Ireland contributed yearly £600,000 (nearly three shillings per head) to the Revenue duty on tea. Mr. Chamberlain proposes to reduce the tea duty by 75 per cent., which involves a reduction of Ireland's contribution to Imperial Revenue by no less a sum than £450,000 a year. Assuming, then, that a Liberal Government does not come in to upset the preferential system and re-impose the tea tax, this sum, capitalized at 3 per cent., represents a bonus to Ireland of fifteen millions sterling, a sum equal to the payment of *more than three yearly instalments under the Land Act on all the land in Ireland*, a sum in excess of all the profits earned by all the railways in Ireland during the past twelve years.

"Again, the proposed reduction in the duty on sugar will save Ireland at least a shilling per head per annum, or a further sum of £225,000 a year, and it may be possible out of the revenue derived from the ten per cent. duty on imported foreign manufactures to considerably reduce the duty on tobacco, to which Ireland contributes at present not less than a million sterling yearly.

"Of late years, Ireland, while exporting her own pigs, has been a large buyer of American bacon and American maize, for food and feeding stuffs. MR. CHAMBERLAIN PROPOSES THAT BOTH BACON AND MAIZE SHALL CONTINUE TO BE IMPORTED FREE OF DUTY.

"IRISHMEN! VOTE THE WHOLE CHAMBERLAIN TICKET! YOUR FUTURE AS A PROTECTED PEASANT PROPRIETARY, ENJOYING A MONOPOLY WITH OUR COLONIES, OF FREE EXPORTS TO THE RICH BRITISH MARKET INSURES YOU A FUTURE OF UNEXAMPLED PROSPERITY."

Astounding as this leaflet is in its shameless effrontery,

and in its contrast to all that was being told simultaneously to the "dwellers in the cities" of England, Scotland, and Wales, the most remarkable thing about it is that after a time it was withdrawn from circulation. And so little has been said about Ireland all through this Protectionist campaign that it may be convenient, before taking our eyes off this dazzling leaflet, to observe that, long after, in 1911, the *Morning Post* (May 27) recorded that "there is no doubt that considerable anxiety has been caused among Irish Tariff Reformers by what appeared to them to be a tendency to whittle away the original agricultural policy of Tariff Reform under the influence of Unionist Free Traders," and Mr. Austen Chamberlain endeavoured to calm the anxiety of the Irish Protectionists by saying to an interviewer from the same paper, "You may rest assured that the interests of Irish agriculture will not be overlooked by any Government which has to frame a reformed tariff." A great fall, that, from the definite promise of six shillings an acre more profit!

In writing, early in 1912, on another political subject,[9] Mr. L. S. Amery, M.P., though he admitted the enormous advance in the prosperity of Ireland under Free Trade, felt obliged to observe that "after all, the prosperity of Ireland is only relative." He said that because he wanted to add that "Tariff Reform will restore to Ireland the lost millions of her population, and restore them at a level of true well-being such as Ireland has never known." How? "To give adequate benefit to Ireland," Mr. Amery explained, "the Unionist Tariff of the future must be one which benefits agriculture."

When he went on to answer his own question, "To what extent can such a tariff benefit agriculture—and particularly Irish agriculture?" he set out the familiar programme of Preferential duties. He took upon himself, however, the responsibility of making considerable alterations in detail. "Very possibly," he hinted, the tariff "may not include any duty against Empire-grown beef, mutton, or bacon"; and there was to be also "a really substantial duty on barley," which Ireland produces in considerable quantities. If the brewers kicked—as they had already done in England when a barley-duty that was not "substantial" was proposed—Mr. Amery suggested that they be "compensated for any rise in price by a reduction of existing taxation," a confession, by the way, that duties do, indeed, raise prices. The Tariff Reform leader himself went over to Belfast on April 9 of the same year to repeat Mr. Amery's wise sayings. The return of a Unionist Government to power, Mr. Bonar Law observed, "will mean a change in the fiscal system of this country. And of all parts of the United Kingdom there is none which, in my opinion, will benefit more from such a change than Ireland. That system," he added, "will be framed with special and anxious regard to the interests of Ireland."

Mr. Amery made many foolish admissions in his book; but he did not make himself quite so ridiculous as did Mr. A. Bigland, M.P., who, speaking in his English constituency, where there are many Irish voters, made a courageous attempt to translate the value of this shadowy preference into figures. Mr. Bigland said that a "real settlement of the Irish question" could be reached only "by a 5 per cent. duty on poultry, eggs, and bacon that Ireland produces, as against foreign supplies," because then they would "get back from five-and-a-half to six million people within ten years." [10] The figures have a comfortable sound; but when it is remembered that our present total imports of poultry, eggs, and bacon from all sources, foreign and colonial, amount in value to about £24,000,000 a year, a little exercise in division will measure the prosperity to be enjoyed by Mr. Bigland's returned emigrants to a fraction!

The "interests of Irish agriculture" are now, apparently, to be satisfied by no more than a mere preference in the British market, for in May 1913 the Tariff Reform League's *Monthly Notes*, after reminding us that "Ireland is mainly an agricultural country," promised only this for her—that "Tariff Reform would secure for her a preference in her only market, Great Britain, for her agricultural produce."

So much for the Salvation of Erin! She cannot be saved by Protection because she is "mainly an agricultural country."

THE WELBECK SPEECH

WHAT splendid satisfaction would the British farmer have enjoyed if the "Salvation of Erin" gospel had been disseminated through the land. Nothing of the kind was done. The criticisms of Earl Percy and Mr. Lowther represented the opinion of a large part of the agricultural class. They were just a little jealous of the manufacturer, and they were puzzled by the contradictory advertisements of what they were going to get out of the Protectionist hat. In short, they wanted something much more definite from no less a man than "Joe" himself. Their mood was one of disappointed expectancy. They passed no such resolutions as they did when the movement went dead against them in 1913. They simply waited.

There is, however, abundant proof that their discontentment was known at the offices of the Tariff Reform League, and possibly the League felt it necessary, also, to take steps to force Mr. Chamberlain's hand. Early in 1904 (the Tariff Reform leaflets are not dated) the League issued a manifesto [11] which told the agricultural industry that if it failed to get a good "slice of tariff pie," the fault would be its own. "Agriculturists throughout the country must have heard with considerable satisfaction the announcement that Mr. Chamberlain has agreed to address a Tariff Reform meeting at Welbeck in August, and that his address will deal with their industry," said the leaflet. "Farmers have a right to ask how they may expect to get any good out of the changes he proposes in the trade policy of the country. It was natural that Mr. Chamberlain, who has been a manufacturer himself, and who sits for a manufacturing constituency, should make his appeal first to the manufacturers—both employers and workmen, of the country. But he recognizes that his case is not complete until he has shown how his plans will benefit the agricultural industry. It is the most ancient, and still the largest, of our industries. No industry is more sadly depressed; none has suffered more from a stupid fiscal policy."

Then came this advice. "Before Mr. Chamberlain resumes his labours, let farmers and rural labourers consider the outline of Tariff Reform which he sketched at Glasgow. Tariff Reformers will welcome reasonable suggestions from those who know where the shoe pinches. The Tariff Commission has been formed for the purpose of collecting and arranging information given by persons who know the different industries from the inside, including, of course, the great agricultural industry. The great thing is, that all who desire reform should enrol themselves *at once* in the ranks of the Reformers. Then they will have a right to a voice in working out the details of the policy. As a rule, the farmer is not a keen politician. He finds his chief interest in the land he cultivates, and unlike the pushing business man, does not anxiously watch the trend of outside affairs. This will not, however, do in the future. He must take an active part in the political battle which will shortly be raging, and he must make his voice heard in the same manner as do his brethren in the towns. The manufacturer does not hesitate to declare what he wants, and neither does he hesitate to insist on having those demands gratified. The agriculturist has many demands that he can legitimately make, and if he fails to voice them now, when the opportunity has arisen, he will have himself, and himself only, to blame, if he fails to share in the national benefits of Tariff Reform."

Agriculturists were bidden to "adopt a definite programme. Let them say, 'This is necessary to revive our industry.' Let them decide on their plan of campaign, and having done so, let them adhere to it through thick and thin. When the candidate comes in their midst, then is the time for them to decide whether he is the right or the wrong man to represent their interests. Let them discover whether he is an ardent Tariff Reformer; let them decide whether he is really prepared to support Mr. Chamberlain's proposals; whether he is, in fact, prepared to demand for agriculture the conditions which make for success, in the same way as will the representative of the manufacturing districts." Repeating Mr. Chamberlain's words, "You have an opportunity!" the agriculturist was told that it was he who has the deciding vote, and it was the agriculturist who should actively fight this battle. "He has more to gain than even the resident in the town, but he will have to buckle on his armour and make a good fight. . . . It is for the farmer to decide whether unfair foreign competition is to go on unchecked, whether in the face of agricultural depression, and a rural exodus which renders the obtaining of necessary labour impossible, he will 'take it lying down,' or whether he will rise, a fitting descendant of the sturdy British farming class, and insist on participation in the prosperity which we may well look for under a new financial policy."

The man who wrote that manifesto was one of the most skilful of all the plausible penmen the League has ever employed. It was a cunning blend of Chamberlainistic warning, flattery, and promise. It avoided blaming Mr. Chamberlain for having said so little; but suggested that he would say more if the farmers made him. It praised the boldness of the "sturdy British farming class," called on them to save their country, and told them they will have only themselves to thank if they failed to get their share of the national plunder. In a word, it bade the farmers "Squeeze!" The way to get what you want is to join the Tariff Reform League!

Nevertheless, the manifesto did not stay the clamour. The leafleteer was wrong when he assumed that the farmer was not "anxiously watching the trend of outside affairs." He was watching them very closely. Voices still protested loudly against the shameless official neglect of the great industry. It was more than neglect; to the farmer the ill-balanced policy, as far as it had been stated, was an attack on his business. A host of assurances was being sent forth to other classes, declaring over again that prices would not be increased to the consumer; and the manufacturer was being constantly reminded of the advantages of Tariff

Reform to his business.[12] But the farmer had to make the best of the unsatisfying 2s. duty on foreign wheat; and a 2s. duty on corn "was not much, but it was something," said Mr. Jesse Collings.[13] Even Lord Heneage, who from the first appears to have doubted Tariff Reform's ability to help, asked: "Where does agriculture come in?" And Mr. Richard Jebb, in a letter to *The Times* [14] sought to answer his lordship by saying that he himself, "as one dependent upon agriculture and a pre-Chamberlain Tariff Reformer, anticipated the following benefits from the proposed duties: (i) Relief of local rates; (ii) cheaper food; (iii) cheaper machinery; (iv) better markets."

That was a curiously intelligent forecast by Mr. Jebb of the meagre list of "benefits" upon which Tariff Reform has had to fall back, after all, in 1913. But the agriculturist believed in them no more in 1904 than he does to-day. It was not his ambition, as a class, to sell more produce at a cheaper rate. What about the extra "six shillings an acre"?

All this while nothing came out of the mouth of Mr. Joseph Chamberlain. Between his Glasgow speech and the much-advertised speech about to be delivered at Welbeck, the best the farmer could get from him was a casual but extremely significant observation in his speech at Cardiff [15] that "we have got so far that the best hope I have for the agriculture of the country is to be found in the increasing prosperity of the home market, in the increasing demand which will flow out from the town towards the country"; and a letter on January 5, 1904, in response to an easily imagined cry for something really useful, to the Unionist candidate in the Mid-Devon by-election. "The adoption of my proposals," he wrote, "would not add a penny to the cost of living, while it will ensure a moderate preference on corn, and especially on meat and dairy produce, which will help the farmers and the holders of allotments. If nothing is done—and I see that your opponent has nothing to propose—the greatest industry of the country will continue to decline." Even at that date—three months after his pig-programme at Glasgow, Mr. Chamberlain could do no better than announce that the preferential encouragement of Colonial competition in corn would "help" the British farmer. But by mid-summer he had pulled himself together for a more determined effort, and being by that time well practised in the performance of promising relief to every sufficiently noisy applicant, he made a bolder bid for favour than anything hitherto attempted.

Mr. Chamberlain's Agricultural Speech was delivered on August 4, 1904, in the Duke of Portland's Riding School at Welbeck Abbey. If the farmer rode him on the snaffle, the landlord rode him on the curb. "The watchword of the new policy which I recommend for your acceptance," he said, "the watchword in the agricultural districts is this: 'More profit for the farmer, more employment for the labourer, and cheaper food for his family.'" About the landlord, silence.

He covered his own blameworthy delay in starting to hoe the agricultural row by grumbling at the inadequacy of what was at that time taken to be the policy of Mr. Balfour's Government, upon which Mr. Chamberlain had ostentatiously turned his back: the "policy of retaliation," which, as he rather contemptuously said, was "a very good policy as far as it goes. But where does agriculture come in? The policy will help the manufacturer of this country to recover and to maintain his position, but how does it help the farmer, and how does it help the labourer? Yet, if you look, it is the farmer and the labourer who have suffered more than any other classes from the system to which I have referred."

There again, at the outset, was the customary indirect implication that the new fiscal system would directly benefit the farmer and his men, as nothing else ever had done or would do. It has always been possible for Mr. Chamberlain's supporters to take isolated passages like these from his speeches and print them in leaflets for popular consumption. They help to create the desired atmosphere, it is thought. As a matter of fact, Mr. Chamberlain found it no easier in August 1904 to deal explicitly with the agricultural problem than he found it before, or than has ever been found since.

How, for instance, did he deal with farm wages ? The labourers were told that the cause of the miseries of the Corn Law days was " not the price of corn, but the lack of employment and the lowness of your wages." The bait of higher wages was dangled more than once in the speech. " What you have to find is employment, plenty of employment, and the best wages you can get for that employment." Again, " My point is this—and I beg you to consider it—what you have to do if you want to improve your position is to see what system, what policy, will give you most employment and most wages." He declared that " the effect of Free Trade upon the labourer of this country had been disastrous," yet he was bound to admit that under Free Trade the wages of the labourer had risen, though not so much as the wages of all other industries combined ; and the labourer was left to infer—there was no definite statement to that effect—that Tariff Reform would increase those wages. Only, however, if the farmer were enabled to make more profits !

" As long as the farmer can make no profit, he cannot afford to pay you more wages, and, therefore, let me say that the interest of the labourer in this question is the interest of the farmer." " If the position of the labourer is to be improved," he explained, " the position of the farmer must be improved with it ; and the real point therefore is, will the proposals I make improve the condition of the farmer, and, under those circumstances, will the farmer be able to improve the condition of the labourer ? "

It has been urged by the wariest of Mr. Chamberlain's supporters that when he promised " more profit " to the farmer out of which " more wages " were to be paid to the labourers—nothing was said of more rent to the landlord—he did not mean that farm produce would be sold at a higher figure. It has been urged that his meaning was only that more produce would be sold, that the farmer's turnover would be greater, that he would be obliged to employ more hands, and so on, because the exclusion of part of the overseas supply would leave more mouths for the home producer to fill (though, to be sure, it had already been said that Tariff

Reform would also encourage the Colonies to fill those same mouths). That, however, was not Mr. Chamberlain's form of the argument. It was developed later in the controversy to a point far beyond Mr. Chamberlain's use of it at Welbeck. There, he felt it safer to say that his 2s. duty on corn would not raise " to any substantial degree the price of corn, and I do not think, therefore, that the farmer is going to get a great deal out of that." There were other means of profit for the farmer. "I attach more importance to a duty on flour," he said. " I propose to put such a duty on flour as will result in the whole of the milling of wheat being done in this country. From that I expect two advantages. In the first place, I expect more employment. This trade, which to a certain extent we have lost, will be revived. There will not only be the milling of wheat in the great ports, but we may expect to see mills started again in the country towns, giving employment to a large number of labourers in the district, and to that extent benefiting the whole of the labourers. The second advantage is that we shall keep in this country all the bran and all the offal, and, as you know better than I do, that will have the effect of cheapening feeding stuffs."

He repeated his illogical exclusion of maize and bacon, because " in any scientific tariff we must try to keep raw materials as cheap as possible," and the way to keep maize cheap was to keep the duty off it. He added to his list of excluded items manure, " whether it be natural manure or artificial manure " ; but he proposed to add dairy produce and preserved milk, poultry and eggs, and vegetables and fruit to the dutiable list. And once again, in the perpetual presence of the necessity of declaring that the producer was to be benefited without loss to the consumer, Mr. Chamberlain was compelled to take refuge in the statement that his proposals with regard to agriculture might " slightly raise the price of the articles affected. It does not at all follow that because they raise the price of the raw produce —of wheat, for instance—that they will necessarily raise the price of the manufactured article—of bread—but they may raise it somewhat, although only to a very small extent;

and that will, besides giving the farmer a slightly better price for his produce, help him to increase his production and to cheapen the cost of it."

It cannot be doubted that here Mr. Chamberlain meant that the farmer's costs would go down and his selling prices go up, even though slightly, and that, therefore, his margin of profit would be greater. A moment later he seemed to say the opposite. He argued that " any duty placed on the products of agriculture does not necessarily increase the price of food. . . . But if it does not increase the price of food, it does, in all cases, extend the production of food, increase the employment of labour, and cheapen the ultimate cost to the consumer; my proposals, therefore, I say, will bring to the labourer more employment, and will not raise the cost of his living."

There was a third stage of this delusive process. In this speech, wherein Mr. Chamberlain said that prices of food might be "slightly raised" and yet would not "necessarily" raise prices, he actually promised to get the increases paid by the foreigner! Again addressing the labourers, he said, " I want to do something more for him and for all the poor in this country. I want to reduce the cost of the living, and I believe it can be done under this system. These duties that I have spoken of will be paid in the main by the foreigner; they will be the foreigner's contribution—and it is a very small one—to our expenditure; but they will bring in a great number of millions a year. All these millions which come from the pocket of the foreigner we will give you back in reductions upon your tea and your sugar, and, I hope, upon your tobacco. We can afford to take off 4½d. per lb. on tea, and ¼d. a lb. on sugar—which is half the tax—and, as I have said, something on tobacco also. Now we will put tobacco on one side, and ask, What is the effect of the reduction upon tea and sugar alone? . . . I am assured that on an average every agricultural labourer's family uses two-thirds of a pound of tea and 6 lbs. of sugar in the week. If that be true, the saving upon the reduction on tea and sugar alone would be 4½d. per week to every labourer's family, and although that is not a great deal, I venture to say it is a great deal more than anybody else has ever promised you."

A good deal of space has been given to this far-off Welbeck speech, chiefly because it is the best that the Tariff Reformers have ever said for the agriculturist; but also because it is the richest example of the fratricidal confusion into which the application of Tariff Reform arguments to the agricultural case always impels the advocate. The peculiarities of those arguments soon became familiar to everybody. The foreigner would pay the tax on all food except maize and bacon. Nevertheless, the British consumer would certainly lose, and his losses were to be balanced by remission of taxes on tea and sugar. Millions paid by the foreigner would be handed over to the British public to make up losses which would never be incurred! In addition to this gift there were to be higher wages. Higher wages would be possible because the farmer would be getting better prices; yet the higher prices would not increase the cost of food because there would be so much more produced that it would be cheaper in the long run; and if his wages did not increase to each individual labourer, there would be more of them employed, and so the total amount paid in wages would be higher. The factors were never cancelled out in this way. Protectionist arithmetic is all millions and multiplication and muddle. In the programme of Tariff Reform it was asserted that the agricultural labourer would get

> Millions from the pocket of the foreigner;
> Higher wages;
> The benefit of lower prices;
> and 4½d. a week besides!

It was certainly "a great deal more than anybody else has ever promised you." Let it be registered as the high-water mark of Protectionist bribery to the man on the land.

There were many fussy and well-meaning attempts to explain Mr. Chamberlain's peculiar attitude toward maize and bacon. It is perhaps the best-remembered part of the Welbeck and Glasgow references to the nation's food supplies. Over and over again Tariff Reformers have been asked to say why the foreigner would pay the taxes on wheat and beef and not on maize and bacon. Mr. Chamberlain's reasons for exempting them was that the one is the food of pigs and the other the food of the poor. In neither case was the reason wholly accurate. In later years, however, a totally different reason for the exemption of maize forced its way to the platform. Mr. George Wyndham told a Liverpool audience in 1908 [16] that "last year we imported from foreign countries 50,000,000 cwts. of maize, and imported from our own British possessions only 3,000,000 cwts., and we cannot grow maize, I believe, in this country at all. So it would be foolish in this case, just as it is wise in the case of wheat, to make the foreigner pay in order to stimulate our colonies to provide for our needs at home. Now that difficulty is really over," added Mr. Wyndham, with a sigh of relief. But it isn't. To this day nobody has explained the bacon exemption. Mr. Wyndham's fatuous maize excuse does not apply to it, because even Tariff Reformers acknowledge the possibility of producing bacon in this country, and have actually promised to double the pig population by taxing flour, so that the pigs may have cheaper wheat-offal to feed on. Later on the Tariff Commission decided, possibly as the best way out of the difficulty, that maize and bacon must both be taxed.

One thing Mr. Chamberlain forgot to mention in the Welbeck speech. Hops! Accordingly, the Kent and Sussex farmers and hop-growers, in conference at Tunbridge Wells on August 19, "regretted that Mr. Chamberlain in his speech at Welbeck avoided all reference to the English hop industry, which employs more labour and capital than any other branch of agriculture." It turned out, however, that Mr. Chamberlain did not think it necessary to talk about taxing hops outside the hop-growing districts. "You will find," his secretary wrote to a correspondent, "on reference to his Welbeck speech, that Mr. Chamberlain spoke of the importance of placing a moderate duty on all agricultural produce except maize; and this, of course, would include hops, as well as fruit and vegetables. The district round Welbeck is not a hop-growing country, and there was no necessity to allude to it specially. Mr. Chamberlain assumes that hop-growers have taken the necessary steps to bring their case fully before the Agricultural Committee of the Tariff Commission."

That was one of the earliest examples of what may be called inter-industrial envy. In later years it developed one of the most despicable forms of the appeal to selfishness, fitting the promise according to local expectations. In the following year Mr. Chamberlain wrote to the Member of Parliament for the Tunbridge Division of Kent, that if the "new fiscal system were successful the hop industry should not be neglected"; and on this very conditional promise the Kentish Protectionists have tried to keep their spirits up ever since.

The year 1904 provided two instruments wherewith to test the efficacy of Mr. Chamberlain's proposals. An examination of them will enable us to understand the wail of Lord Heneage, who, writing to *The Times*[17] as an agriculturist, said, "I should be inclined to Mr. Chamberlain's views. . . if I could only learn where agriculture came in!" "In his speech at Welbeck," Lord Heneage added, Mr. Chamberlain "did not attempt to deal with the agricultural problem of the farming interest, or to show how the producers of corn, beef, and mutton will be affected by the scientific tariff to be framed by a powerful commission of trade experts in their own interests, and on which every trade is represented except the farming industry."

Before the Welbeck speech, as early in the year as January 25, the Lincolnshire Chamber of Agriculture passed the following resolutions:—

"(1) That it is inadvisable to support the proposition to place taxes upon foreign manufactured goods unless there is at the same time an undertaking that corresponding duties would be placed upon the products of agriculturists; that the meeting, therefore, supports the propositions of Mr. Chamberlain in their entirety;

"(2) That the undermentioned fiscal propositions be advocated upon manufactured goods: Articles of luxury, 10 per cent.; necessaries, 5 per cent.; certain raw materials (if any), 2½ per cent. *ad valorem*; upon farm products, wheat and barley, 2s. per qr.; other grain, 1s. per qr.; wheat flour, 2s. per cwt.; other grain meal, 1s. per cwt.; wool, meat, poultry, and dairy produce, 5 per cent. *ad valorem*;

"(3) That all colonial produce be admitted free ;

"(4) That local taxation be revised ;

"(5) That agricultural land be freed from taxation for roads, police, and education (houses and premises being charged with their proportion as heretofore) ;

"(6) That tea, coffee, drugs, dyes, and similar articles not in competition with home growers be admitted free of duty ; and

"(7) That to encourage farms to grow more wheat, and to hold it with a view to preclude 'cornering' and to prevent scarcity or famine prices, 5s. per qr. be allowed by the Government to all farmers holding their wheat in stock and threshing it out between April 30 and September 1 in every year—rural district councils to look after such allowances in every parish on behalf of the Government."

This is a frank attempt to see that the balance between the rival claimants for legislative favours was maintained. It was comprehensively in favour of the agriculturists who framed it ; and it was thoroughly Protectionist. It even included a duty on wool ! The suggestion of a "bounty" of 5s. per quarter was a revival of an old idea that was afterward rejected by the Tariff Commission, though that rejection did not terminate its adventures on the Protectionist platform.

A comparison of the Lincolnshire budget and the muddled proposals of Mr. Chamberlain at Welbeck will give some measure of the dissatisfaction prevalent in agricultural circles throughout 1904 and 1905. But before setting down the detailed evidence of that dissatisfaction, it may be well to refer to the collective opinion of another wholly agricultural county. On November 19, the Dorset farmers met at Dorchester, and the Joint Committee of the Farmers' Clubs of the country presented their report.[18] The Committee reported that the imposition of a duty of 2s. per quarter on wheat would not materially increase the growth of wheat in this country. They were of opinion, however, that a substantial duty on flour, not less than 2s. per cwt., would have the effect of reinstating the milling industry, while not increasing the price of bread. The report favoured the admission of all feeding barley free, but recommended that an import duty of 6d. per quarter should be imposed on all barley and other grain used for malting and distilling purposes. The Dorset farmers also asked that maize and oats should be admitted free except when used for malting and distilling. The Committee were of opinion that a 5 per cent. *ad valorem* duty should be imposed on meat, both dead and alive, and that, contrary to Mr. Chamberlain's proposal, bacon should be included in the term meat. The reason advanced for this was that the whole of the pork required for consumption could be produced in this country, and that, although the poor man is the consumer of bacon, he is also the producer. Mr. Chamberlain's proposal to impose a 5 per cent. *ad valorem* duty on all dairy produce was endorsed. The Committee advocated preferential treatment of the Colonies in respect of flour, but not in respect of malting barley, meat (dead and alive), and dairy produce, which should bear the same duty as foreign. A duty on roots used for distilling, and also on poultry and eggs, was advocated.

Thus the Dorset farmer, like his Lincolnshire colleague, made it quite clear that he wanted to be protected, if at all, quite as much against the Colonies as against the foreigner. He saw the futility of hoping for an artificial price that was worth anything to him for wheat, and concentrated his demand on higher prices for meat and dairy produce. It will be observed that neither in Lincolnshire nor Dorsetshire was any reference made to the wages question. That matter was contemptuously left by the practical farmer to the Tariff Reform politician. It would do to catch votes; it was not a subject for a moment's consideration in chambers of agriculture, where the labourer has no seat.

With the Welbeck speech and two typical farming counties' opinions before it, how did the agricultural class receive the scheme now? Naturally enough, the rank and file wanted to know a great deal about details. For instance, would the promised Protection stop at 2s.? Mr. Chaplin's attitude on that point was very significant. He took care not to close the way to an increase. At Sleaford [19] he refused to pledge himself to oppose any proposal to increase "Mr. Chamberlain's suggested tax of 2s. on foreign corn," or to oppose "the taxation of colonial foodstuffs."

Would feeding-stuffs be taxed? A vital question this,

in view of the determination of the Dorset farmers, for example, to protect the pastoral side of their industry rather than the arable. On December 23, 1904, Mr. Chamberlain wrote to a Devonshire correspondent to say that the question of putting cotton-seed and other feeding-stuffs on the free list was a very proper one for the consideration of the Tariff Commission. The Agricultural Committee of the Commission left it to the other Committees, which left it alone, and it was not till 1911 the Tariff Reform League issued a leaflet [20] declaring that "Tariff Reform will admit feeding stuffs and manures Free of Duty."

There had been plenty of references to the cheapness of wheat offals when the rural mills should be re-opened under Tariff Reform, and the Tariff Reform League had translated them into glowing promises like this: "Farmers, do you know what Tariff Reform means to you? It means cheaper feeding-stuffs for live stock." [21] But the farmer knew, if the Tariff Reform League did not, that there are other, and even more expensive feeding stuffs, besides wheat-offal. Cotton-seed, for example, mentioned by Mr. Chamberlain in the letter just referred to; and other seeds and beans from which the oil has been expressed. A huge trade is done in this "cake," as the agriculturist generally calls it. Perhaps, too, the farmer had read speeches like that of the Tariff Reform candidate for Hull, one of the seaports where the seed-crushing industry is carried on. "He would tell them," he said, "how the seed-crushing industry would be affected. In Manchuria, the place of the new Soya beans, seed-crushing plant was being laid down, and he warned them that unless they took steps to protect their industry by Tariff Reform, they would soon have in East Hull great competition from Manchuria. Was it unfair to ask the foreigner to pay a 10 per cent. duty? He thought not." [22] Hull evidently expected Protection in its own interests, and against the interests of the British cattle-breeder and grazier. At any rate, Hull Tariff Reformers thought it good business to hold out such a hope to the Hull electors.

Then, what about agricultural machinery? The agricultural machinery makers were represented on Mr. Chamberlain's Tariff Commission. Were they sitting there in their own interests as manufacturers, or in self-sacrificing behalf of their customers, the farmers? Not only that, but at this time the agricultural-implement makers were loud in their complaints at the low prices at which American machinery was being sold, in competition with their home-made articles. There was even talk of combinations of implement makers refusing to repair American machines, and so on. Farmers' organizations found it necessary to protest against these threats. The possibility of Tariff Reform sending up the price of ploughs and mowers and reapers and harrows was vividly present to the minds of the men who had to purchase such articles. One of them wrote to *The Times* early in 1904, demanding heavy duties on flour against all comers, foreign or Colonial, but "no duties on machinery, cakes, or manures."[23]

There is on record no protest by the British agricultural implement makers against these proposals to leave them "out in the cold." They felt confident in the promised Protection of manufacturers. From that category they could not by any means be dislodged. Tariff Reformers generally realized the strong position of implement makers, and tried to allay the alarm of the farmer by pointing out to him that he would make money enough under Tariff Reform to buy his machinery, to whatever price it might rise. This was seven or eight years before Mr. Bonar Law's faltering excuse at Edinburgh that home competition among the implement makers would keep down prices. In the early years the agriculturist could only be cured of his fears of having to pay out higher prices, by making him listen repeatedly to the assurance that he would make more money himself—an evanescent "benefit," anyway, but a definite encouragement of the belief that selling prices would rise under Tariff Reform. Still, this kind of argument did not satisfy the farmer. Either he was to pay away his extra profits in higher-priced purchases, or he was to get no more for his produce, while paying more for his needs. No; it was not convincing enough. On the other hand, the Tariff Reformer could not promise the farmer higher prices without jeopardising the town vote, and he could not exclude agricultural machinery from a protective tariff without making the agricultural engineers indignant, and generally playing false to "manufacturers." Accordingly, the Tariff Reform League took the line of trying to cover its weakness by strong language. It published an article [24] entitled "The Agricultural Machinery Bogey," declaring that "Cobdenites who attempt to humbug the farmer into the belief that a small duty would increase the price of agricultural machinery are neither ingenious not ingenuous." They were neatly dealt with, said the leaflet, by a recent correspondent of the *Chamber of Commerce Journal*, "who justly described the idea as 'absurd,' and gives the following example to prove it, 'Take the case of binders. If a farmer can buy an American binder for £30—they cost a bit more, but we will say £30—he can also buy an English binder for the same money. Now suppose a duty of 10 per cent. was put on the American machine,—it may be more, it may be less, Parliament will fix it—Mr. Chamberlain's figures are only suggestions,—that would raise the price of the American machine to £33 unless he paid the duty himself. Now does any sane person believe that the English maker will be such an utter fool as to raise his price up to the level of the American? Certainly he will not. If he can make machines at a profit now, he will be able to do so when the American has to pay £3 duty; and having that advantage he will be able to undersell the American, secure more orders, and thus make more profit without raising his prices. So the American will pay the duty, and thus relieve our internal taxation.' "

"Let the farmer remember," the leaflet went on, "that the foreigner will pay the duty, just as his own manufacturers pay the foreign duties on goods they want to sell in America or Germany. Let him remember, also, that the foreigner does not pay a penny of our present Cobdenite taxes on imports. He does not pay a penny of the duties on our tea, our coffee, our sugar, our cocoa, our tobacco. He does not pay our Income-Tax, nor does he pay a penny towards our local rates and taxes of every description. Is it not about time he contributed something towards the prosperity of the farmer's best market, which he has exploited so long unchallenged ? "

The foolish futility of this official editorial is proved by the knowledge that in 1913 it had not sufficed, even after eight years of currency, to remove the fear of unfair treatment from the farmer's mind. As a whole it was itself absurd ; for every farmer knew that a generous margin of £3 would never be maintained by the British maker ; and in detail it was contradictory, for the British maker was to secure the home market by underselling the American, yet the American was to leap the tariff wall by paying the duty and undersell the Briton ; and moreover, the contributions of the American competitor to our customs revenue were to " relieve our internal taxation." The market was to be ringed round by a tariff for the benefit of the British implement maker ; but the ring was to be broken down by the American competitor for the benefit of the British farmer. Opposing classes that had been in sore conflict over prices, were both to be profited by the same means.

It is one of the vices of Tariff Reform that it imagines the British farmer stupid enough not to see through the intentional deception of a jumbled-up argument like that.

The Dorset resolution demanded the protection of malting barley against all comers ; and it may be recalled that in 1903 Mr. Henry Chaplin—speaking in a malting district [25]—said " he was happy to think and remember " that Mr. Chamberlain's 2s. duty included barley. " He was informed by those who were best able to judge," he said, " that the soil of the Colonies was not suited to the growth of barley and was not likely to be so for a great number of years to come." But the protection of barley affected the users of malt, the brewers, who evidently did not accept the common assurance that duties do not increase prices. Messrs. Rhodes, Freeman, & Co., brewers, of Sheffield, wrote to the *Standard* to say, " We do not think it is understood, especially by the working classes, who are beer-drinkers, and we would therefore draw attention to the fact, that if Mr. Chamberlain's fiscal changes were carried out, the price of barley would be considerably augmented.

In addition to the proposed 2s. duty, competition, being narrowed, would have the effect of raising prices, and the poor man's glass of beer, besides his loaf, would be burdened with an additional tax"; and Messrs. Boorne & Co., of the Wallington Brewery in Surrey, in declining to supply information to Mr. Chamberlain's Tariff Commission, said, "We are quite satisfied that the proposals made by Mr. Chamberlain would burden us with about 2s. per quarter on malting barley and oats, and something on hops, perhaps, and would increase the price we now pay for plant, machinery, utensils, etc. If you say we shall be compensated for all that by a reduction on the beer duty, we answer that we are already entitled to the 1s. per barrel which was imposed as a war tax. Anything the House of Commons is likely to concede beyond that will be much more than counterbalanced by the loss of trade (home) which would result owing to the purchasing power of the great majority of our customers being diminished by the proposed taxes on corn, meat, and dairy produce, and the 10 per cent. protective duty on manufactured goods."

Mr. Bonar Law, in 1913,[26] imagines that the narrowing of competition will increase its intensity. Practical men of business know the opposite to be true. The barley-grower can only be protected at the expense of the beer-drinker.

The market gardeners, the fruit-growers, and the horticulturists felt sadly neglected by the Welbeck programme and the demands of the broad-acre agriculturists. Little had been said for them. So here again the leafleteers sought to repair the omissions of responsible men whose silence made the market gardeners uneasy. In 1903 the market gardener was not thought of. In 1904 the Imperial Tariff Committee[27] reminded him that "when trade is brisk there is more money spent by townsmen and others in the purchase of articles grown by small holders, market gardeners, etc.," and went on to ask, "Why should the foreigner, for example, send us so much of his asparagus, tomatoes, lettuces, potatoes, fruit, etc., when he will not let us send him these and other articles except at a prohibitive rate? Mr. Chamberlain's proposal for Tariff Reform will, if adopted, alter this in favour of the Britisher." In July of the following year the official organ of the Tariff Reform League,[28] in a summary of the Report of the Board of Agriculture Departmental Committee on Fruit Culture, grudgingly admitted that it was "quite conceivable that imports of oranges and bananas, and even of some competitive fruits, when British fruits of the same class are out of season, may have all the beneficial and stimulating effects ascribed to them," but went on to say that "there is all the difference in the world between such 'blessings of Free Trade' and importations of highly competitive foreign fruit, landed in this country in immense quantities, free of all duty, during or just before our own fruit season, and often at prices ruinously below our own cost of production."

That, again, was a clear enough hint that Tariff Reform would raise the prices of fruit. The same suggestion was made by the same authority [29] earlier in the year when it said, "It is difficult to understand how any market gardener can be found who prefers our present system of taxes on tea and coffee, and chicory and cocoa, and sugar and raisins—things we don't grow in this country—to a system which would transfer part of such existing taxation to articles like apples, tomatoes, or onions, upon which an import duty would be of some practical use to him, without in any way increasing the cost of living to the people of this country." In other words, the Tariff jugglers would reduce the price of tea and increase the price of potatoes. Such an advantage to the potato-grower was specifically promised by a Tariff Reform speaker in a potato-growing district of Lincolnshire, who pointed out that the German could sell "for £2 or £2 10s. per ton potatoes which cost the Englishman £3 per ton to grow." [30] Obviously, the Englishman would want much more than the German when the potatoes reached the market.

The standard summary of all these promises to the discontented elements among the cultivators of the soil was pronounced by Mr. Austen Chamberlain in 1906, in a speech at Canterbury dealing mainly with hops and small fruit.[31] "The question is," he said, "will Tariff Reform help you? I think it would. In the case of wheat-growing, I tell you frankly that no such small duty as proposed would, in my opinion, lead to the growth of any more wheat in this country. . . . But in the other articles which I have spoken about—in meat, in dairy produce, in bacon, in hops, in fruit—I think that by Tariff Reform we might give great encouragement to the producer, a great stimulus to native industry; that we might encourage the investment of energy and capital in this country, which is now going away to our Colonies or to the United States; that we might find employment for men in this country who are now forced to seek it elsewhere; that we might revive not only a great part of the cultivation which is ruined by the fluctuation and uncertainty caused by the operations of the foreign nations working from behind their own tariff laws—that we might revive a great part of that industry, and, in so doing, that we might bring a new prosperity to the little country industries, and to the country towns which draw their life from the prosperity of the agricultural districts in which they were situated."

Mr. Austen Chamberlain, without waiting for the Report of the Tariff Commission to which his father referred the hop-growers, did not scruple to paint the Protectionist future in those glowing colours. Apparently he was unconscious of his own flat contradiction of his father and of the Tariff Reform organizations. For while they held out prospects of a greater production of corn in this country, such as would bring "thousands of acres of derelict land" back to cultivation, Mr. Austen Chamberlain frankly admitted that the small duty proposed would not lead to the growth of more wheat.

Before leaving this review of the first volume of Tariff Reform promises and palliatives, it is necessary to say a few words about two other matters—the revision of taxation in favour of the farmer, and the granting of bounties. Both subjects were mentioned by the representative farmers' resolutions which have been quoted. The first important party statement on the revision of existing taxation was made at the annual meeting of the Unionist Party, held at Southampton in October 1904. At this meeting Mr. MacIver moved: "That, in the opinion of this Conference, the burden of local and other taxation presses unduly upon the food-producing and manufacturing industries of this country, and should as far as practicable be transferred to foreign importations of competing productions." This was seconded by Sir Carne Rasche, M.P., who consolingly described Mr. Chamberlain's proposals as being "good in parts." They were good in nine points out of ten, but the 2s. duty on wheat would not do much good. What was required was a 10 per cent. duty on all imported manufactured articles, and the proceeds devoted to taking rates and taxes off the land. Mr. Hope was afraid the last words of the resolution would be taken to mean full-blooded Protection, so Mr. MacIver accepted Mr. Hope's suggestion to delete the words "of competing productions," and in that amended form the resolution was adopted.

How the promise grew was well shown in a speech of Mr. Chaplin's nearly three years later, when he said that "with the revenue gained from taxing foreign goods it was proposed to relieve the burdens which now rested so heavily upon agriculture."[32] The proposal was, however, based upon the same slippery slope as the sister promise to pay bounties to British grain-growers out of revenue gained by the taxation of foreign importations—a proposal that the Tariff Commission rejected later on. For, if Tariff Reform was to keep competing manufactured goods out—and this was always to be one of its main objects—then the more those goods were kept out the less revenue, they would yield to pay agricultural taxes and bounties. Conversely, the more they yielded the revenue the less the manufacturer would be protected. The foreigner would, in fact, as the *Birmingham Post* pointed out long ago, "gradually cease to find the fund" from which the subventions were to be drawn.[33] It was a mirage. It was a confession that the Tariff Reformers were not courageous enough to insist through thick and thin upon the only thing that would convince the agriculturist of their sincerity, namely, an effective protective duty upon all the produce of the farm.

Conscious of this weakness, the Tariff Reform League did its best to restore the vitality of the programme. It loudly cried that the proposals already before the country were only "a first step." The *Agricultural World* had said that "while there is a great deal to rouse their enthusiasm in the Imperial idea which it sets forth, there is nothing to rouse agriculturists to much enthusiasm so far as their own industry is concerned."[34] Whereupon the organ of the Tariff Reform League "strongly demurred" to the statement. "It comes," said the League,[35] "of a too exclusive contemplation of the actual agricultural proposals of Mr. Chamberlain's scheme—the 2s. corn duty, the preferential duties on flour, meat, dairy produce, and the rest. Mr. Chamberlain has himself said that, except in the case of the flour duty, he does not expect any miraculous benefit to the farmer from those duties. On the other hand, we have never yet heard of the farmer who did not admit that each and all of them are distinctly better for him than the pure, undiluted Cobdenism of absolute free imports. Half a loaf is always more than no bread. And Mr. Chamberlain's proposed duties on agricultural produce may certainly recommend themselves to the farmer as a first step—the only step that has yet been proposed—towards placing his industry in a fairer position towards that foreign competition in respect to which Cobdenism leaves him absolutely defenceless. Give the farmer his choice, and he will prefer a 5 per cent. advantage to nothing at all. That is only business common sense."

To-day, the farmer is fuming at being offered a 10 per cent. *dis*advantage or nothing at all, and he is prudently asking for the latter.

THE TARIFF COMMISSION'S BARREN REPORT

SERENELY indifferent to all the unseemly wrangling going on outside, Mr. Chamberlain's Tariff Commission was diligently preparing its portentous Report on Agriculture. After considering the evidence of no fewer than 2251 witnesses, the Committee on Agriculture published its Report at the end of 1906. Its principal recommendations are reprinted here :—

"We are of opinion that, for removing the disabilities under which British agriculturists suffer, a change in the fiscal policy of the country is absolutely necessary, but if this change is to be permanently effective, it must be combined with measures dealing with transport, the enlargement of the powers of the Board of Agriculture, and local taxation. We are also of opinion that the position of the industry generally would be improved if means could be found to create further facilities for land purchase in the United Kingdom.

"We recommend in the first instance the restoration of the 3d. per cwt. duty (or about 1s. per quarter) imposed on cereals by Sir Michael Hicks-Beach. We propose, however, a preference to the Colonies, and recommend that the duty on wheat imports from all foreign countries to be 6d. per cwt. (or about 2s. per quarter) ; we also recommend that there be no rebate on the exportation of offals from imported wheat. The experience of this rebate during the year of its operation showed that considerable quantities of offals were exported to Denmark and other countries, thus benefiting their agriculture at the expense of ours. That no increase in the cost of living would follow from such a scale of duties is, we think, shown conclusively by the following diagrams, giving the prices of wheat, flour, and bread for the last eighty years. Here it is seen that although, taking the periodical movement of prices, the price of bread follows generally the price of wheat, the connection between them is not immediate; the price of bread lags behind the price of wheat, and the general tendency is for the price of bread neither to rise nor to fall so much as the price of wheat.

"Maize should, we think, be treated on similar lines, as in the case of other cereals, to those adopted by Sir Michael Hicks-Beach when the 1s. duty was imposed, provided that a preference be given to the Colonies by the levying of proportionately higher duties on foreign maize. Scarcely any proposal has excited greater interest amongst the agricultural classes than that for a duty upon imported flour and meal, which should be slightly higher than the wheat duty. All the witnesses we have examined attach the greatest importance to this proposal, and anticipate a great advantage by the cheapening of offals and feeding-stuffs. The evidence we have taken shows that in regard to milling machinery and the organization of the milling trade generally, the United Kingdom is not behind any country, but the industry would enormously expand and a great revival would take place were the above-mentioned proposal carried into effect. We recommend, therefore, a duty of 1s. 3d. per cwt. on foreign flour, the duty upon Colonial flour to be substantially lower, the exact rate of duty to be a subject of negotiation with the Colonies, provided that the duty as finally arranged gives an advantage to the milling industry of the United Kingdom.

"With regard to meat, including bacon, we propose the levying of import duties, the general level of which should be equivalent to about 5 per cent. *ad valorem.*

"The foregoing recommendation differs from the outline scheme submitted by Mr. Chamberlain to the country in one important particular, namely, the proposed imposition of an impost duty upon bacon. We have gone at considerable length and in great detail into this question, and we have taken evidence from all the interests affected. The general trend of the evidence is to the effect that even a very moderate duty on pork and bacon would encourage agricultural labourers and other inhabitants of the rural districts to breed and fatten pigs in greater numbers than at present. We are the more disposed to attach full weight to these representations because a policy which had this result could not fail to be of general advantage, especially to the poorer classes, who could find a profitable occupation in this branch of agricultural industry, and so add considerably to their earnings. It has further to be considered that the possibility of giving to the Colonies a preference on bacon would be a very great advantage in the arrangement of a preferential scheme, especially with regard to Canada, and the evidence we have examined shows that the arrangement we suggest would not be likely to lead to a rise of prices.

"We recognize that the United Kingdom will probably depend more or less upon imported food supplies, and that any material improvement of agriculture can be the outcome only of an expansion in the home demand. In these circumstances, British agriculture has much to gain from the extended Colonial market for British manufactures which would result from a system of reciprocal preference and the consequently increased demand for food produce in the British industrial centres. In the case of all the proposed duties on agricultural produce, we recommend that a substantial preference should be given to the British Colonies, thus opening up a wide area for negotiation. The exact amount of the preference on all articles except wheat must obviously depend upon the value of the return preferences which the Colonies are willing to grant, and are, therefore, matters for negotiation with them. We have recommended a registration duty on Colonial as well as foreign wheat, because by this method a large permanent revenue is guaranteed, and, as we have already indicated, we think the increase of revenue from the duties proposed would remove most of the difficulties in the way of adopting the new fiscal measure of agricultural reform which we recommend."

The foregoing summary is taken with purpose from the Tariff Reform League's special publication, *Monthly Notes*, for December 1906. It is part of an article fifteen pages long, prefaced by an "earnest hope" that all Tariff Reformers will buy the full Report for themselves at half a crown a copy, and make a point of studying the "abundance of valuable information which we cannot reproduce here." Among the items which the League could not reproduce was this short but marvellously pregnant paragraph No. 375) :—

> "The average price of British wheat for 1906 has been 27s. 9d., and *the evidence we have received is to the effect that no considerable extension of wheat-growing can take place unless the price is at least 40s. per quarter*, and to restore the growth of wheat to anything like its old proportions a rise in price to 50s. per quarter would probably be required. This would mean duties as high as, and in most cases higher than, those which prevail in the most highly protected foreign countries."

Little penetration is needed to see why the League left that significant admission of the meaning of the evidence it had collected lurking in the bulky volume, and feared to expose it to the popular gaze in its penny magazine.

"The Provisional Scale of Duties" with which the Report concluded will be found at the end of this review.[36]

On the subject of bounties, to which reference has been made above, the Committee, in paragraph 374 of its recommendations, stated: "We agree that no real improvement in the agricultural situation can be effected without considerable expenditure, but we may point out that although the decline is most marked in the case of wheat, it extends to nearly every other branch of agriculture, and in these circumstances it would be difficult to resist the claims of these other branches of agriculture for similar treatment. Secondly, if the bounty is so limited, it appears to us impossible to arrange any scheme under which the production of wheat would necessarily be extended. We also see the gravest practical difficulties in the way of administering such a bounty. While, therefore, we are heartily in sympathy with the end in view, we are unable to accept the suggestion for a bounty on wheat."

The Committee was careful to point out that the provisional scale was " only an indication of the nature of the scheme which may hereafter be recommended " when the Commission's inquiry into other " trades and interests " should have been completed and the Final Report of the Commission prepared. And, above all, the Agricultural Committee did not deal with two points which were of especial interest to the farmers. To the table of " provisional duties " was appended a very significant note saying that " the subject of agricultural machinery will be dealt with in the report on the Engineering industry, and in the Final Report. In regard to feeding-stuffs and fertilizers, the general rule would be that they should be imported free; but the subject belongs in the main to the Chemical industry, and will be dealt with in the report of that industry, and in the Final Report."

The Engineering Report succeeded that on Agriculture; but having by that time learned the danger of publishing details, the Commission wisely refrained from printing any " provisional scale of duties " on the implements of agriculture, or any other of the products of the engineering industry. In a summary of the evidence taken by the Engineering Committee, however, the Committee quoted the statement of a witness that " we think that a 15 per cent. to 20 per cent. tariff on agricultural implements would enable our British makers to command the home trade." The Chemical Report has never appeared. As for the " Final Report," which the Commission at this time confidently referred to with capital initials, it is not likely to be seen, if ever, until after the Tariff Reformers bring in their first Protective Budget, so that the farmer is not yet in a position to make even a prospective balance in his accounts. As a scheme of Protection for British agriculturists the Tariff Commission Report thus carries its own condemnation. Tariff Reform was " absolutely necessary," but could only be " permanently effective " if it were accompanied by many other reforms, such as cheaper and readier transport, lower rates, bigger grants from the Board of Agriculture, assisted purchase of land.

In this programme Tariff Reform looked like the cart put before the horse; and so it was regarded by the agricultural classes. Men who had thought 2s. useless, viewed with contempt the trumpery 1s. duty on the competitive products of the overseas Dominions. The difficulties of the Commission in framing a tariff that would go down with the electorate were exhibited in its anxious pleading that nothing it proposed would increase the cost of living, while all the time it had to make a good showing for the farmer, whose sole desire was to get higher prices and not to be compelled to pay the extra profits away on his purchases. The Commission's Report, if it can be accepted as the deliberate conclusions of an honest inquiry, was a condemnation of all the preceding promises of higher profits, better prices, and better wages. The only forecast of better times for the labourer lay in the claim that he would be able to add to his earnings by keeping more pigs. How often had the pig been called into save the situation? This time pig products were to be taxed. Mr. Chamberlain had promised they should not be taxed. The Commission's explanation of the change in the policy was that "even a very moderate duty on pork and bacon" would secure higher prices—they did not put it in exactly those words, but that is what they wished to be understood by the pig-keeper—and further, that such a duty would extend the basis of preferential negotiations with the Colonies. But the British agriculturist did not want any encouragement of competition in anything, bacon or wheat, from the Colonies.

Several witnesses before the Commission were strong on this danger. "A Colonial Preference," said Captain E. G. Pretyman,[37] "means selling manufactured goods to these Colonies, and buying agricultural produce from them—*i.e.*, benefiting the home manufacturer at the expense of increased competition for the farmer. I feel strongly that if a tariff is framed it should not put agriculturists in a worse position than they now occupy. I do not consider that these proposals are adequate." Indeed, an impartial reader of the Commission's Report could not help but see how unreal was the relation of the recommendations to the evidence. Perhaps that is why the Tariff Reform League has never sought to popularize the evidence. The official publications of the League have printed the conclusions (and not all of those); but people who wish to get at the mind of the Protectionist farmer must sift the statements of the 2251 witnesses for themselves. Doing so, they would come across such illuminating items as these :—

"Nothing but a bounty of 10s. per quarter on home-grown wheat will be of any benefit to us." [38]

"I am distinctly in favour of a bounty of 5s. per quarter on English-grown wheat provided the farmer kept it in stock until April." [39]

"There should be a higher duty on foreign, say 5s. per quarter, and 2s. 6d. on Colonial wheat." [40]

"A 5s. duty should be put on all foreign corn other than from the Colonies, putting a duty on them of 2s. per quarter." [41]

"Two shillings per quarter upon foreign barley is not nearly sufficient. Foreign flour should pay 5s. per sack to benefit the British farmer." [42]

"Put 10s. per quarter duty on corn and let the farmer have power to purchase his farm, and Government lend him money at 2½ per cent., repayable in thirty years." [43]

"Ought to be increased to prevent the price ever going down to less than 10s. per sack, as a few years ago." [44]

"If a duty of from 15 per cent. to 20 per cent. be put on meat and dairy produce, it would be of some substantial benefit to me." [45]

"Mr. Chamberlain's suggestions don't go far enough to benefit agriculture, but I regard them as the first step in the right direction." [46]

Again, fifty-three farmers in various parts of the United Kingdom state in so many words that the proposed duty would be of no benefit to them, and some of them oppose the change in the general interests of the community.[47] Forty-eight farmers state in so many words that the proposed duty would make very little difference to them; [48] while several farmers make the general statement that in their opinion the proposed duty would only benefit them if rates and taxes were reduced by the proceeds.[49]

The other side of the ledger is remembered by many.

"I fail to see any advantage; if we get a little more for our corn, other things we have to purchase will cost us more."[50]

"Anything that makes corn, cake, or any feeding stuff dearer will handicap me in producing meat; also manures, such as guano, if taxed, would handicap me growing fruit and hops. Any duty is so much more freight or railway carriage to pay. As I have no desire to go back to corn-growing, any duty will do me harm."[51]

"The recent 1s. duty on wheat took £50 per annum out of my pocket, because it raised the price of all my purchased feeding stuffs from 5s. to 8s. per ton, without any corresponding benefit to me."[52]

"Looking at it broadly, it seems to me the farmer stands to lose in any case."[53]

"Mr. Chamberlain's proposal would put us in the position of the farmer of the Western States of America. He lives under high protection for everything he has to buy, and Free Trade for what he has to sell."[54]

"There would naturally be higher rents, dearer labour, and everything which I purchased would be dearer. I should be in a worse position than I am at present."[55]

And the agriculturists' attitude toward Colonial competition was clearly marked out.

"I protest against any Colonial preference. Colonial corn ought to be taxed equally. The Colonies don't help to pay our taxes and heavy rates."[56]

"The admission of Colonial corn free is the weak part of the scheme. I do not believe in giving preference to relations in matters of trade."[57]

"From a farmer's point of view, there should be no preference to the Colonies."[58]

"The admission of Colonial produce free would be a serious disadvantage to our agriculturists, who pay rent, rates, and taxes, whereas in the Colonies there are no such burdens on the land."[59]

"The preference given to the Colonial farmer as against the foreigner may so stimulate Colonial production as to make competition with home produce in time even greater than it has been hitherto."[60]

"Supposing Colonial corn was admitted free of duty, English farmers would be quite as much swamped as at present." [61]

"I would not let in Canadian cattle free. How would you prevent American cattle being shipped from Canadian ports?" [62]

"If the Colonies are able to take full advantage of this preference, the British farmer will reap no benefit, as the Colonies will supply England with corn instead of the Americans." [63]

Nor did they leave the Commission in any doubt as to their opinions on the ultimate destination of the increased profit.

"If the land made more rent the landlords would get the advantage, not the tenant;" [64] and there is much other evidence of the same opinion in these passages :—

"The landlord would be able to get a little more rent as the effect of all the duties combined." [65]

"If prices are raised on an apparent permanent basis, their increase will in great part be discounted on any re-arrangement of rent." [66]

"Any duty would tend to make landlords demand more rent." [67]

"Labour and rents will rise." [68]

Even the witness who thought that he would benefit if the duty increased the price of his produce, "and it most decidedly would if big enough," said when asked about the labourer, "I do not quite know how the labourers would obtain a share of that benefit, for with farming as it is now I should say decidedly their wages could not rise for some considerable time." [69]

One is almost led to sympathize with the labours of a Committee that had to frame proposals to meet every objection, every expectation. Imagine the disappointment of Colonel Sharman-Crawford, of Crawfordsburn, Co. Down, Ireland, Chairman of the Council of the Royal Ulster Agricultural Association, who said in the course of his evidence that "the members of my council have all kinds of political opinions, but 95 per cent. are in favour of Tariff Reform. Mr. Chamberlain's scheme would benefit the whole country, and farmers, labourers, and all of us must get some of the profit. Ireland would gain more than any other part of Great Britain. It would enable us to open up land for the growing of wheat, flax, etc. . . . Much land which has been going out would come back into tillage again; more labour would be employed, and farmers would be in a position to give better wages, paying high wages if labour is scarce. This would stop families going abroad and into towns, as there would be employment for all the members." [70]

Colonel Sharman-Crawford evidently remembered well "The Salvation of Erin" leaflet. He could find small consolation in comparing the prospect of "six shillings an acre" with these apologetic and incomplete proposals of the Tariff Commission. The Commission's report was a tombstone for the Agricultural Protectionist's hopes. Many queer things are contained in it, and if it were possible here, they should be repeated. Let it suffice to refer to the ambition of a famous Lincolnshire potato-grower to increase the area under potatoes in order that a potato-spirit might be produced to be used as in Germany for street lighting, for house lighting by the poorer part of the population—how beneficent is the philanthropy of Protectionism!—and "as an ingredient in the manufacture of potable spirits." [71] In this way the Protection of potato-growers might even found a useful industry that does not yet exist in this country, add to the profits of spirit-sellers and the sensations of spirit-drinkers, and possibly even cheapen the price of lamp oil. It were stingy to refuse such a thoughtful potato-grower a little of the profits of Protection for himself.

Yet the outstanding surprises of the Commission's Report were, first its throwing over of the undertaking that there should be no tax on Colonial wheat, and second, its provision for a much heavier tax on flour than on wheat. It did not take long for the country to realize that these proposals would inevitably raise the price of bread, for they would increase the cost of the millers' supplies yet would protect him by a tax on all the flour from which bread is made. In 1910 an effort was made to repair the tactical blunder of the "registration duty" on Colonial wheat. But in 1907 it merely had the effect of turning the Tariff Commission's Report into political waste paper. The Report, in other words, left the Tariff Reform movement, in respect to agriculture, in as sorry a mess as ever. Anything like a water-tight scheme for the Protection of British agriculture is still to come.

Some prominent agricultural reformers have never ceased to recommend as principal measures those which the Tariff Commission set down as subsidiary. Mr. Jesse Collings, for example, has been one of the staunchest advocates of the first and foremost necessity of a system of land purchase for small farmers. Pursuing this cause, he has entirely subverted the accepted Tariff Reform argument that a 2s. wheat duty would help the farmer. In 1905 [72] he declared that "the farmer cannot grow corn in face of the competition of the whole world. If Protection were given him—and nothing short of 6s. or 8s. per quarter would be of any use—it would, I fear, be of no use to the tenant farmer. As soon as prosperity comes to the tenant farmer through Protection, the landlord takes advantage of it to a large extent, and sometimes wholly, by raising rents. Therefore Protection to an amount to be of any use, is impossible under our present system. My remedy is that contained in the Land Purchase Bill—namely, to turn the tenant farmer into the yeoman owner of his farm." Three years later [73] Mr. Collings raised his figure to 10s. "They could not help the tenant," he said. "If they were to give him a 10s. duty to-morrow on every quarter of wheat he raised, what would happen? In a very short time that 10s. would appear in the rent. It always had done so, and the consequence to the labourer was that when farming was most prosperous and rents highest, the labourers' wages were lowest; the farmer had as much as he could do to pay his rent and make a profit."

These admissions, made, as it appears, in order to emphasize the priority of another branch of agricultural reform, had their counterpart in various warnings that the British farmer must not expect too much from Tariff Reform. As if, after the Commission's Report, he was likely to!

Listen, for example, to the Rt. Hon. W. S. Kenyon-Slaney, M.P., saying in the House of Commons that "the last thing for which a man should support Tariff Reform was the idea that he was going to get an increased profit on his corn. It might give him advantages in other ways, but not an increased price for his corn," [74] and to the purely electioneering point of view courageously put by another Conservative Parliamentarian, Mr. H. E. Duke, K.C., who reminded an Exeter audience that a great majority of his countrymen declined absolutely to submit to a 2s. duty upon foreign corn, and that therefore "to my mind it would be idle and mischievous at the present time for the Conservative Party to introduce proposals for a duty on corn in the event of its being returned to power, say, within the next twelve months. There is no credit or advantage in being an advocate of a duty upon corn." [75]

There were many others who sought to avoid the stigma of price-raising, as Mr. Balfour's subsequent removal of the 1s. duty on Colonial wheat showed. The agriculturist found his crop of Protectionist promises badly set back by such a succession of frosts. Moreover, he heard leading Tariff Reformers, like Mr. Bonar Law, Mr. Austen Chamberlain, Mr. Wyndham, and Mr. Amery, affirming that the wheat duty was only proposed for the good of the Empire, and that it would encourage the competition of Colonial growers, and so actually keep the farmer from realizing those higher prices on which his heart was set.[76] Mr. Wyndham, indeed, was amongst those who swung right over to the side of the consumer—who, after all, is the electorate—and definitely foretold as a result of Colonial Preference, "a fall in the price of bread," and that "the price of meat will go down." [77] It mattered nothing to Mr. Wyndham that two years later [78] he was declaring that "only by Tariff Reform could they "safeguard the products by which small owners made a living." The compass had been boxed too many times to cause any surprise.

The straitened path into which the Tariff Commission Report thrust the Tariff Reform League brought the latter to a state that would have earned general pity if the sufferer had deserved any. Of course the League went on circulating most of the leaflets which have been referred to here. It continued to lay particular stress on the denial of bigger profits to the farmer. Politicians like Mr. F. E. Smith, who appeared to take his cue from the League's leaflets, repeated the assurance that "there must be a tariff designed to help agriculture just as much as manufacturing industry." [79] But the state of mind of the League's supporters was most accurately reflected in the "Answers to Correspondents" in the official journal of the League. Two examples from the post-bag may be cited, the one insisting with pathetic vigour on the "absolutely essential" necessity of Colonial Preference to the future prosperity of British agriculture,[80] and the other scarifying the farmers' feelings by picturing his condition if the wicked foreigner eventually (and before Tariff Reform saved the situation) "wiped out" the British manufacturers of agricultural machinery! "Such a consummation would inevitably be followed by a raising of prices." [81] No wonder the British agricultural engineer cried aloud for Protection.

The Secretary of the Tariff Commission, Mr. W. A. S. Hewins, went down to Lincoln [82] in the heat of this cross-examination to address the Lincolnshire Farmers' Union, a body that came into existence soon after the beginning of the Tariff Reform campaign and has since developed into a National Union of great influence. Mr. Hewins had had a chief hand in drafting the popular literature of the Tariff Reform League, as well as the sober reports of the Tariff Commission Committees. Face to face with critical agriculturists, however, he seems to have realized the impossibility of taking the popular line, for in the forefront of his address he put the necessity of raising revenue for the State. For this reason he refused to be bound by Mr. Joseph Chamberlain's speeches, and for this reason only, said he, the Tariff Commission had proposed a duty on Colonial wheat. The Commission proposals as a whole were, naturally enough, the text of his speech, and he warned his hearers that they must not expect a return to the high duties of former days, because there was no prospect of getting them, because they were not as advantageous to farmers as was often thought, and because it was desirable to dissociate the Tariff Reform movement from any such claim. What he meant, apparently, was that the farmers could not even begin to get what they wanted—could not even take the " first step "—so long as the country thought they were " on the make." There was one passage at " Question Time " that was illuminating. Mr. T. Robinson, one of the members of the Union, said he thought it was " a very unwise thing to give a preference to Canada, who was going to be their greatest competitor," for the preference might lead to Canada " flooding their market, and making the prices lower than they were at the present time." To this all Mr. Hewins had to say was that they could not prevent Canada becoming a powerful competitor either by adopting or rejecting his policy. Which was quite true.

The necessity of finding words to describe the condition of the Tariff Reform movement in these later years is saved us by the worried utterance of Major Coates, M.P. Speaking at the City Carlton Club in March 1910, he complained that " when his own election was complete, he went north, south, east, and west to help other Unionist candidates, and he found that the party needed a definite policy with regard to food taxes and Colonial Preference. In one place he was told to say nothing about such taxes ; in another, to declare that no duty would be put on Colonial corn ; and in a third, that a 1s. duty would be placed on that corn. There was no definite policy, and speakers did not know what to say. That confusion must not be allowed to continue. The party must have one clear policy on Colonial Preference."

It should be said, for those who like to observe the looseness into which all Tariff Reform speakers generally fall, that this use of the words " Colonial Preference " was a wrong use. Colonial Preference, by which the Colonies place lower duties in the way of British imports, already exists. What Major Coates meant was Imperial Preference, by which the United Kingdom would place duties on food now admitted free, in order to admit Colonial produce on lower terms than foreign produce. One of his worries was soon to be removed. In the following month (April 1910), Mr. G. L. Courthope, M.P., wrote to Mr. Balfour to say that "in the course of the last General Election there was some divergence of opinion among Unionists and Tariff Reform candidates and speakers upon the question of the 1s. duty on Colonial wheat. As you are well aware, the original proposal was to admit Colonial wheat free of duty, but some authority for a small tax was found in the recommendation of the Agricultural Committee of the Tariff Commission. In these circumstances it was not unnatural that a variety of opinions prevailed upon this question of policy. Without any desire to press you unduly for a decision on the point, if in your judgment the time has not yet come for a pronouncement, it has occurred to some of us that you may not be unwilling to give us an indication of your opinion, as the matter stands upon a somewhat different footing to the general details of a tariff scheme."

In reply Mr. Balfour wrote: "You are perfectly correct in stating that there has been divergence of opinion among members of the party as to whether wheat grown within the limits of the Empire shall be imported free or whether it should be subject to a small preferential duty. I have been giving the subject much consideration, and, after consultation with my colleagues, I have come to the conclusion that it should be imported free. This policy will, I believe, commend itself to the judgment of the British community, and will certainly be received with favour in the Colonies. It will not in the least interfere with the general agricultural policy of Tariff Reform, it will assist preferential arrangements with the over-seas dominions, and it ought to dissipate any lingering alarms lest the policy of Tariff Reform should have any material effect upon the price of bread."

As a matter of fact, the agriculturists had counted the 1s. corn duty as so little a thing—it is only a drop in the bucketful of taxes their representatives at the Tariff Commission had pleaded for—that they had no protest to make against its disappearance, not even when the Tariff Reform League, on April 26, unanimously welcomed the statement of Mr. Balfour, and pledged itself "heartily to support this policy." True, there was some discussion of the change in agricultural circles, but mainly because the farmers thought it a good opportunity for a political bargain, as, for example, when the Hampshire farmers [11] decided "to offer no opposition" to Mr. Balfour's proposals, but only "on the distinct understanding that a substantial duty is put upon imported flour from every source, so that the farmer and small holder shall have the advantage of cheap offal in local centres, and also that the country milling industry shall be encouraged." Evidently the flour duty proposed by the Tariff Commission was not considered "substantial" enough to double the pig population. And as the 1s. proposal pleased nobody, so its disappearance failed to satisfy anybody; for the *Morning Post* (June 21) bitterly complained that "the value of Tariff Reform as an agency of national union has been seriously impaired, if not wholly destroyed, by a concession which is unnecessary Imperially, and useless as an electioneering weapon." That is to say, there was not a single farmer who would say "Thank you" for nothing!

"THE WHOLE POLICY" OF SUBSTITUTES

TO go over the ground between 1910 and 1913 in detail would be merely to repeat, *ad nauseam*, the pitiful record of duplicity and disappointment. In these later years the Tariff Reformers have still circulated their promissory notes to the farmer and gone behind his back to discredit them in the ears of the payees. More and more has the preferential treatment of Colonial food produce been exalted as the only way to save the Empire, and British agriculturists have been bidden to look for salvation, not to 6s. an acre, but to those other reforms which the Tariff Commission so tenderly invoked. Emphasis has been laid on the building up of the Overseas Dominions on terms that would tie them to the mother country as customers for our manufactured goods, and so, by increasing employment in our factories, give the British farmer more mouths to fill.

Yet even on this point there has been the inevitable discounting from a prominent Tariff Reformer. For in a little book, written by the Editor of the *Rural World*, from which we have already quoted, there is a section dealing with "Mr. Cobden's Agricultural Sayings." The writer reminds us that in 1843 Cobden said: "The home market for food will be doubled," which is very much what the Tariff Reformers tell the farmer to-day. "Yes," retorts the Editor of the *Rural World*, "but of what avail is it to the British agriculturist when the foreigner supplies the market, which is what happens under the present system?"[84] In the eyes of the British agriculturist it matters little where the competing produce comes from. Mr. Bonar Law said almost the same thing as the Editor of the *Rural World* when he told a Manchester audience that though in his opinion Tariff Reform would benefit the farmer, "I do not think the proposed duty on corn would benefit the farmer in the least."[85] Lord Milner, too, when he was asked how Tariff Reform would benefit agriculture, replied: "It was true that in the only shape in which it was possible to propose it in this country, Tariff Reform would not directly benefit agriculture as it would benefit other industrial and manufacturing interests. Agriculturists, however, would secure a larger and more stable market, and would be indirectly benefited by the increased prosperity of the community." [86] And lastly, Mr. W. A. S. Hewins, the Secretary of the Tariff Commission, indicated that, as the time had at last arrived for something definite to be announced, he thought "a combined policy of Tariff Reform and agricultural reorganisation" would be both "practical and desirable." "In looking at the movement of opinion during the last ten years, he had no hesitation in saying that the adoption of an agricultural policy would be absolutely certain." [87] That was in 1910. Even Mr. Hewins could not foresee what would happen by 1913.

Another indication of the coming modification in the programme was given in 1912 by Mr. A. D. Steel-Maitland, M.P., the chief of the party organization, at Heath Hayes, Staffordshire. Outlining the two main proposals of Unionist policy, Mr. Steel-Maitland said the party thought they ought to tackle the industry and the land of the country together, and that they ought to tackle them by a Tariff Reform policy on the one hand and by a land policy on the other. The two policies ought to work in and out with one another to make the surest foundations for what ought to follow. He (being, please observe, on a public platform addressing voters) placed Tariff Reform in the forefront. They had to make industry firm and self-supporting, not subject to attacks from outside. Then they could build firmly and securely. He did not believe, however, that the farmers could really expect to sell their corn at a shilling a quarter more because of Tariff Reform, for so much was coming in from Canada.[88]

That this reversion of the order of Protectionist procedure was the measured decision of the Tariff Reform Party was also indicated by an editorial article in the official organ of the League in October 1912.[89] This article showed that the "machine" was very uneasy about the agriculturist. Tariff

Reformers had nothing definite to offer him except the prospect of lower prices for his products and heavier out-goings for his purchases. Consciousness of the inadequacy of this offer as a vote-catcher led the Editor of the League publication to go a little further than usual, and say (on page 231) in an article addressed to agriculturists, that " Tariff Reform, as applied to agriculture, means not only the imposition of a small tariff on foreign products, but includes the whole agricultural policy sketched out by the Tariff Commission and adopted by the leaders of the Unionist Party. It involves measures dealing with small ownership, with transport, with local taxation, and generally with the removal of the disabilities under which British agriculturists suffer. While British agriculture would be thus fostered and developed, the policy of Imperial Preference would encourage Colonial production by giving a tariff preference in our market to the products of the Empire."

On page 234 of the same issue, in an article addressed to industrial working-men, who must not be alarmed by the prospect of dear food, the alleged effect of Imperial Preference on British agriculture was said to be that " by means of Imperial Preference they (Tariff Reformers) would develop the food resources of the Empire, and thus secure an abundant supply of wheat and other foodstuffs. It is obvious that increased supplies must mean cheaper food. More food cannot mean dearer food."

On page 238 (in an article on the German agitation against food prices) it was tantalizingly and truthfully pointed out that " the high German duties (on foodstuffs) were imposed with the deliberate object of protecting German agriculture by the limitation of imports." How such an admission must have made the British Protectionist farmer's mouth water! But his hopes were coldly dashed on the same page by the stout declaration that " no responsible Tariff Reformer has ever suggested the imposition of duties high enough to raise the price of food to the consumer."

No; the farmer must be content with a flat denial of the " benefits " of Protection for which he had voted so often. " The prosperity of agriculture in this country must depend not so much upon a protective tariff as upon the carrying out of the whole agricultural policy of the Unionist Party, and on the larger *and more profitable* markets which increased industrial prosperity under Tariff Reform must bring" (page 239). The addition of the words italicised to this well-known and worn-out argument indicated the anxiety of the Tariff Reformer when he wondered again what in the world he could promise to do for the British farmers. How could cheaper food be more profitable to the food producer? The first con structive work of the party, remember, was to be a protective tariff, and the first effect of the tariff, in their view, would be to enable the Colonies to beat down the price of foodstuffs in the British market. Thereafter the British farmer must wait till the party find time and opportunity to turn the pious opinions of the Tariff Commission into realities, alter the land-purchase system, lower the cost of transport, reform local taxation, and "generally remove the disabilities under which British agriculturists suffer." It was a painfully slow way round, when the short cut of a thumping tax on wheat might have made it so much quicker.

There is ready to hand a very convenient test of what the agricultural industry thought of the majority of the non-fiscal reforms that were now becoming the substitute for the wheat duty. Mr. J. L. Green, who has spent many years of his life in association with Mr. Jesse Collings in advocating the extension of the allotment and small-holding system, has written a book (which has been already quoted) enthusiastically in favour of Tariff Reform. It is entitled *Agriculture and Tariff Reform.* It deals with most of the agricultural problems on large and small farms, as well as on allotments, and deals with them consistently from the Protectionist point of view. The greater part of the book was written before Mr. Chamberlain spoke at Welbeck in 1904; but a second edition was published in 1911, and that edition may be taken as a fair statement of the Tariff Reform policy as applied to agriculture in that year. The author is the editor of *The Rural World* and Secretary of the Rural League, of which the Rt. Hon. Jesse Collings, M.P., is the President.

In his preface, Mr. Green writes that "it would appear that

there are those who hold the opinion that so long as the urban trades and manufactures flourish, all is well." He makes it clear that this is not his opinion, though whether his opinion will undergo the same alteration as that of Mr. Bonar Law, we shall probably see in a later edition, which, it is understood, is now being prepared. A section of the book to which it is necessary to draw particular attention is a scornful summary of many of the alternative proposals which the Tariff Commission placed *after* Tariff Reform, but which subsequent events have placed *before* Tariff Reform. This section, therefore, which Mr. Green entitles, "Objections Answered," provides a useful standard wherewith to test the sincerity of the latest revision of the Protectionist agricultural programme.

"Of what avail," asks Mr. Green, "is *Education*, whether to a townsman or to a farmer, if, when he has obtained it, he is driven out of the market by the foreigner? Education will not get one over the foreigner's tariff wall! . . . So long as a foreign farmer makes a good price at home in his own country, he can undersell the Britisher, and gradually wipe him out of existence." So much for this agricultural authority's estimate of the value of education compared with the value of Tariff Reform. He goes on to say that it is "a favourite suggestion of some people," that the farmer should *Farm Better*. It is a maxim which he thinks may be applied to small holdings, "but it is not applicable to any general extent to the average farmer or to the farm lands of this country." As to *Railway Rates*, he thinks it would be a mistake to suppose "that a slight reduction on the carriage of milk, or on that of other produce, would at the end of the year put the farmer in the position he ought to occupy, namely, one of fair competition all round with the foreign producer." He does not think it possible that *Rents* should be lowered; *Co-operation* and the extended use of labour-saving implements he regards as of no avail without Tariff Reform; no *Amendment of the Agricultural Holdings Act* dealing with tenure and improvements "could by any stretch of reasoning enable the farmers to compete with the foreigner under our present absurd fiscal conditions"; and as to the suggestion that "a sufficient remedy for agricultural depression is to adopt the *Small*

Holdings system," Mr. Green emphatically, though without a shred of evidence to support him, says that "if we had a huge increase in small holdings, the cultivators of them here, as abroad, would take precious good care that they had Tariff Reform, because to them Tariff Reform would be of special utility!"

One thing is clear above all others in this sordid story of Protectionist shuffling. It is that the Protectionists dare not promise the agriculturist the one thing he has demanded most insistently. The united genius of the party has failed to find a formula to please the farmer and not offend the general public. The dilemma that Mr. Balfour saw in 1903 confronts them as mockingly as ever in 1913. Mr. Balfour, in the meantime, had given place to Mr. Bonar Law in the leadership of the party. When Mr. Bonar Law tried his hand at framing programmes to please everybody he blundered woefully, and he blundered most of all on the question of the protection of agriculture. Now, Mr. Bonar Law had already declared "that the Protection of agriculture is past, that the time for it has gone."[90] Still, everybody realized his vain-glorious confidence in his own ability to popularize Tariff Reform, and the Tariff Reformers were quite cock-a-whoop when, on November 14, 1912, at the Albert Hall, first Lord Lansdowne and then Mr. Bonar Law declared that they still stood by food taxes. To the agriculturist, however, these courageous declarations were more than usually disappointing. Consistently had they been told that the money raised by "taxing the foreigner" would be devoted to relieving the farmers' rates. Both Lord Lansdowne and Mr. Bonar Law now reverted to Mr. Chamberlain's original idea, and undertook to divert them to the "working classes," who, by the way, had thrice rejected a similar bribe.

Lord Lansdowne said: "We will undertake that any revenue raised from taxes of this kind on food shall not be treated as ordinary revenue, but shall be used for the purpose of alleviating other burdens falling on the shoulders of the working classes." To this Mr. Bonar Law assented. "We shall not treat any revenue derived from so-called food taxes, whatever they are, which may be imposed for preference, as ordinary revenue. We shall use it to diminish the burdens which in other ways are falling upon the poorer class of this country. It will not be an addition to taxation, it will be a readjustment of taxation. And owing to this revenue, and owing to the expansion which I am certain will come with this change of system, I say that, instead of adding to the cost of living, the adjustment which we shall make will make the burden smaller and not larger that falls upon the working classes."

Neither of them, however, cared to specify what these food-taxes should be, nor even whether they meant to admit Colonial produce free or not. It became necessary to put a very pointed inquiry to them. Accordingly, Sir John Simon publicly asked: "What we want to know is, whether or not the responsible leaders of the Tariff Reform Party propose to put a tax upon any Colonial products—for instance, do they mean to tax Colonial flour, or beef, or mutton, or barley, or oats, or fruits, or cheese? Mr. Bonar Law is going to make a speech on Monday; and as Lord Lansdowne asserted the other day that Unionists desire to put the policy 'plainly and frankly before the people of this country,' we look forward to an explanation from Mr. Bonar Law as to whether it is his policy to tax any, and which, Colonial products." [90a]

Rudely pushed aside as he had been, yet this question remained one of moderate interest to the British farmer, because he still felt that Colonial competition against him ought not to be definitely encouraged by any change in our fiscal laws. And though Sir John Simon put the question more in the interest of the whole public, it is necessary to deal with it here because it led up to the blind plunge in which Mr. Bonar Law frantically threw off all pretence of protecting agriculture, and brought the Tariff Reform movement to a temporary standstill. He made a speech at Ashton-under-Lyne on December 16, 1912, but he did not attempt to answer Sir John Simon's question. Instead, he took another step towards the destruction of the agricultural hope. He undertook that if they were returned to power as the result of a General Election, the Tariff Reform party would at once proceed to impose an "average 10 per cent." tax on manufactures; but that the agriculturist, who, like everybody else, would have to begin to pay extra prices for his requirements as soon as those taxes were imposed, must wait an indefinite time for Protection for himself. The "remission" argument was not found convenient in this connection. Summarized, the astonishing idea Mr. Bonar Law put forth at Ashton-under-Lyne was this: We have not abandoned the food taxes. What we intend to do is to call a conference of the Colonies to consider the whole question of preferential trade, and the question whether or not food duties will be imposed will not arise until those negotiations are completed. Unless the Dominions regard them as essential for Preference, then also the food duties will not be imposed. All we ask is that our countrymen should give us authority to enter into that negotiation with power to impose certain low duties on foodstuffs within strict limits, which will never be increased. Long before the next election comes you will know precisely within what limits we want authority. Those limits will never be exceeded by us in any Parliament until we have received the express sanction of the people of the country. If the Dominions do not think these duties necessary they will never be imposed.

Mr. Bonar Law's only allusion to Sir John Simon's question was that it was impossible "to give in detail really what we mean to do." "The details will only be known," he said, "after the negotiations have been completed."

The present section of this record deals, remember, only with such parts of the Tariff Reform record as have affected the agriculturist. The bungling speech at Ashton called forth a unanimous protest from overseas. "The Dominions, without exception, do not wish Great Britain to tax corn," was the *Daily Mail's* summary of that protest.[91] Away went the last straw of hope that the Tariff Reformers meant business with the British agriculturist. Promptly the Farmers' Union registered the determination of its class to have nothing to do with a fiscal policy that left their position "in doubt." At the annual meeting of the Lincolnshire branch of that Union, held in January 1913, it was unanimously agreed that, "In view of the resolution passed by the National Farmers' Union, and the recent statement by Mr. Bonar Law on Tariff Reform, which leaves the position of agriculture in doubt, this committee declares that it will be no party to any change in our fiscal policy that excludes agriculture from its benefits." On February 26, the central body, the National Farmers' Union, passed the same resolution, which was afterwards adopted by branches all over the country.

As one of the Lincolnshire speakers to the resolution in which this determination was embodied said, "Mr. Bonar Law had declared that the taxation of food should not be part of the Conservative programme for the next General Election. They could not afford to ignore this. For if this idea was carried they would be in an infinitely worse position than they were to-day under Free Trade. Whilst he had his own opinions on Tariff Reform in general, a one-sided Tariff Reform of this kind would be one of the most detrimental things that could happen to the English farmer. He would have to pay more for the things he imported, wages would rise, and he would have to sell his produce in the open market of the world. If the farmer was to keep his head above water, he must see that no Tariff Reform should take place which did not include agriculture." [92]

The general political effect of Mr. Bonar Law's speech was explosive. There was a full month of angry recriminations in the Tariff Reform press and on the Tariff Reform platform. The food-taxes became once more the centre of a vivid storm; and the agriculturist sat by helplessly watching the lightning and listening to the thunder, and fearing for his crops and herds. Some of the paper disputants remembered him occasionally. The *Pall Mall Gazette*, for example, on December 19, insultingly tried to console him by an offer of the customary bunch of thistles. "The Unionist policy, as expounded by Mr. Bonar Law at Ashton-under-Lyne," said this fire-eating Protectionist paper, "is manifestly incomplete in its bearing on the agricultural community"; and, after condemning *laissez-faire*, and suggesting the possibility of giving bounties to grain-growers, the journal added that the Unionist policy of agriculture could not be too soon presented to the country with all necessary force and clearness. Some papers, like the *Nottingham Guardian*,[93] which has always been a faithful friend of the farmer, told him frankly that "Mr. Bonar Law's speech marks the end of the proposal to place a tax on either foreign meat or foreign corn so far as the present generation is concerned." Others saw in the situation signs that the Tariff Reform party "will be out for twenty years"; [94] and Mr. J. L. Garvin [95] reminded Mr. Bonar Law that even Bismarck "explained, in a famous speech, that when there is a tariff for manufacture there must be a tariff for agriculture—the 'parallel' system, as he expressed it—and that agriculturists will never support a tariff which excludes them from its benefits;" following that obvious truth with the declaration a week later that "rural voters will never tolerate a tariff only on what they buy with none for what they produce. Without a reasoned agricultural scheme as part of it, the whole Tariff Reform policy would be impossible."

On the day the resolution of the Lincolnshire Farmers' Union was published, the Nottingham paper already quoted advised farmers that they "had better leave the subject of Tariff Reform where it is for the moment." *The Times*, a little more encouraging, pointed out that "the two chief conditions which make them (food-taxes) undesirable as well as unpopular at the present moment, will first have to be modified. There will have to be, that is, a change in the general movement of food prices, and there will have to be a great increase of agricultural production in these islands." In the meantime, 232 Tariff Reform Members of Parliament had presented a memorial to Lord Lansdowne and Mr. Bonar Law, to which those "leaders" replied on January 15, 1913, agreeing "that if, when a Unionist Government has been returned to power, it proves desirable, after consultation with the Dominions, to impose new duties on any articles of food, in order to secure the most effective system of Preference, such duties should not be imposed until they have been submitted to the people of this country at a General Election."

But even here there was nothing to reassure the agriculturists. They had now definitely become the scapegoats of the party's frenzy of food-tax fright. Many attempts were made to mollify them; but nothing could get over the grievance that their interests had been postponed to those of the manufacturers. To deepen their resentment at this unfair treatment, Mr. Bonar Law made another clumsy attempt at Edinburgh, on January 24, to demonstrate how much better it would be for the agriculturist to leave his fate in the hands of the party that for nearly ten years had not shown pluck enough to propose out-and-out Protection for the most-talked-of industry of them all. In this speech Mr. Bonar Law thought to encourage confidence by declaring that "if the present scheme of Tariff Reform does exclude agriculture from its benefits, every farmer will be justified in opposing it."

That was his soft answer to the Lincolnshire resolution. How little it availed to turn away wrath may be gathered from the statement of Mr. Dean, the Chairman of the Lincolnshire Farmers' Union. "Yet another matter of extreme and pressing importance to farmers of every shade and condition," wrote this representative agriculturist, "is the sudden change of policy on Fiscal Reform which, if carried into effect, will place the agricultural interest in a very grave position, and not the least serious feature is the scant consideration which has been given to those interests, if, indeed, any serious consideration has been given at all. Imperial Preference has been abandoned, and a preference for manufacturers and their workmen substituted. Could a more inopportune moment have been selected for that change, seeing that manufactures are in a state of great prosperity, their workmen fully employed at remunerative wages, whilst agriculture, the only depressed industry in the country, is thrown over. We may readily draw our own inference from that sudden change of policy. The Farmers' Union never had a greater opportunity of asserting itself, and, indeed, would have been false to the interests of those it seeks to represent had it not taken immediate action, which, I am glad to state, the Lincolnshire Farmers' Union did in forwarding the following resolution to Mr. Bonar Law: 'That this Union will be no party to any change in the fiscal policy of this country that excludes agriculture from its benefits.' Justice demands that all shall be treated alike, or else not treated at all. If, then, we cannot have Imperial Preference, we had better remain as we are, under the system of Free Trade. That resolution has elicited a lengthy reply from Mr. Bonar Law in his speech in Edinburgh. Whether it will satisfy the farmers is another question; to my mind, his alternative benefits, which he foreshadows in that speech, are purely imaginary and nothing decisive."[96]

There is an indication in this dignified request for equal treatment for both, or none for either, that the agriculturist is not now in the mood to press for Protection as keenly as in former years. His ardour is damped. In 1913, Mr. Chaplin, full as he is of sound and fury signifying nothing, is no longer the ideal representative of the British farmer. Agriculture has become, under the management of strong men of business, as so many farmers now are, a profitable industry. The protective prop is no longer really necessary to save them from ruin; they have as good a home market as any food-supplier can desire, and they understand the science of farming better than their fellows, as a class, in any part of the world. While for ten years Tariff Reformers have been fumbling for a formula that would tickle the farmer's fancy, the farmer has gone about his work in quiet contempt of such trumpery platform tricks, until at last his attitude has become one of fixed, almost stern, disregard. To-day he does not ask for Protection, because, first of all, he does not need it, and also because he has calculated that any attainable measure of Protection is just as likely to harm as to benefit him; his better business methods have led him to realize that there are two sides to his ledger. But he is determined to see that no other class shall secure State benefit at his expense. Instead of being a clamorous advocate of Protection, the farmer has become its most watchful critic. In the hands of a party that cuts its programme into all sorts of shapes to meet the varying demands of all sections of the electorate, a tariff is exactly what Mr. Taft called the United States tariff, a hit-or-miss affair.

At present—and as long as the memory of the past ten years' evasions remains—Tariff Reform is suspiciously regarded by the farmer as his enemy. That is all Mr. Bonar Law has done for his party. In side-tracking food-taxes he has written first on his list of beneficiaries, not the agriculturist, but the manufacturer. And the former therefore cries, " Equal treatment or none."

Specifically, Mr. Bonar Law postponed the direct fiscal benefit of food taxes to a second election. To that the farmer would perhaps agree if the benefits of other taxes to other industries were postponed likewise. The indirect benefits Mr. Bonar Law mentioned, though he probably meant to include all the others we have recorded, were that if his party came into power it would foster sugar-beet growing, encourage small owners, assist tenants to buy their farms, and relieve rates! A paltry list, that may take many years to carry out —while the other industries would all the time be getting their hands in the farmers' pockets—and a list, moreover, that arouses no spark of enthusiasm in the farmer's breast. He is not a faddist; what does he want with beet?

Inadequacy and injustice are not the only faults of Mr. Bonar Law's new policy. He was foolish enough to make excuses. He said, " We are told that everything that a farmer buys will cost him more, and in what he sells he will get no benefit. What truth is there in that? The farmer does, it is true, buy agricultural implements, but he does not buy them very often in the course of his life, and they are mostly made at home, and after the change, as before, there will be free competition in the home market." But does the farmer only buy agricultural implements? And does he always buy British ones? Has it not been often told how the poor British machine-maker is being dumped out of existence by the protected foreigner; and that a 15 to 20 per cent. duty is necessary to keep imported machinery out? Does the farmer not sometimes buy manufactured oilcake, and manure, fencing, and twine, and tools, and other things of this sort, to say nothing of the manifold needs of his family? Are they all of British make? If so, the Tariff Reform League will have to make a big bonfire of those leaflets which assure us that foreign competition is stifling our home producers. For here was its own great champion actually belittling the extent of foreign competition in agricultural machinery! Moreover, he sought palliatives, and used them in so timid a way that the whole country laughed at him. Compare the following halting passage from Mr. Bonar Law's Edinburgh speech—noting its " ifs " and its " tends "—with the strident, though forced and insincere Welbeck utterance of his predecessor, the man who had definitely said his policy could not be carried out without a tax on food : " If the result of a tariff is as we believe it will be, and if we did not believe it we should not advocate it—if it is to improve employment, to tend to raise the level of wages, then by increasing the earning power of the people, and so increasing their buying power, the one market open to the farmer will be increased and made infinitely more valuable than it is at present."

And, last of all, Mr. Bonar Law held up to the British agriculturist the splendid examples of Denmark, where " there is an industrial tariff, though a very small one, and practically no duties on agricultural produce " ; and Belgium, where also " there is an industrial tariff higher than we mean to impose and there is no duty on wheat and very few and small duties on any other agricultural produce ! " The promised protection had vanished quite away !

There was a sort of dying spasm of protest ; but it counted for little more than a register of the utter failure of the Tariff Reformers to keep their promises. Agriculturists raised their voices once more against this definite exclusion from the expected " benefits " of Protection. They did not use that word in a general, hypothetical sense. Other people's money in their pockets was their idea of Protection. When the tariff pie is cut up every clamorous industry must have a slice. The Protectionist *Globe* [97] drove home this point when it assured the farmer that " the Unionist Party, through its leader, offers him a policy of real betterment, which will do much to tide him over those first years of Tariff Reform," during which there is to be pie for the manufacturer, but only sour grapes for the farmer. And Mr. George Wyndham, M.P.,[98] admitted the same ignoble sentiment when he said that "the permanent welfare of our industrial artisans cannot be assured if we leave agriculture in the lurch." At the annual meeting of the Shrewsbury Branch of the National Farmers' Union, Mr. E. Goodwin Preece said : " The direct financial benefits farmers were going to get from those proposals (Mr. Bonar Law's Edinburgh proposals) would not be equal to the benefits manufacturers would get." [99] There was no sentiment about that. At the Alton, Hants., branch of the same Union, Mr. Block, the Hon. Secretary, declared that "they as farmers were not going to be deprived of any favours when Tariff Reform did come forward." [100] An agricultural journal, *Farm and Home*,[101] demanded that the Unionist Party should definitely state without loss of time what *quid pro quo* the farmers were to get. The Worcestershire Chamber of Commerce passed a resolution that the exclusion of agriculture would be "unfair." [102] The Staffordshire Chamber of Agriculture boldly used the fearsome little words, "food-taxes," in a resolution declaring that "no system of Tariff Reform can be supported by landowners, farmers, or agricultural workers which does not provide for a rearrangement of the food taxes." In Kent, the Tonbridge branch of the National Farmers' Union declared by resolution that "agriculture in all its branches should receive an equal share of any benefits that may accrue to other industries." [103] In the same fair county Mr. G. Mallion said at the annual meeting of the Kent Tariff Reform Federation that "tenant farmers should organize so that they would ensure a fair share of the benefits when Tariff Reform was adopted." [104] The West Sussex Farmers' Union also protested against agriculture being "excluded from its benefits." [105]

The recurrence of these terms showed only too plainly what farmers had expected from Protection. Even Mr. Charles Bathurst, M.P., one of the farmers' chief champions in Parliament, talked of the State conferring upon agriculture "a *quid pro quo* for the protection afforded to its urban industries by duties upon foreign manufactured goods." [106] It is possible to sympathize with the sorrows of that brave knight of the shires, Mr. Henry Chaplin, M.P., who said as long ago as 1903, when his party took off the corn tax because it made bread dearer, that "he began to think he should be ashamed to belong" to such a party, and who now finds himself in "a difficult position" because "in no other country is agriculture treated as is now proposed" by that same party. The only solace that can be offered to Mr. Chaplin is that his mantle seems to have fallen upon the worthy shoulders of Lord Willoughby de Broke, who at Liverpool declared that "until some Government was strong enough boldly to institute a tariff which would keep the price of corn steady at 40s. a quarter, they had better leave the agricultural industry alone to work out its own salvation."[107] It may be added that Lord Willoughby de Broke said "they would not see it in their day." That sounds true. But it still remains the Protectionist ideal. There can be no Protection without taxes on food.

III.—THE EMPIRE

THE IMPERIAL SENTIMENT

SACRIFICE OR GAIN ?

THE TWO MEANINGS OF PREFERENCE

A SELF-SUSTAINING EMPIRE

THE COLONIAL "OFFER"

EXPLOITING THE COLONIAL CONFERENCE

THE ATTITUDE OF THE COLONIES

THE GREAT BETRAYAL

THE MODIFIED PREFERENCE

EMIGRATION

THE IMPERIAL SENTIMENT

"THERE is a quixotic nobility about Imperial preference in strong contrast to the selfishness of manufacturers' protection," wrote Mr. Winston Churchill in 1903 to the Birmingham Secretary of the Postal Telegraph Clerks' Association.[1] "When we are told that the result of all these food-taxes will be to make living cheaper, anyone can see that that is humbug. But if they had been put forward, as Mr. Chamberlain was first inclined to put them forward, as a sacrifice for the sake of the Empire, I can well believe there are thousands of postmen and telegraph clerks who would have been willing in such a cause to make contributions from their weekly earnings."

That is a true statement, generally and in detail. Mr. Chamberlain rang his first peal on the Imperial *carillon*. Ten years of jangling on all kinds of bells in all kinds of changes have intervened. To-day the Tariff Reformers are pathetically trying to recapture the note of the first fine careless rapture. Is not that sufficient proof of the wisdom of observant men of affairs who have always held that the Imperial sentiment was the best asset of the Protectionists? The Tariff Reformers have done their best to make Imperialism a synonym for Protectionism, and they have only succeeded in depreciating the value of their principal asset.

Events that were fresh in the public memory gave a vivid setting to Mr. Chamberlain's original appeal to the country. The South African War was ended, and Mr. Chamberlain had just returned from a grand tour of the Colonies that have since been brought into the Union. Another event, now almost forgotten, was the action of Germany in withdrawing most-favoured-nation treatment from Canada because Canada had given a preference to certain goods imported from the Mother Country; and Mr. Chamberlain, who in his earlier days regarded such incidents as not worth making a fuss about, tried hard to work up a feeling of resentment. "Germany," he cried, "insists upon treating Canada as though it were a separate country, refuses to recognize it as part of one empire, entitled to claim, as I have said, the privileges of that empire, regards this agreement as being something more than a domestic agreement; and it has penalized Canada by placing upon Canadian goods an additional duty. Well, now the reason for that is clear. The German newspapers very frankly explain that this is a policy of reprisal, and that it is intended to deter other Colonies from giving to us the same advantage. Therefore it is not merely punishment inflicted by Germany upon Canada, but it is a threat to South Africa, to Australia, and to New Zealand; and this policy, as a policy of dictation and interference, is justified by the belief that we are so wedded to our fiscal system that we cannot interfere, that we cannot defend our Colonies, and that, in fact, any one of them which attempts to establish any kind of special relations with us does so at her own risk, and must be left to bear the brunt of foreign hostility. In my mind that is putting us in a rather humiliating position." [2]

"We should have power," said Mr. Chamberlain, "to put duties on certain things if we are to retaliate in any way where our Colonies are injured by the reprisals of foreign countries." A month later he tried to pile on the agony by speaking of Germany as having "penalized" Canada, and indignantly asserted that "so long as the policy of this country is to *lie down* under that treatment, so long we have no complaint either against Germany or against any other nation which treats our Colonies in that way." [3] The country, however, refused to lose its temper over the affair.

The speech Mr. Chamberlain delivered at Birmingham soon after his return from "the solitude of the illimitable veldt"—the speech which the first President of the Tariff Reform League ran with to Mr. Chaplin, saying, "Here is something worth fighting for!"—contained something much more likely to arouse the attention of the nation, then in a very sensitive Imperial mood. "You are excited at home about an

Education Bill—about Temperance Reform—about local finance," he said. "Yes, I should be if I had remained at home. But these things matter no more to South Africa, to Canada, to Australia, than their local affairs matter to you. On the other hand, everything that touches Imperial policy, everything which affects their interests as well as yours, has for them, as it ought to have for us, a supreme importance. And our Imperial policy is vital to them and vital to us. Upon that Imperial policy, and upon what you do in the next few years, depends that tremendous issue whether this great Empire of ours is to stand together, one free nation if necessary, against all the world, or whether it is to fall apart into separate States, each selfishly seeking its own interest alone—losing sight of the common weal, and losing also all the advantages which union alone can give."

"I have read with care and interest all the speeches that have been made by the leaders of the Liberal Party," he went on, "and in none of them do I find a frank acceptance of that National and Imperial policy which, I believe, is the first necessity of our time. As long as that is the case, however anxious I may be personally for rest, I confess I cannot look forward without dread to handing over the security and existence of this great Empire to the hands of those who have made common cause with its enemies, who have charged their own country-men with methods of barbarism, and who, apparently, have been untouched by that pervading sentiment which I found everywhere where the British flag floats, and which has done so much in recent years to draw us together. The Empire is in its infancy. Now is the time when we can mould that Empire, and we and those who live with us can decide the future destinies." [4]

There is in those sentences a sign that the new Imperial policy of Mr. Chamberlain was to be used as a battering-ram against the Government then in power. It was a deliberately strategic movement. That estimate of it is supported by a letter Mr. Chamberlain himself wrote to Lady Dorothy Nevill in the following year.[5] The new Imperial policy was to be the means of "turning" the Opposition criticism of the Government's management of the war. The loyal part which the contingents of Colonial troops took in the war—"our new-found pride and faith in our distant kinsmen"[6]—called forth a response that was fully exploited by the Protectionists. The echo of it is still heard in places of public meeting; for just as Mr. Chamberlain ended most of his speeches on the Empire note, so to-day do Tariff Reform orators depend upon it to arouse a spurious enthusiasm for their selfish Protectionist ideals. It was quite true, as Mr. C. A. Vince once pointed out,[7] that "the term Imperial Federation has now been in the mouths of politicians for fully thirty years." But when Mr. Vince went on to ask, "Is the adornment of perorations the first and last use to which it is to be put? Is it never to be translated into fact?" he only exhibited the simple faith of those who never looked beyond the speech of May 15, from which considerations of sordid gains were absent. "The issue, as raised by Mr. Chamberlain," declared Mr. Vince, "is primarily an issue of Imperial, not of fiscal policy."

Mr. Vince was the Secretary of the Imperial Tariff Committee which "looked after" the Birmingham area while the Tariff Reform League looked after the rest of the country, in the manner indicated in a previous chapter. The Imperial Tariff Committee looked after Mr. Chamberlain himself as well as his political territory, and helped the manufacturers to pull him into the Protectionist pit. While he was preparing his October speeches Mr. Chamberlain wrote two letters. To the Duke of Devonshire he wrote:[8] "You refused to look at my proposals for Preference, which are put forward solely with the object of ensuring Imperial Unity, and which under no circumstances would lead to any substantial or indeed perceptible protection of a home industry. It is ridiculous to suppose that 2s. a quarter on corn would restore prosperity to agriculture, although the farmers might possibly support it as drowning men will catch at a straw. For my own part, I care only for the question of Imperial Unity; everything else is secondary or consequential. But for this—to quote a celebrated phrase—I would not have taken my coat off."

To a Nottingham manufacturer he wrote almost at the same time:[9] "I have taken up this subject chiefly in the interests of the working people of this country, whose livelihood is seriously threatened by the changes which have taken place in our commercial position and relations. My policy has always been to do more for friends than for enemies or rivals. The Colonies are our best friends, and largest customers for manufactured goods, and the greatest potential source of supply for our food. They are ready to make profitable arrangements with us, while the foreigners are gradually closing every outlet of our trade." It should be observed, by the way, that the self-governing Colonies, which must be the Colonies Mr. Chamberlain referred to, were not, and never have been, our "largest customers for manufactured goods." He appeared to include India, and that has been a favourite miscalculation of the Tariff Reformers ever since.

The main purpose of recalling these two letters is to show that when writing to a recent colleague in the Cabinet Mr. Chamberlain regarded his proposals as "put forward *solely* with the object of ensuring Imperial unity"; while in the letter to a manufacturer he declared that he had taken the matter up "chiefly" in the interests of the manufacturers and working people "of this country." Here, then, is the first sign of the degradation of the Imperial sentiment to Protectionist uses, and the first example of the rich confusion of motives upon which the Tariff Reform movement has endeavoured to subsist ever since.

The new Imperial policy thus became frankly a trade policy. The bonds of commerce were exalted above all the other interests of the "common ideal." British trade with one Canadian, Canadian trade with one Australian, Australian trade with one New Zealander, was held to be worth more to the Empire than the trade of any of them with two score customers outside the Empire. The Imperial Tariff Committee labelled all the first flight of its popular leaflets, "Trade and the Empire," and the burden of them was the attempt to prove that the Empire's only safety lay in the development of its inter-Imperial trading.

The October speeches of Mr. Chamberlain condemned the Empire to the same doom as it condemned the pearl button trade to. "We have reached our highest point. Our fate will be the fate of the empires and the kingdoms of the past." [10] "If you choose to remain unprotected, no statesman, however wise, can save these Colonies for you." [11] "Our foreign trade, much of it, is gone and cannot be recovered, but our Colonial trade remains with us." [12] "The Colonies are no longer in their infancy. They are growing rapidly to a vigorous manhood. Now is the time—the last time—that you can bind them closer to you. . . . We can, if we will, make the Empire mutually supporting. We can make it one for defence, one for common aid and assistance." [13] With all this there was a sorry attempt to make it appear that "the men who advocated Free Trade in this country" considered the Colonies "as an encumbrance which we should be glad to get rid of" [13]—a wilful distortion of historical fact which will be dealt with fully on a later page.

The sordid link between the Imperial sentiment and the selfish interests of certain British manufacturers was hammered on by the Tariff Reform League in a publication [14] that appeared immediately after these October speeches. "The majestic vision of a great Confederation of British States girdling the world, and all owning the sway of the British crown, must appeal," said the leaflet, "to anyone with the slightest gift of imagination. But it appeals not only to the imagination, but to the pocket. A real system of Imperial Federation is not merely a majestic vision; it is good business." On another page of the same publication [15] it was pointed out that though the Colonies gave us a preference in their tariffs, "there is abundant evidence that they regard a one-sided preference as both inexpedient and unjust. Are they not right in this feeling?" it was asked. "Why should we expect something for nothing in a commercial transaction?"

But these were the crudities of the unpractised penman. The vulgar references to the "pocket" and to "something for nothing," silently disappeared from later editions of the Tariff Reform League handbook. To-day, instead of talking of "good business," and "commercial transactions," and "profitable arrangements," the phrase goes that we are to "complete the circle" by granting the Colonies "some reciprocal preference in any tariff we see fit to adopt in our national interest."[16] It is further evidence of the gradual hiding away of the real Protectionist purpose of the Tariff Reform campaign behind carefully moulded phrases. The "profits" of which Mr. Chamberlain spoke can only come —if they come at all—with the tariff, and it is of this part of their contract with the public the Tariff Reformers most vehemently refuse to give any details.

When in full sway Mr. Chamberlain talked more at random about the "profitable arrangements" he was anxious to bring about. "Let them send me as Ambassador to the Colonies with full powers," he said, "and I am perfectly willing to risk my reputation on my being able, not merely to satisfy the Colonies that we have something to give them which is worth their acceptance, but also to secure from the Colonies equal measure in return."[17] At the Guildhall in the following month he bade the nation learn to "think Imperially";[18] for this "Imperial aspect of the question" was, he said, "the steam which keeps the engine going"[19] —a rather frank confession of the need of using Imperialism to push the interests of the Protectionists. Indeed, being out for profit for his "friends," he scorned sentiment as altogether insufficient. Addressing 200 M.P.s who entertained him at a Hotel Cecil Banquet,[20] he said: "We are told that we ought to 'trust to sentiment' by those who can always find an excuse for doing nothing, and especially when all they are asked to do is to make this Empire great. Sentiment, yes. Sentiment is indeed a great and potent factor in the history of the world, and how splendid that sentiment may be which unites men of kindred blood and kindred faith was seen in the late war, when wherever the British flag floated we had the moral support, and, where it was possible, the material assistance of all of British race. Without sentiment we can do nothing. But sentiment alone is not enough. Sentiment without organization is no better than courage without discipline. Let us unite the two. Let us use sentiment, this all-powerful sentiment, to remove the difficulties in the way of practical organization." In other words, the Imperial sentiment, properly worked, might be "all powerful" in organizing a Protective tariff. It was in this speech also that he spoke of the danger of "the British Colonies turning their backs on the Empire." "I think," he said, "the Colonies will never want for suitors; and if you do not pay your court to them, while still they are willing to receive your addresses, you will find that in the time to come they will have made some arrangements, and you will no longer be welcomed in the house of those who are now your greatest friends." But it was the trading instinct, after all, that led him, after describing himself as an ambassador, a missionary, a matchmaker, and an exploiter of sentiment, to apply to himself the description of a commercial traveller. He began a speech in the midsummer of 1904 by saying that "the Chairman has introduced me to you in the character of a commercial man, and, indeed, I think I am. I am not only a commercial man, but in a technical sense I am a commercial traveller. Wherever I go I try to dispose of my wares, and my wares are the Imperial sentiment, upon which, as I believe, the future of this county absolutely depends." [21]

It is advisable to give the closest attention to this presentation of the Tariff Reform case in view of what followed much later, and it is also necessary because the chastened phase through which the Tariff Reformers are passing in 1913 indicates how sorry they are that they ever permitted anything else to take precedence of the Imperial sentiment. They could not, of course, go on talking for ten years about the danger of living in an Empire bound together by so thin a tie as sentiment and sympathy, as Mr. Chamberlain called it, "that a rough blow might shatter it and dissolve it into its constituent atoms;" [22] because the strain that he said might be placed on it "at any moment" [23] has shown no sign of occurring. They contented themselves by recording their belief that a change in the fiscal policy would "tend to consolidate the Empire;" [24] and that is the vague kind of formula in which this tender sentiment has been enwrapped ever since. It was impossible to keep up the excitement without running the risk of making themselves look foolish.

That is not to say there have not been many foolish things said about this slender Imperial sentiment, which instead of snapping has grown stronger every day. Very early in the controversy Lord Selborne, who has distinguished himself more than once by his "quixotic nobility," observed that "to think Imperially, as Mr. Chamberlain has suggested, was to think intellectually;" [25] and Sir Gilbert Parker, M.P., a man of prolific Imperial imagination, speaking at Cape Town about the same time, said that "love and sentiment were the basis, but he asked for the marriage lines," by which he meant something visible in the way of "an increase of trade within the Empire." [26] It was a pretty way of putting it, and Sir Gilbert Parker fancied it so well that he repeated it on his return to England, when he said that "by the closer linking of the commercial interests, by free and open bargaining for Preference to each other's goods, they would not only have the protestations of affection but also the marriage lines." [27] A few years later the same phrase-maker spoke of Preference "as much a moral stimulation of energy as a concrete benefit." [28] But when it comes to definitions it would be hard to beat that of Mr. Wyndham, who said he "deduced, with the inevitability of a proposition in Euclid, that the only way towards the goal of a united Empire was the way of Tariff Reform." [29] The precision of that utterance may be contrasted for effect with the beautiful language of Captain Grogan, who when he was seeking the suffrages of the electors of Newcastle-under-Lyme, published a book on the fiscal question,[30] in which he said that "Preferential trade between England and the Empire would mean that, concurrently with the individual integration of each State towards organic self-sufficiency as to its own intrinsically defined functions, there would be a process of integration of all the States towards organic interdependent self-sufficiency as to all functions. Imperial Preference means that each of the component States will make the exploitation of its own sun-frontage primarily relative to its own actual or potential population, and secondarily relative to the entire Imperial population."

It is not desired to give the impression that this exploitation of the Imperial sentiment has ever been forgotten in the course of the Protectionist campaign; though it has for long periods at a time sunk into a secondary place. Spasmodically it has enjoyed occasional returns to prominence, as when in 1908 Mr. Joseph Chamberlain wrote to Mid-Devon to warn the country of the danger of the Empire sinking "into the fifth rôle among nations." [31] In 1911, a year of great political activity in the United Kingdom, Mr. Jebb swept everything but the Empire into the bucket of negligible items. "Even the constitutional revolution is secondary," he wailed, "because what is Single Chamber or Double Chamber government, national unity or Home Rule, Republic or Monarchy, to a Britain bereft of her Imperial future?" [32]

In 1912, Mr. H. Page Croft, M.P., who runs a little organization like those that got between the feet of the Protectionists of 1903, deplored the fact that "a multitude of circumstances" had recently proved that any further delay in getting Tariff Reform "may now prove fatal to the supremacy of the British race," [33]—the whole race! And last of all, when Lord Lansdowne and Mr. Bonar Law in 1913 agreed to postpone the food-taxes issue to the General Election after next, and in so doing brought down on their heads the scorn of the class known as "whole-hoggers," Mr. J. L. Garvin declared that "we must not be asked to acquiesce in a policy of silence, or to join in hoodwinking the electorate by suppression of what we believe to be the essential part of Mr. Chamberlain's policy. We must not be asked to whittle down a high Imperial cause into a mere device for adding to the profits of those engaged in the manufacture of certain goods. We are not 'out' for that. If we did not believe, earnestly and sincerely, that only by commercial union can the eventual union of the Empire for policy and defence be brought about, we should never, in Parnell's phrase, have 'taken off our coats' in this cause." [34]

Mr. Garvin's hot words may stand for the present mind of the Tariff Reformers, so that, in the end, the wheel has turned full circle again, and "the high Imperial cause" is divorced from mere profit-seeking, because it had become too plain that Preference meant profits for the few and food taxes for the many.

SACRIFICE OR GAIN?

THE conflict of opinion among Tariff Reformers as to whether Preference is good for the pocket or "a high Imperial aim" has never been resolved into a convenient formula for the misguidance of the public. It has been shown in the preceding section on Agriculture how completely the consciousness that Preference involves food taxes has prevented the realization of the Protectionist hopes. Mr. Chamberlain himself provided a perfectly logical statement of the obstacle. A month after he made the Opposition "a present," as he described it, of the declaration that "if you are to give a Preference to the Colonies —I do not say you are—you must put a tax on food," [35] he repeated his "opinion that a system of preferential tariffs is the only system by which this Empire can be kept together." [36] That seemed thorough enough. But he went further. In a "letter to a working man," published midway between the two speeches already recalled, he explicitly associated Preference and food duties.[37] "It will be impossible," he wrote, "to secure preferential treatment with the Colonies without some duty on corn as well as on other articles of food, because these are the chief articles of Colonial produce. Whether this will raise the cost of living is a matter of opinion, and there is no doubt that in many cases a duty of this kind is paid by the exporter, and it really depends on the extent of competition among the exporting countries. For instance, it is, I think, established that the shilling duty recently imposed was met by a reduction of price and freights in the United States of America, and that the tax did not therefore fall in any way on the consumer here. But even if the price of food is raised, the rate of wages will certainly be raised in greater proportion. This has been the case both in the United States and Germany. In the former country the available balance left to the working man after he has paid for necessaries is much larger than here. These are facts which we have to bring to the notice of the working men generally."

In this letter, which appeared simultaneously in all the Protectionist journals, nothing is said about the balancing of the new food duties by the remission of some of the existing duties, on tea and sugar for instance. It was a letter to a "working man," and money in the pocket was supposed to be the thing to touch him! Hence the balance was to be restored, and more than restored, by wages so much higher that even when the extra duties had been paid the working man would have a greater sum left. It is impossible to think that even if this had been the only argument brought "to the notice of the working men generally" it would have succeeded in deceiving them: they have, as a rule, so keen a sense of money in the pocket that they would choose to see the wages first and the taxes after. But the Protectionists have not been content to simply follow the lead of Mr. Chamberlain and the Tariff Reform League in chinking the coin. They have gone to the other end of the emotional scale and played on the "working man's" love of sacrifice.

It is necessary to get back to the origin of this appeal. In his Glasgow speech of October 6, 1903, Mr. Chamberlain talked at large of trade with the British Possessions (not the self-governing Colonies only, be it observed) finding "subsistence" for 3,075,000—"nearly four millions" he called that—of our population. He feared that the Leader of the Opposition would describe that as "a squalid argument." "I have appealed to your interests, I have come here as a man of business," he said; but "now I abandon that line of argument for the moment. I appeal to something higher, which I believe is in your hearts as it is in mine." Thereupon he spoke of the greatness of the Empire; of the way in which the men of the Empire "when the old country was in straits, rushed to her assistance," giving us both material and moral assistance. "Is such a dominion, are such traditions, is such a glorious inheritance, is such a splendid sentiment—are these worth preserving?" he asked. This great ideal had cost us much in lives and treasure. " I am not likely to do you the injustice to believe that you would make these sacrifices fruitless, that you would make all this endeavour vain." A few moments later in the same speech Mr. Chamberlain, having as yet said nothing definite on the point, continued: " Well, we have to consider, of course, what is the sacrifice we are called upon to make. No; let me first say if there be a sacrifice; if that can be shown, I will go confidently to my countrymen, I will tell them what it is, and I will ask them to make it. Nowadays a great deal too much attention is paid to what is called the sacrifice; no attention is given to what is the gain. But, although I would not hesitate to ask you for a sacrifice if a sacrifice were needed to keep together the Empire to which I attach so much importance, I do not believe that there would be any sacrifice at all. This is an arrangement among friends. This is a negotiation among kinsmen. Can you not conceive the possibility that both sides may gain and neither lose ? "

Then he asked, in the words of Mr. Cecil Rhodes, " Can we invent a tie—which must be a practical one—which will prevent separation? " To this question he made the same answer as Mr. Rhodes, " that it is only by commercial union, reciprocal preference, that you can lay the foundations of the confederation of the Empire to which we all look forward as a brilliant possibility." * And once again he asserted that the Colonies must be given " a preference on their principal products." It would be " futile to offer them a preference on manufactured goods." And " what remains ? Food."

This may seem a long way round to connect sacrifices with food duties in Mr. Chamberlain's mind; but then, when they are analyzed, Mr. Chamberlain's arguments always do go round about: his bold verbal finger-posts direct nowhither. Yet there, at any rate, is the genesis of the idea of sacrifice. The next night at Greenock, Mr. Chamberlain declared that the Colonies were " not asking you to make any sacrifices for them. They think that something can be done which

* This was not a complete interpretation of Mr. Rhodes' views. See an article by Mr. Samuel Evans in the 21st anniversary number of the *South African Mining Journal*, 1912.

may involve concession on both sides, but which in the long run will be good for both." And in the same speech he said, quite unabashed, that he had not hesitated to preach that Colonies and Mother Country "alike must be content to make a common sacrifice if that were necessary in order to secure the common good." It was not enough to "shout of Empire."

It is a tempting exercise to follow the tortuous evolution of this idea. There was to be sacrifice. There was to be no sacrifice. Everybody must be content to make a common sacrifice. It would all come back in cash. "Surely," said Mr. Chamberlain to a Liverpool audience,[38] "you need not be afraid of trying my prescription, which, after all, only involves, if it involves anything, this small transference of taxation from certain kinds of food to certain other kinds of food, and this small protection against foreign manufactured goods, which I think can be justified entirely by the circumstances under which these goods are imported into this country. I admit that sometimes I almost feel as if this were the weak point in my whole argument. I have to say to you—because I believe it to be true—that I ask you to make this change for your own good, for the good of the Empire, and that you will not be called upon for any sacrifice. I declare to you I wish I could say that you would be called upon for a sacrifice. I declare I would rather speak to you here and appeal to you as Englishmen, and ask you whether you are not willing to do what your fathers would have done, and what, in fact, they did do, whether, for some great good, in which, indeed, you might have no immediate personal or squalid interest—as we are told to consider it—you may yet be willing to make a sacrifice for great Imperial results."

Three weeks later, at Newport, his scheme would "put money into the pockets of everybody."[39] Next year at Stafford House[40] he declared: "We are not asked to make sacrifices, unless it be a sacrifice of ancient prejudice and dead superstition. Not a single man among us is asked to make any personal or pecuniary sacrifice." At Gainsborough the Empire could "only be maintained by sacrifice."[41] At St. Helens, "This arrangement with the Colonies would necessitate not a tax on food, as you are told—that is false—but it might entail a transfer of taxation from one kind of food to another kind of food. It is not much of a sacrifice, but it is capable of the grossest misrepresentation." [42] For that misrepresentation who was to blame but Mr. Chamberlain himself? Yet he seemed blissfully unconscious of his own meanderings, for at the annual meeting of the Tariff Reform League in 1905 he actually rebuked lesser men for shirking the difficulties he himself had created. "It is of no use for a man to go down into the country," he said, "and to profess to be an advocate of preference with our Colonies, to put forward the importance of union of the Empire, and at the same time to boast that he is unwilling to pay the price. It is not a large price, but he will find it better policy to face all the difficulties of the situation than to attempt to escape them, as I am sorry to say some politicians have done. I do not think that is doing justice to the intelligence or to the patriotism of the people of this country." [43]

Lord Lansdowne very early realized the necessity of being more exact. At the 1904 meetings of the Liberal Unionist Council, when the Free Trade members refused to walk in Protectionist ways with their old colleagues, Lord Lansdowne, one of the Council's Vice-Presidents, impressed upon his hearers [44] that they must tell the Colonies "exactly what sacrifices, if any, you ask them to make"; and "with regard to our people at home," to them too, "you must be able to explain exactly what it is that you intend. You must be able to tell them with absolute frankness what sacrifice, if any, you ask them to submit to." At the end of 1907 [45] Lord Lansdowne had begun to think that this sacrifice might after all prove "greater than our people are willing to bear," showing that he was quite prepared to drop the Chamberlain proposals, as indeed he attempted to do five years afterwards.

There is mention in some of the speeches that have been quoted of a sacrifice on the part of the Colonies as well as on our own part. It is almost forgotten that the Colonies were originally asked to sacrifice their own industrial development to the interests of the Empire! It was a much greater act of self-denial to ask of them than anything ever asked of us; and because it was so unreasonably disproportionate, so utterly unnatural, the suggestion was very early thrown on the Tariff Reform scrap-heap.

In his Glasgow speech Mr. Chamberlain said: "Canada has been protective for a long time, and a protective policy has produced its natural result. The principal industries are there, and you can never get rid of them. They will be there for ever. But up to the present time the secondary industries have not been created. There is an immense deal of trade that is still open to you, that you may still retain, that you may increase. In Australasia the industrial position of the country is still less advanced. The agricultural products of the country have been first of all developed. Accordingly, Australasia takes more from you per head than Canada. In South Africa there are, practically speaking, no industries at all. Very well, now I ask you to suppose that we intervene in any stage of this process. We can do it now; we might have done it with greater effect ten years ago. Whether we can do it with any effect or at all twenty years hence, I am very doubtful. But we can intervene now, and we can say to our great Colonies: 'We understand your views and conditions. We do not attempt to dictate to you. We do not think ourselves superior to you. We have taken the trouble to learn your objections, to appreciate and sympathize with your policy. We know you are right in saying that you will not always be content to be what the Americans call "a one-horse country," with a single industry and no diversity of employment. We understand, and we can see that you are right not to neglect what Providence has given you in the shape of mineral or other resources [not to neglect profiting by any natural aptitudes which you may have]. We understand and we appreciate the wisdom of your statesmen when they say that they will not allow their country to be solely dependent upon foreign supplies for the necessities of their life. We understand all that, and therefore we will not propose to you anything that is unreasonable or contrary to this policy which we know is deep in your hearts. But we will say to you: After all, there are many things which you do not now make, many things for which we have a great capacity of production. Leave them to us as you have left them hitherto. Do not increase your tariff walls against us, pull them down where they are unnecessary to the success of this policy to which you are committed. [Let us in exchange with you have your products in all those numberless industries which have not yet been created.] Do that because we are kinsmen without injury to any important interest, because it is good for the Empire as a whole, and because we have taken the first step and have set you an example. We offer you a preference. We rely on your patriotism, your affection, that we shall not be the losers thereby.' "

There are at least three editions of this Glasgow speech. The passage quoted above is from the reprint entitled *Imperial Union and Tariff Reform*, containing the speeches from May 15 to November 4, 1903, to which Mr. Chamberlain himself wrote an introduction. From that edition the passages set in brackets above are omitted. In the same speech Mr. Chamberlain said, according to the reported version, "The Colonies are prepared to meet us. In return for a very moderate preference they will give us a substantial advantage. They will give us, in the first place—I believe they will reserve to us the trade which we already enjoy. *They will arrange for tariffs in the future in order not to start industries in competition with those which are already in existence in the Mother Country.*" But in the revised version appearing in the book referred to, that passage is altered. "The Colonies are prepared to meet us," it runs, "in return for a very moderate preference they will give us in the first place—I believe they will reserve to us—*much, at any rate,* of the trade which we already enjoy."

Thus it is seen that Mr. Chamberlain himself speedily became aware that this "schedule of forbidden industries," as Lord Rosebery described it, involved a sacrifice that would not prove acceptable to the Colonies. Indeed, he changed his tone very promptly. A fortnight after asking the Colonies to stay their own development, he was pretending that he was not the kind of man who could ever have thought of such a thing. "No, sir," he told a Tynemouth audience,[46] "The Colonists, I think, know me. They know that under no circumstances do I want to interfere with their commercial freedom any more than I should like them to interfere with our commercial freedom. We have given them full power to decide for themselves what their fiscal policy should be. When we come together in negotiation we shall see how far we can arrange our fiscal policies to suit mutual interests. Neither has the right to say to the other, 'You shall do this, or you shall do that, or you shall be blamed if you do not do it.' And in the second place, they know that I would be the last man to want to stereotype their progress. They will be great nations in the future. Small nations now, but in imagination cannot you see what they are certain to become?" And so on.

Yet the notion that there was to be some kind of mutual sacrifice persisted. Mr. Chamberlain himself changed his meaning without altering his words. "We find at the present time," he said, "that all our children in Canada, in Australia, in South Africa, are moved by a strong unity of feeling and are prepared to make sacrifices in order to secure both for themselves and for us this great advantage of a real and organized union";[47] and this doubtless encouraged some Tariff Reform candidates to persist in representing that under Tariff Reform "India and all parts of our Empire shall remove the duties upon British goods."[48] From time to time, however, it has been found prudent that prominent Tariff Reformers should repudiate these hot-headed proposals. Lord Lansdowne, for example, who had already expressed the desire for "absolute frankness" in this matter, confessed in 1907 that "in reference to the Colonies the day had long passed for anything which could properly be called Imperial Free Trade. The four great Colonies had made up their minds to have industries of their own, and to protect them, and to protect them if necessary against us;"[49] and in the following year Mr. Bonar Law erroneously alleged that "no one who advocates Colonial preference has ever suggested that the result of it will be to induce the Colonies to cease to develop their own manufactures, to confine themselves simply to the production of raw material, and to buy their manufactured goods from us." [50] Later that year Mr. Austen Chamberlain felt compelled to make the position clearer still. "Our great white Colonies," he said, "were not going to sacrifice their industrial development any more than we were going to sacrifice ours." [51]

The stalwart *Morning Post* [52] in 1909 stumbled very much as Mr. Chamberlain had stumbled. In an article on "What Real Preference would mean," the journal gave this "specific example": "Australia at present has rich lands for cotton-growing, but no cotton mills. An arrangement by which Great Britain stimulated Australian cotton-growing in return for Australia allowing free entry of British, and only British, cotton goods, would now be recognized as mutually advantageous. A few years hence Australia may have set up cotton mills, and the problem be made much more complex. The ultimate ideal is inter-Imperial Free Trade. Each year's delay on the part of Great Britain in adopting Tariff Reform puts fresh difficulties in the way of that ideal."

That was exactly the idea of Mr. Chamberlain's Glasgow speech; and just as Mr. Chamberlain excised it when reprinting his speech, so the following day the *Morning Post* wrote: "Discussing Preferential Trade in this column yesterday, the writer strayed from practical politics to suggest a future possible development of Preferential Trade which, whilst it would be welcome in some of the Dominions, would not have their unanimous support, and is consequently not part of the programme of Tariff Reform. . . . It is not—let it be quite clear—part of the policy of Preferential Trade to suggest to any oversea Dominion a limitation of its industries, present or future."

This final destruction of the suggestion that the Colonies should sacrifice their future to ours, rather disturbed the delicate balance of the Protectionist ideals. There was now to be only one sacrifice, and that on our own part. The benefit, moreover, was quite problematical. Mr. Austen Chamberlain in 1909, for instance, "appealed to the people of the country to make a little sacrifice in order to secure a better market for their labour," [53] the suggestion being that the Colonies would open their markets to our products if we closed our markets to foreign products. But even this did not satisfy the high Imperialists, who have set themselves the task of saving the Protectionists from themselves. Their temper and spirit were nicely shown by the *Daily Mail* in the midsummer of 1910,[54] when it pleaded that "as Prussia became the head of a united Germany because her citizens were prepared to show sacrifice for a great ideal, . . . so England should be ready to sacrifice something, and to eschew the temper that counts the value of Preference in terms of farthings gained or lost," and thus prepared the ground for the last great change of all.

It was Lord Selborne who brought the sacrificial sentiment to its final testing. As long ago as 1904 Lord Selborne said that preference represented a "noble ideal." [55] "In this matter of Empire," he told us a year later, "we had not only to think of ourselves to-day, but of our children and our children's children in time to come. Russia, France, and Germany were in the future going to be numbered by hundreds of millions of people; and if we were to remain at forty millions how were we going to compare with these nations of hundreds of millions? We could not be in the same class with them. It was numbers that told," he went on, "but if the British Empire by a high ideal of Imperial unity were to be made one, then we could hold our heads on the same level." [56] The "noble ideal" was, after all, it appeared, based on millions. Yet the passages quoted enable us to understand the depth of Lord Selborne's fear of our outnumbered future, and the sincerity of his feelings, when he said at the end of 1912: "The spirit at the bottom of Tariff Reform is the noble spirit of self-sacrifice. On the one hand you have the appeal of Mr. Chamberlain to patriotism and to the spirit of self-sacrifice, on the other the party of gammon and mammon. It is for you to choose." [57]

The Tariff Reform League had up to this time regarded the covering up of the mutual sacrifice idea as fairly complete. True, there is a page in the League's official handbook [58] entitled "No Sacrifice in Preference," whereon are quoted the asseverations of Colonial Premiers at the 1907 Conference, like that of Sir Starr (then Dr.) Jameson who said, " We have no idea of imposing any burden upon the poor men of this country." But that only served to show that the League took sacrifice to mean food-taxes, as everybody else took them to mean. And when Lord Selborne committed his fearsome indiscretion the Tariff Reform League published a manifesto [59] quoting some of the speeches of Mr. Chamberlain and proving to its own satisfaction thereby that he " expressly repudiated the suggestion that he asked for any sacrifice whatever " other than that of an " ancient prejudice " and a " dead superstition." [60] The *Morning Post* [61] went a step farther and said that " self-sacrifice was a term which does not apply. What Unionists ask the nation to agree to is good business," a reminiscent sentence that was improved on later in the year in the same journal when it declared that " there is no sacrifice expected. . . . It is solid gain." [62] The notion that there was anything to be given up, anything to be lost, by the adoption of a Protective tariff was ridiculous ! Everybody remembered a thousand occasions on which Tariff Reformers, high and low, had promised, in the ear of the public, to " improve trade, increase employment, raise wages, lower the poor rates, and lighten taxation ; " [63] and the net effect of Lord Selborne's noble absurdity was to fix attention more sharply than ever on the fact that Protection was a device for putting money into some people's pockets and taking it out of other people's pockets. The attempt to make the country forget that Preference meant the sacrifice of free food failed utterly.

THE TWO MEANINGS OF "PREFERENCE"

SIDE by side with this denial of the certainty that there was something to be lost by the adoption of a Preferential Tariff ran the deliberate attempt to confuse the public mind on the meanings of Imperial Preference and Colonial Preference. The former does not exist: to bring it into existence a Protective, food-taxing tariff in this country is first of all necessary. Colonial Preference does exist in the self-governing dominions.

The distinction used to be clearly set forth in the official Tariff Reform publications. For example, in the first edition of the *Speakers' Handbook,* issued by the Tariff Reform League in 1903, there stands the definition [64] that "under a Preferential Tariff (1) England would charge a duty on foreign goods, and admit Colonial goods into the British market either free or on the payment of a lower duty than the foreigner. (2) The Colonies would admit British goods into their territories either free or on the payment of a lower duty than the foreign goods."

That was a correct statement of the difference. But it was much too plain to stand. Accordingly, in later editions of the *Handbook* the reference to the "duty on foreign goods" was watered down, and the definition now runs [65] that "Preference means that our Colonies should charge a smaller duty on goods coming from England than on goods coming from foreign countries; and that England should allow goods from the Colonies to come in at a lower rate than from foreign countries. Canada, South Africa, Australia, and New Zealand already give us such preferential terms in their markets."

The change in those essential and tell-tale words was not the only change. Originally it was confessed that the first step towards Imperial Preference would be taken by

"England." In the later version, first place is given to the Colonies. To say the revised version is a garbled one is not hard enough; the suppression and subversion are evidence of a deliberate endeavour to blind the country to the real meaning of a Preferential Tariff. The *Handbook* to-day is silent on the vital distinction between Imperial and non-existing Preference, and Colonial and existing Preference. What it does say about it is intentionally misleading. It quotes speeches made at Colonial Conferences by British Free Trade Ministers [66] who acknowledged the undoubted advantages of the preference to British goods now given by the Colonies, and leaves it to be inferred that they were speeches in favour of Imperial Preference involving British food-taxes.

The example of the Tariff Reform League has been faithfully followed by the orators of the movement. Mr. Bonar Law, for example, just after his election to the leadership,[67] asked the country to "remember that while the British Government defended that treaty (the Canadian-American Reciprocity Treaty) on the ground that it would destroy Preference, Sir Wilfred Laurier defended it always because, in his belief, it would not injure Preference," therein speaking of two utterly different things as though they were one and the same thing. Indeed, it is hardly possible to read a Tariff Reform speech through all the ten years without finding proof of the way in which the Tariff Reform League has deliberately sought to confuse this important issue. Once more, to be explicit is to be found out.

A SELF-SUSTAINING EMPIRE

AT a lunch given to a number of Canadian manufacturers in Birmingham two years after the opening of his campaign,[68] Mr. Chamberlain ejaculated, "You have an Empire: your Empire, that is what I wish to impress upon you—your Empire as much as ours—you have this Empire, and there is nothing that man can want, there is no necessity of our lives, nothing which adds to our comfort, no luxury which is desirable, which cannot be, if you will have it, produced within this Empire and interchanged within it. If you are willing, and the other branches of the Imperial race, you may have a self-sustaining Empire. And think—although I have not time to develop it—think what a self-sustaining Empire would mean, and what an unique and absolutely unparalleled position it would give to the British Empire in the future. Ladies and gentlemen, it sounds a simple saying, let us take it as a motto, let us buy of one another."

The Tariff Reform League thought it possible to "increase trade enormously" by thus buying of one another.[69] "The spending power of the people of the Empire is lessened every time an order is given to the foreigner which could be done as well by British and Colonial workmen," was another form of this taking-in-one-another's-washing argument.[70] "What do we mean by Preference?" asked the official publication of the League.[71] "Surely we mean absolute fair play as between our Colonies and ourselves. They do not want a one-sided bargain; neither do we. They can give us, if they like, to-morrow a preference which would throw into our hands something like thirty millions of trade, and trade that is going in ever-increasing proportions to our competitors on the Continent and elsewhere. Are we going to ask them for this, and are we going, at the same time, to tell them that we will give them nothing in return? We must have reciprocal preference. If we have a preference in the goods we are manufacturing, we must give them a preference in the goods they produce."

It has been a favourite pastime of the Tariff Reformers to reckon up what the trade of the Colonies is worth, and what it might be worth under different conditions. Sometimes they have quoted figures including British trade with India and other Crown possessions; sometimes they have confined their arithmetic to the self-governing dominions, the only parts of the Empire that give a Preference to British goods. Contrasts between the purchases of our goods by "Americans" and by "Colonials" "per head" have been printed to show that the former buys 6s. worth of our goods while the latter buys £5, 18s. worth, and that therefore "trade follows the flag."[72] There were attempts to show that things would have gone ill with us if customers in the Colonies had not come along to take the place of customers in foreign countries. When our exports were declining, "fortunately for us, the Colonies have been buying more and more from us, and that partly made it up."[73] When our exports were increasing, the swelling purchases of the Colonies were set forth in fat millions as though they were wholly due to the Preference, for no account was taken of the enormous increase of the population of the Colonies.[74] The natural fact that more people need more goods was quietly ignored; and the growth of business was put down to the artificial device of tariffs such as those held up for our imitation. There has been such a wild scrambling for statistical foothold that in the official journal in the first three months of 1906[75] it was stated, in January, that "the foreign competition which has been so detrimental to our trade with foreign countries has already begun to operate detrimentally on our trade with our own Colonies. This is Mr. Chamberlain's leading argument: we are in danger of losing our Colonial trade for the same reasons that have impaired our foreign trade"; and in March, that "the year 1905 was a record year for British exports. The analysis, however, shows that the gradual changes described by Mr. Chamberlain at the outset are still operative, *i.e.*, that a further loss of trade with protective countries is counterbalanced by a gain of trade with British Possessions." The first statement was based on returns up to 1903; the second on those of 1905. In two years the trend had changed, and the Tariff Reform argument had swung round with it.

"Free Trade throughout the Empire" was another of Mr. Chamberlain's "ideals." "I hope," he said,[76] "we all have ideals which are higher at times than anything to which we can possibly attain. That is my ideal, but I know as a practical statesman that you cannot realize any such ideal as that in the twinkling of an eye, by the waving of a wand. You must proceed to it step by step, and the proposal which I make to you is a step—and a great step—towards the Imperial Free Trade throughout the Empire which is no doubt the ultimate object of our aspirations, but which at the present moment is impossible." Mr. Vince went so far as to call this ideal "hopeful." [77] The League, however, agreed with Mr. Chamberlain that it was "impossible," [78] wisely basing its opinion on the resolution of the 1902 Annual Conference, with which Mr. Chamberlain was as familiar as itself. "But Preference," said the League, "is possible, and would be the first step toward Imperial Free Trade, which is, indeed, the ultimate goal of Tariff Reform."

The ideal, therefore, is as far away as any of the others. To-day it is defined in the *Speakers' Handbook* [79] thus: "Free Trade throughout the Empire, in the Cobdenite sense, *i.e.* the adoption of free importation by all the Colonies from all countries, is impossible and out of the question. Free Trade within the Empire, *i.e.* the adoption of free importation by the Colonies from each other and the Mother Country, with a tariff against foreign countries, is at present impracticable, and has been recognized as such by the second resolution passed by the Colonial Conference of 1902, which runs as follows: 'That the Conference recognizes that in the present circumstances of the Colonies, it is not practicable to adopt a general system of Free Trade as between the Mother Country and the British Dominions beyond the seas.' This resolution was unanimously reaffirmed at the Colonial Conference of 1907."

The ultimate goal is now in a different spot. The Colonies, it is asserted, "ask us for some tariff advantage, however small, over foreign countries in our market." [80] And at this tariff advantage the modernized ideal stops short. Its present position may be summed up in the words of Lord Milner,[81] that "I am somewhat doubtful of the advantages of such a general system of Free Trade;" or, as Mr. Lyttelton had it still later: [82] "My own belief is that there is far more danger of friction from a system of Free Trade than there is from a system of Colonial Preference between ourselves and the Dominions overseas." It was considered unwise even to promise the realization of the first little step that Mr. Chamberlain sighed for. "Tariff Reformers," said the *Morning Post* in 1910,[83] "would do well to avoid telling the electors that if they consent to the proposed 'food duties' Canada is certain at once to extend the preference already accorded to British trade."

Yet, though this ideal, which visionaries like Mr. Vince regarded as hopeful, ultimately gave way to a plain confession that the Tariff Reformers wished to multiply Protective barriers within the Empire, they still held up the examples of Germany and the United States, which have Free Trade within their borders. "The policy of Bismarck" (the unification of Germany), said Mr. Bonar Law in 1907,[84] "would not have been possible if, long before that policy was adopted, the different German States had not been brought into close commercial union by a common system of tariffs throughout their borders." "The common system of tariffs" which helped to unite Germany was of course the total abolition of tariffs between component and contiguous States. The Tariff Reform method of uniting the British Empire is to set up tariffs in this country against the different parts of the Empire abroad, which have existing tariffs against one another. The pages of Tariff Reform publications may be searched in vain for any recognition of this vital distinction. The "ideal" is rudely thrown down, but the nations that have achieved it are exalted.

There is yet another illustration worth recording of the

delicacy with which Tariff Reformers have found it advisable to treat this ticklish subject of the Preference.

"Will any duty be put on manufactured goods from the Colonies under Mr. Chamberlain's scheme?" Mr. Vince was asked in 1904.[85]

"No," he replied. "If the Colonies are willing to lower tariffs against us we shall probably give them Free Trade. If the Colonies refuse to give us better treatment, then, of course, *we shall treat them as we treat foreign nations*."

But, persisted the questioner, "if we consent to have our food taxed for the benefit of the Colonies, will the Colonies allow our manufacturers to compete with their manufacturers on equal terms?"

"What is proposed is a reciprocal arrangement," said Mr. Vince. "If the Colonies will not give what we want, we shall not give what they ask."

"You think they will let our manufacturers trade on equal terms?"

"I would not go so far as that," Mr. Vince answered. "The Colonies have a few manufactures which have been established, fortunately or unfortunately, as protected industries, and they will be obliged to continue protecting these industries."

That mild threat, to treat recalcitrant Colonies "as we treat foreign nations," by taxing their manufactures, was rather more felicitously phrased by Mr. Chamberlain. Once he dropped into poetry over it, and sang—

> "Those friends thou hast, and their adoption tried,
> Grapple them to thy soul with hooks of steel." [86]

"Let the Empire be self-sustained," he cried, "let us trade with one another and with our own relations sooner than with foreigners, who may be competitors and even foes; let us treat them a little better than those who are not so near and dear to us, and they will reciprocate, and with the bond of commerce binding us together we shall find all the rest follow. We will have an Imperial Council, an Imperial Defence, an Imperial Navy, an Imperial Army, and the peace and prosperity of those who come after us." [87] The

Tariff Reform League tried to stereotype the sentiment in leaflet No. 332 thus: "The Colonies treat *us* better than they treat the foreigner. Tariff Reform means treating the Colonies better than we treat the foreigner." But Mr. Bonar Law entirely spoiled the effect of the pretty phrases when he added in Parliament in 1913: "We intend to treat the Colonies better than we treat any foreign country, *but we do not intend to treat them as we treat ourselves*." [88]

That completion of the argument showed how far the Tariff Reform movement had travelled from its goal of Imperial Free Trade.

It has been shown already that another claim made on behalf of Preference was that it would "guarantee cheap food" [89]—"the only possible guarantee," indeed, "of real and permanent cheapness." "By giving a preference to Canadian wheat Mr. Chamberlain will make food in England cheaper. He will increase the supply, and the price will necessarily fall. It has been estimated that 100,000 square miles of very moderate wheat country would grow enough to feed the whole United Kingdom. There are, in Canada alone, at the very least 500,000 square miles of magnificent wheat lands still unscratched. New railways are being pushed out to them, and will be pushed out all the faster if Canada gets a preference in our market. In ten years Canada should be able to supply all the breadstuffs wanted by the Mother Country from abroad." [90] It was pointed out that these wheat lands would be developed—and inferentially that this would be the only way to develop them—if the United Kingdom gave Canada "a secure market for her surplus production of wheat." [91] What Canada would do with her produce when she extended the grain-growing area beyond the 100,000 square miles no Tariff Reformer has ever deemed it worth while to consider. The future will solve its own problems, just as the years that have passed since 1903 have solved the problems which the Tariff Reformers regarded with such artificial anxiety at that time.

"Consider!" one of these early leaflets bade us. "At this moment one foreign country sells to us more than **one-half** of all the wheat and wheat stuffs which we import, and not far from one-half of all we consume. Is this right or safe? Be sure that some day, if you allow this to go on, that foreign country will make you pay dearly for your wheat and for your bread. Seventeen millions of people in these islands are living on the wheat stuffs of one foreign power. Are you satisfied with this?"[92] "That foreign country" was the United States, which now sends us practically no meat and very little wheat. Indeed, the way of the world is against the Protectionists. Nature has killed their favourite arguments; necessity has smashed their ideals. The Colonists are steadily increasing their hold upon the British market without Preference; and all that is left to the Protectionists to-day is the scare-cry that if war broke out and we could not obtain all our food from Empire sources, it might perchance go ill with us. When Mr. Bonar Law maintained, as he did in 1908,[93] "that the Liberal Party are responsible for some part of the rise in the price of bread, because it is the result of a shortage of supply which would have been obviated had this country years ago given a preference to the wheat-growing portions of the Empire," he was merely trying to frighten the country. Inter-Imperial commerce develops more surely every year. The experience of the past has proved a stumbling-block to the Tariff Reformers. They can only look to the vague future. In a brochure published in 1911,[94] entitled *A Self-Sustaining Empire: Its Value to Great Britain*, the trade and potentialities of the Colonies are set forth in glowing terms. "Do you realize what our Colonies mean to you? Do you know what they are doing for you now? They are providing you with a quarter of your food; they are sending you raw materials to feed your factories; they are giving you protected markets where you can sell your goods; they are giving you battleships and helping to maintain the Navy; they send you soldiers to help fight your battles; they are offering a home and a chance of fortune to thousands of your fellow-countrymen who have been driven from the Mother Country by cruel circumstances." All accomplished, let it be observed, without Imperial Preference. The chagrined Tariff Reformers do not make this observation. They point to the achievements of the past to excite fear of the future. "If we continue our present policy of refusing to make preferential trade treaties with them we may lose them, lose all that vast wealth of natural resources with which our Colonies are brimming; they will be forced to seek elsewhere commercial alliances, with the inevitable consequence that we shall be faced with the danger of the British Empire falling apart, divided by separate interests, leaving Great Britain a solitary little island ringed about with powerful hostile nations."

Poor little island! In 1903 she was told that her trade with the Colonies would be lost without Imperial Preference. In 1913 her trade is found to have increased enormously. What of that? In the eyes of Tariff Reformers the more we gain the more we stand to lose. Any increase of trade that is not brought about by means of their Protective system is held to be insecure. The greater the trade, the greater the danger. There is no naïver way of putting it than as it was put in the booklet already quoted. "Are you, as a citizen of the British Empire, prepared to lose it all; or worse, are you prepared to lose all that the future offers?"

There have been notably few departures from the safe rule of vague generalization which has guided the Tariff Reform movement along the Preference line. Now and then, however, the sordid calculations that are behind it have accidentally been made apparent. In the early days of the decade leaflets were distributed showing how a Preferential tariff would benefit certain trades. The boot trade, for example. "If we give our Canadian friends a small advantage over the Americans in selling us their corn and cheese, they will give to our bootmakers, and other manufacturers, such an advantage as will enable us to compete with the Americans in spite of the disadvantage of longer distance."[95] And the monthly journal of the movement in 1905, in an article showing that our exports of carpets to certain foreign countries had declined, while to Canada there had been an increase, observed that "the importance of retaining and encouraging this Colonial trade must be obvious to every one, and how there can be any hesitation in the carpet trade over the fiscal question is not easy to understand. To the ordinary mind Mr. Chamberlain's policy offers our carpet manufacturers and their workpeople the one chance they have of saving their industry." [96] That is far from being a complete statement of Mr. Chamberlain's case. The late Sir Alfred Jones, K.C.M.G., a member of the Tariff Commission, at a meeting in London under the auspices of the West India Committee, said, "The British people were beginning to realize that they had an asset in their Colonies. For that thanks were due to Mr. Chamberlain. It was he who had brought sugar up from £6 to £16 a ton." [97] The real measure of the value of the Imperial sentiment to the Protectionist cause is perhaps better indicated in those words than in all the leaflets of the League.

THE COLONIAL "OFFER"

IT has been insisted on with almost pathetic force from 1903 onwards that the Colonies have held out an "offer" to the Mother Country. It is not only insisted that they have offered to give us a bigger preference in their markets if we give them a preference in ours. The Imperial sentiment is exploited here as elsewhere to cover up the real design of the Protectionists and to make it appear that the Mother Country is acting unfaithfully to her children in refusing to grasp their outstretched hands. More than that, all the eloquence of the movement has protested that the Colonies are ready to make something like a sacrifice for the sake of the old country, and that we are foolishly blind not to see it. Misquoting a passage from a speech by Mr. Winston Churchill, Tariff Reformers roundly accused their opponents of having "banged, barred, and bolted the door" upon the offer, though what Mr. Churchill said was strictly true. "They were told," he said, "the Government had banged the door. Upon what had they banged it? They had banged the door upon Imperial taxation of food. Yes, they had banged it, barred it, and bolted it." [98]

The origin of the alleged "offer" has been digged out by the Tariff Reformers themselves. "The first important specific proposal," says the official organ of the movement,[99] "was submitted by letter to the British Government by the then Premier of Queensland, Sir Samuel Griffith, who in March 1887 said: "I hope that an opportunity may arise during the Conference of discussing the practicability of consolidating and maintaining the unity of the Empire by adding to the existing bonds a definite recognition that her Majesty's subjects, as such, have a community of material interest as distinguished from the rest of the world, and on considering how far effect may be given to this principle by the several countries forming part of her Majesty's dominions affording to each other commercial concessions and advantages greater than those which are granted to subjects of other States. Without for a moment suggesting any interference with the freedom of each legislature to deal with the tariff of the country under its jurisdiction, I conceive that such freedom is not incompatible with a general recognition of the principle that when any article is subjected to a duty on importation a higher duty should be imposed on goods coming from foreign countries than on those imported from her Majesty's dominions." And the same authority [100] reminds us that in April 1892 the Dominion Parliament resolved "that if and when the Parliament of Great Britain and Ireland admits Canadian products to the markets of the United Kingdom upon more favourable terms than it accords to the products of foreign countries, the Parliament of Canada will be prepared to accord corresponding advantages by a substantial reduction in the duties it imposes upon British manufactured goods."

"To the ordinary mind," comments the League, "that is an offer of the most unmistakable kind—an offer, moreover, made ten years before it was repeated by all the self-governing Colonies at the Colonial Conference of 1902." The "repetition" by the Colonial Conference of 1902 was in the form of a resolution: "That with a view to promoting the increase of trade within the Empire, it is desirable that those Colonies which have not already adopted such a policy should, as far as their circumstances permit, give substantial preferential treatment to the products and manufactures of the United Kingdom." And "That the Prime Ministers of the Colonies respectfully urge on His Majesty's Government the expediency of granting in the United Kingdom Preferential treatment to the products and manufactures of the Colonies."

It will be observed that all these declarations were made in a strongly conditional mood. But the Tariff Reformers have invariably overlooked the "ifs" and "whens." They have even overlooked what Mr. Chamberlain himself said at the 1902 Conference, over which he presided as Secretary for the Colonies. "While we may most readily and most gratefully accept from you any preference which you may be willing voluntarily to accord to us," he said, "we cannot bargain with you for it. We cannot pay for it unless you go much further, and enable us to enter your home markets on terms of greater equality." Representatives of Canada, Australia, and New Zealand emphatically declined to concede Mr. Chamberlain's demand for "greater equality"; but no mention of this fact can be found in Tariff Reform literature. Instead, its pages are filled [101] with records of the existing preferences, followed by the statement that "these facts show that the Dominions have not merely offered, but have already given us preferences, to which, as yet, we have made no response. But in addition to these gifts of preferences," the Handbook goes on, "the Dominions have also made us an offer. They have offered to go on and extend the preference already given us, if we can see our way to give them in return some commercial advantage over the foreigner in the markets of their Mother Country."

Since 1902, then, the boot has been put on the other leg. Mr. Chamberlain asked for greater preference in the Colonial tariffs, and said he would not bargain for it. To-day the preferences already given are held to be big enough to justify "reciprocal action" on our part. There is still no inclination to state the price this country would have to pay for an extension of the privilege." Many extracts from the speeches of Colonial statesmen are printed by the Tariff Reform League. They are vague enough. For instance, "If a preference were given on Canadian products," said Sir Wilfrid Laurier, "we should be prepared to go further into the subject and endeavour to give to the British manufacturer some increased advantage over his foreign competitor in the markets of Canada." Those are the words also of the memorandum presented to the 1902 Conference by the Canadian Ministers present thereat.

There is nothing more substantial; yet upon such a foundation the Tariff Reformers have builded high. "If we do nothing in return," said the first edition of the *Speakers'*

Handbook,[102] "these things will surely happen: (1) Canada will withdraw her preference and make a treaty with the United States, by which each will admit the other's goods at a lower rate of duty. (2) The other Colonial Parliaments will withdraw their offers unless we meet them half-way. (3) Britain will lose a present advantage in the only markets where her trade is advancing. Business will be bad in England, and both employers and workmen will suffer. There will be less work to do, and wages will fall." And Mr. Vince, in his book on *Mr. Chamberlain's Proposals*, declared that if we "refuse to meet the Colonies in their present advance," we should "find this trade rapidly passing away under the influence of higher protective duties, and of reciprocity agreements with foreign countries, which do not share our fiscal scruples."

Mr. Chamberlain himself talked vehemently of this so-called "offer."[103] "Made by the Colonies, it came from them," he said.[104] "There is no doubt about the offer, it is in writing and it is public to all. Sir Wilfrid Laurier, on behalf of Canada, has made an offer, which will be supported by every other Colony, that we should come together and make a treaty of commercial union upon the principle of preference and reciprocity. Now, shall we accept that offer? Or shall we in our self-sufficiency reject the proffered hands?"[105] All that need be said is that if the offer was in writing, Mr. Chamberlain's successor at the Colonial Office did not find it; nor did Mr. Balfour, the Prime Minister; nor Lord Lansdowne, the Leader of the party in the House of Lords; nor the Duke of Marlborough; for we have their explicit statements that no such "offer" existed.

In 1904, Mr. Buchanan asked the Secretary for the Colonies whether the Colonial Office had at any time received any offer from any of the self-governing Colonies to open the home market of such colony to British manufactures on equal terms with colonial manufactures, or on terms better relatively to colonial manufactures than those now existing; and, if such an offer had been received, from which colony or colonies had such offer been received and what were the conditions accompanying it. To this Mr. Lyttelton replied that "no offers have been made of the nature indicated in the question. The general attitude of the self-governing Colonies in respect to this matter was defined in the resolutions passed at the Colonial Conference in 1902. Steps have since been voluntarily taken by several of the self-governing Colonies to give effect to this policy, but without any negotiation or correspondence or bargaining with the Mother Country." [106] Lord Lansdowne threw no light on the subject. All he could say in 1904 was that "it seems to me impossible to arrive at any conclusion but that something which may not be unfairly described in general terms as an offer has been made by the Colonies." [107] The Duke of Marlborough, at the same time and place, was a little more explicit. "The Colonies in general," he said, "had not made us a definite offer in the sense that they would give us something if we gave them something in return, excepting the case of Canada; but they had in a practical manner invited us to enter into reciprocal relations by giving us, as a pledge of their goodwill and desire in this matter, preferences which were neither inconsiderable nor by any means valueless." [108] Mr. Balfour was most definite of all. "The Colonies have never themselves put forward, so far as I know, any plan," he said in 1905.[109]

If it be objected that none of these was present at the Conference where the "offer" is supposed to have been formulated, the inquirer is referred to the very decided statement of one who was present. At the end of 1903 Mr. Deakin was asked in the Commonwealth Parliament "whether Mr. Chamberlain is trying to deceive the British public, and, if not, what 'offer' has been made by the Australian Government?" He replied that Mr. Chamberlain probably had in mind the resolutions in favour of preferential trade passed by the Colonial Conference. Mr. Reid, the Free Trade Leader of the Opposition, pointed out that as the Australian Premier had received no authority to speak for the Parliament or for the nation, the resolutions of the Conference were "simply an expression of opinion by certain gentlemen then present in London." Mr. Deakin's reply was that "the Leader of the Opposition doubts the application of the word 'offer' to the resolution carried by the Imperial Conference, and therefore I tell the hon. member frankly that I know of nothing that can be so construed."[110]

EXPLOITING THE COLONIAL CONFERENCE

THE 1907 Colonial Conference was made the occasion for a Tariff Reform manifesto so remarkable that it is desirable to print it in full. It was published in the April issue of *Monthly Notes,* which at this time was being temporarily edited by Messrs. C. A. Vince and E. A. Hunt and "published by the Imperial Tariff Committee, Birmingham." The Birmingham Committee did not always, as has been shown, see eye to eye with the Tariff Reform League on all matters ; yet even the League could not have made a more barefaced Protectionist use of an Imperial occasion than this. The manifesto was as follows :—

" THE COLONIAL OFFER.

" The approaching visit of the Colonial Premiers to this country, and the public interest which that visit may be expected to excite, affords a highly favourable opportunity of directing public attention once more to the Imperialist purpose of the policy of Tariff Reform.

It is most important that, for the encouragement of the Colonial Premiers themselves, it should be demonstrated that, in spite of the defeat of the Tariff Reformers in January 1906, the policy which the Colonial Premiers respectfully urged on the Government of the United Kingdom at the Coronation Conference in 1902 is supported by a large and a steadily increasing body of public opinion in this country.

We print below for the use of speakers and debaters, the full text of Resolutions unanimously adopted at the Conference of 1902. It will be useful to supply the audience at any Tariff Reform meeting with printed copies of these Resolutions.

The following topics are suggested for speakers at meetings held before or during the Colonial Conference.

(1) The Resolutions of 1902 embody the unanimous answer given by the representative Statesmen of the self-governing Colonies to two questions of high Imperial importance, namely :—

(*a*) By what means can the better consolidation of an Empire loosely organized and widely distributed over the habitable globe, be most effectually promoted ?

(*b*) By what means is it possible to secure Free Trade — or, failing Free Trade, Freer Trade — within and throughout the British Empire ?

(2) Thus for the first time an Imperial policy was propounded, and laid before the Mother Country by the unanimous voice of all the Colonies. The question of Imperial Preference, hitherto the subject of academic discussion only, was made a question of practical politics by the fourth resolution of the Colonial Premiers. The origin of the Tariff Reform movement is to be sought in the Coronation Conference.

(3) In May 1903, Mr. Chamberlain, then Colonial Secretary, took the responsibility of advising the country to give an affirmative reply to the request of the Colonial Premiers. This judgment of Mr. Chamberlain's was the result of eight years of thorough and sympathetic study of Colonial questions.

(4) The economical questions raised in the subsequent discussion (though many of them are relevant and important) are subsidiary only to the Imperial issue raised by the Colonial Premiers and by Mr. Chamberlain.

(5) The undertaking contained in the fifth resolution has been amply redeemed, New Zealand, South Africa, and the Commonwealth of Australia having since the Conference followed the Canadian example and established tariffs, giving a preference to British products.

(6) These preferences have given us a guarantee of faith in the principle, and are in every case to be largely extended after negotiation, when the Mother Country is ready to give reciprocal preference. The advantages, however, that have already resulted are of no small practical value. (Abundant testimony to the benefits of the small preferences already given can be gathered from the reports and evidence published by the Tariff Commission. Evidence derived from the experience of local industries, especially if supplied to the commission by local manufacturers, is most effective.)"

Perhaps it is only necessary to recall the fact that the Tariff Reform League had said that Free Trade within the Empire was impossible ; and to point out that the Birmingham Committee was true to its character when it professed to trace the origin of the Tariff Reform movement to the 1902 Conference, and to regard all other points in the fiscal controversy as "subsidiary" to the Imperial issue. Its expectation that Colonial preferences would after negotiation be "largely extended" had already been denied by leaders of the movement. What has been written in this section shows in how many other respects the manifesto fell short of the facts.

THE ATTITUDE OF THE COLONIES

IT is no part of the business of this book to deal with the fiscal systems of the overseas dominions of the British Empire. Yet without some reference to the opinions of those dominions on the points raised in our own fiscal controversy the record would be incomplete.

Out of the mass of vague statements made during ten years by the Tariff Reformers there emerge two clear points in relation to the Colonies. First of all, they were asked to relinquish the hope of developing their manufacturing industries. That impudent request was promptly dropped, almost before the comment of the *Sydney Bulletin*, "We will see Mr. Chamberlain boiled first," had reached his burning ears. Secondly, the hope was held out that the Colonies would increase their preference to British goods—"largely extend" it, as Mr. Vince had it. The two ideas had this in common, that the Colonies were to buy more from the Mother Country and manufacture no more for themselves. And the second suggestion was repudiated almost as violently as the first.

Mr. Bonar Law was quite wrong when he said that "neither in Canada nor in any of the other self-governing Dominions" was Imperial Preference a party question.[111] There is a decided Free Trade opinion in Canada, though the only way in which it has yet found expression is in repeated extensions of the British preference. The Canadian Protectionists have never failed to let it be known, however, that they would resist any preference that permitted effective competition with their own products. The purpose of these men is expressed in many resolutions of the Canadian Manufacturers' Association and in presidential speeches at their meetings. In 1903, at the Association banquet, the President said, "We favour a policy of reciprocal trade with the Empire by means of preference against foreign States. To make the present Canadian preference in favour of Great Britain of real value the base of Canada's general tariff must be raised. The orders for many lines of goods now going to the United States and Germany might be transferred to Great Britain. Canada must, however, necessarily provide under all conditions that the minimum tariff should afford fair protection to Canadian producers, so that the high standard of wages and living may be retained on a parity with the wages paid in the United States." All that this meant was that, in the view of the Canadian Protectionists, even the Preferential tariff rates must be raised. In 1904, again, the Association adopted a series of resolutions urging tariff revision and higher duties for the protection of Canadian industries, specially mentioning the woollen industry. In 1905 the President declared: "It is our intention to make in Canada everything which we can advantageously produce: and it is our ambition to make them just as well as they are made in any place on earth";[112] and in the same year, at the annual convention of his Association, he said that all classes in the Dominion "were agreed upon the need of adequate protection for native industries." Their position as to Preference, he added, was this: "We desire to make in Canada everything which we can advantageously produce, and to buy our surplus requirements as far as possible from British sources." Two days later, at the Association banquet the Dominion Premier dwelt on the expansion of Canada and pointed out that so rich a country must soon have a population of 20,000,000 people. "They will require clothes, they will require furniture, they will require implements, shoes, and everything that man has to be supplied with. It is your mission, it is my mission also, that this scientific tariff of ours shall make it possible that every shoe worn in these provinces shall be a Canadian shoe, that every yard of cloth shall be made in Canada, and so on."

Thus the story might be told, year by year, down to the present time; for at the 1912 banquet of the Canadian Manufacturers' Association, with Mr. Borden and Sir Wilfrid Laurier as the principal guests, Mr. Gourlay, the new President, said he had been asked by the British manufacturers recently touring the country if the Canadian manufacturers would favour an increase in British Preference. "We would not," was his reply, "and their best course is to cast in their lot with us and establish branch factories in Canada."[113] The whole matter was shrewdly summed up in 1906 by a powerful Canadian journal, the *Toronto Globe*,[114] when it observed that "the Colonial Representatives at the London Congress of the Chambers of Commerce of the Empire dominated the Congress, and the Colonies are Protectionist. Protected interests demand restrictions not only to foreign but on British competition. They take a certain delight in favouring what might be called a 'Pickwickian Preference'—one accompanied by so high a general tariff that it will still exclude British goods. A familiar declaration favours all concessions to Great Britain that will not adversely affect Canadian industries. That being interpreted, means no real concessions whatever, for British manufacturers cannot sell a dollar's worth in Canada without diverting Canadian industry from one line to another, and the line feeling competition would claim to be adversely affected. . . . The existing preference was established not for the benefit of Great Britain but for the benefit of Canada. In spite of that it is the subject of continuous attack by those who would nullify it by some such device as an increase in the general rate. We may as well admit that British manufacturers want a market, and that Canadian manufacturers will not let them have one in the Dominion."

Resolutions of Australian manufacturers could be quoted to match those from Canada; and in 1907 *The Times* (September 13) had a very frank article on the Australian Tariff, in which it was said that "the tendency of the whole tariff is in the direction of largely increased protection; and although, in a considerable number of cases, the duties levied upon British goods will be somewhat less than those upon goods of the same description arriving from other countries, the general effect of the whole is in a direction which must be detrimental to our trade. . . . We fear it must be admitted, even by those who are most earnest in promoting commercial intercourse with the Commonwealth, that the course taken by Australian statesmen is scarcely calculated to achieve that result."

The South African manufacturers have reported, through a Commission on which they were in a majority, in favour of higher Protective duties all round; and Mr. Seddon once said that "Consideration for the industries of New Zealand prevented a reduction of the duties on British imports."[115]

Nor is there any indication that the Colonies desire the Mother Country to impose duties on food for the sake of giving them a preference, against the interests of the inhabitants of this country. The grain growers of Canada have repeatedly passed resolutions declaring that they do not "look with favour on any fiscal or preferential tariff that will have the tendency to enhance the cost of living to British artisans and labourers"; the Melbourne correspondent of *The Times* tells us that while thinking men in Australia would gladly welcome any change which secured for them a substantial preference in the home market for wheat, wool, and butter; yet, "they would prefer to let matters alone rather than such changes should entail sacrifices on the part of the masses who are the chief consumers of the articles."[116] At the 1907 Conference Sir Joseph Ward declared, "If I were a public man resident in England, and with the general knowledge of economic conditions that I possess at the moment, I should be found on the side of those who are fighting for cheap food for the masses of the people. I believe," he added, "that anything in the way of preference that the Colonies might suggest, if it were calculated to raise the price of food to the masses of the people, ought to be opposed, and rightly so, by the British people";[117] and New Zealand's attitude was, again, clearly summed up by *The Times* so late as May 24, 1913, when in a review of twenty years' affairs in the Dominion the writer stated that the suggestion, attributable to Mr. Richard Seddon, that "New Zealand was snubbed or slighted by the refusal of Great Britain to tax their food for our benefit was an absurd travesty of the fact."

The multiplication of such assertions would be easy,

were it necessary to print them all. Enough evidence has been given to show that the Tariff Reformers have no ground for saying that the Colonies either ask for an advantage in our markets, or offer us even conditionally any further advantage in theirs. The mockery of the pretence was clearly shown in the House of Commons in February 1907 by Mr. Austen Chamberlain when he said, "The hon. member for Leicester (Mr. Ramsay Macdonald) says that the Australian cry is 'Australian work for Australian workmen,' the New Zealand cry is 'New Zealand work for New Zealand workmen,' and the Canadian cry is 'Canadian work for Canadian workmen.' I, for one, am not ashamed to say that I want British work for British workmen in as large a measure as we can obtain it." If Mr. Chamberlain were to think the matter out he would find that this desire he was not ashamed to admit would make anything like inter-Imperial trade impossible, and render all these ten years of talk about increasing the trade by preferential tariffs like so much water run to waste. He only succeeded in proving that Imperial Preference is precisely what Mr. Asquith said of it in 1911, "one of the greatest and most disastrous political impostures of modern times."

THE GREAT BETRAYAL

ALL the evasions and avoidances of the past ten years were outdone by the deliberate, though temporary, withdrawal of the Preference proposals by Lord Lansdowne and Mr. Bonar Law, in the name of the Parliamentary Tariff Reformers, in 1913.

It was temporary, because Mr. Bonar Law had himself declared that " Preferential trade and taxation of foreign manufactures are part of the one idea ; the one is the complement of the other, and the adoption of the one would inevitably lead to the adoption of the other " ; [118] and also because the Tariff Reform League at its annual meeting this year [119] resolved " that the rank and file of the Tariff Reform League adhere to the full policy of Tariff Reform as advocated by their leaders since 1903, and would regard any departure from it as equally disastrous to the cause of Tariff Reform as to the interests of the Unionist Party."

It was deliberate, because the Tariff Reformers had quite made up their minds that they could not get back to power with food-taxes in their knapsacks ; and also because it was the second time in the history of the movement that they had tried to wear the innocent air of having no intention to legislate on food-tax lines.

In 1904, when Mr. Balfour was trying to extricate the Unionist party from the trouble into which it had been brought by the re-introduction of Protectionism, he made a speech at Edinburgh [120] in which he so far complied with Mr. Chamberlain's call for a Conference of the Colonies as to say that, " In my view, we have got to a point when the only possible way of moving out of the *impasse* in which we now find ourselves—an *impasse* dangerous to the Empire as a whole—is to have a free conference with those self-governing Colonies and with India which would enable us to determine, one way or the other, in the first place, whether these great dependencies desire an arrangement, and, in the second place, whether an arrangement be possible or not." In more detail, he defined the plan of the Conference thus : " The policy of this party should be, if we have the power after the next election, to ask the Colonies to join in such a Conference and plainly intimate to them that those whom they send shall come unhampered by limitations in this direction or in that direction, but that as a necessary corollary, an inevitable set-off to the complete freedom of discussion, any plan, or, at all events, any large plan, of Imperial union on fiscal or other lines, ought not to be regarded as accepted by any of the parties to the contract unless their various electorates have given their adhesion to the scheme. I can conceive no objection to that policy except the one that it may take, and, indeed, must take, some time to carry out. Is that a grave objection ? For my part, I am so hopeful that an arrangement would be come to, and I am so fearful if it be come to without having behind it the public opinion of all the free governing communities concerned, that I do not desire, as I long ago said at Manchester, to see this matter hastily forced upon public opinion. We want it to be permanent. What we are aiming at is the consolidation of the British Empire."

It should be recalled that though Mr. Balfour preferred not to mention food-taxes, Mr. Chamberlain had already made it quite clear that " to suggest a Conference on preference, while rigidly excluding all reference to taxes on food, would be, in present circumstances, childish, and almost an insulting proposition."[121] But now, relying on the Prime Minister's prudent avoidance of this essential point, he effusively welcomed his suggestion. " It is the certain precursor of a victory which will give us closer union," he said. There was only one " blemish " in the plan. " Delay may mean the introduction of some new issue. If that part of the scheme were to be insisted upon, I think the Colonies would be justified in accusing us of insincerity, and of saying : ' No, we will not come to a Conference where we shall have disclosed our hands, where we shall have taken all this trouble, where we shall have expressed our willingness to make these sacrifices, and then find that nothing is to be done until after a number of doubtful events have taken place, over which we shall have no control and the performance of which may take many years.' "[122] Much the same was said in the House of Lords by Lord Ridley, then the Chairman of the Tariff Reform League. "It was proposed that two elections should intervene between them and the solution of the question. He thought the solution of the question more pressing than this proposal would indicate. There was a pressing need for some closer relation with the Colonies, and this dissolving view of general elections might involve a dissolving Empire."[123]

Mr. Bonar Law's opinion on the "two elections" idea is of especial interest, for he is the mouthpiece through whom the same proposal was renewed a few months ago. His first suggestion was made five days after Mr. Balfour spoke.

"Mr. Balfour," he observed, "had definitely pledged the party which he led to the summoning of a Colonial Conference, if he were returned to power. He promised, however, that the decision of this Conference would not be carried into effect without a fresh election. Mr. Chamberlain thought a new election was unnecessary; but that was a difference not of principle but of detail, and so far as practical politics were concerned it did not matter a row of pins. Mr. Chamberlain himself had said that he did not expect his policy would succeed at the first election. If he was right, if their opponents obtained power, then after they had ploughed the sands for a year or two, this question would have been thoroughly discussed and the country would probably be ripe, and Mr. Balfour would think it ripe, not only to summon the conference, but to carry its decision into effect. On the other hand, if the Conservatives won, they could not possibly do it by a large enough majority to make so great a change. They could, however, immediately summon the conference, and after it had sat the country would have to decide whether or not its wishes should be carried into effect."[124]

In a later speech Mr. Bonar Law more accurately anticipated the action he was to take when in the seat of authority nearly eight years later. The issue, he said, was really more than that of the dear or cheap loaf. "It was whether electors were willing *without committing themselves to anything*, to hold a Colonial Conference to consider whether preferential trade was desirable and practicable, and whether it could be obtained without injury to the country. If the Colonies were not willing to offer anything under such a scheme, then preferential trade would be dead." The only reason for the objection of the Opposition was that their opponents knew that there was another side of the question. "If the people knew the facts they would realize that there was more than the dear loaf and something else worth striving for, even possibly at the expense of a slightly dearer loaf." [125]

In the meantime, one of the Harmsworth journals had announced that, inasmuch as it had been recognized for several months past "that the country is not yet ripe for a fundamental change in our fiscal policy, it has, accordingly, been arranged that Mr. Chamberlain's war-cry at the next election shall only be : 'Vote for the Colonial Conference.' Electors will not for the moment be asked to go further." [126]

It is a matter of history how that cry fared. It was scarce heard in the din of the conflict, and it was thereafter so definitely dropped that in 1908 Lord Lansdowne spoke these words at its grave : "The suggestion of a double election was made by Mr. Balfour at a time when this question had been little, if at all, considered, and when it was impossible to expect that the General Election then before them would enable them to take a clear and favourable decision from the people upon the issue. The pledge Mr. Balfour then gave was expressly limited to the conditions of that time, was based on the very improbable contingency that they would win the election at that time, and was only intended to bind the party in that particular contingency." Moreover, as Lord Lansdowne reminded the country, Mr. Chamberlain had said "the pledge given in those peculiar circumstances could not be revived now, when none of the conditions by which it was then justified were any longer existing." [127]

The exhumation of political corpses is, however, a common practice of the Protectionist conspirators, and it was not surprising to find the "two elections" plan with a Colonial Conference intervening appearing on the Tariff Reform platform again in 1913. A good deal of what occurred at this time has been related in the section on Agriculture. The leader in the House of Lords and the leader in the House of Commons in speeches delivered on November 14, and December 4 and 16, 1912, definitely withdrew the undertaking that had stood on the records since the second of the 1910 general elections, to submit Tariff Reform to a Referendum, and Mr. Bonar Law undertook that if returned to power the Tariff Reform party would proceed to impose the "average 10 per cent" duties on manufactures; that before the next election took place the "limitation" of the proposed food taxation was, as suggested by Lord Lansdowne, to be indicated, and "in no circumstances" would the next Unionist Government exceed those limits without the permission of the electors; that there was to be no Referendum on Tariff Reform; but an Imperial Conference was to be called, when Imperial Preference was to be discussed; and lastly, that the taxation of food in the United Kingdom, within limits to be laid down before the election, was to be decided by the Colonial representatives.[128]

There was not much difference between this programme and that of Mr. Balfour in 1904; but Mr. Bonar Law has an awkward habit of saying just the little too much that "gives the show away," as the following passages from the speech indicate:—

"We have not abandoned the food duties, for two reasons.

The first is that in our opinion it is essential for this country that we should at least retain, and, if we can, increase the preference for our manufactures which we enjoy now in the oversea dominions of the Crown.

There is another reason. For nine years we have advocated preference as a step towards Imperial unity. For nine years we have kept that flag flying, and if there is any sincerity in political life this is not the time, and at all events I am not the man, to haul down my flag.

If our countrymen entrust us with power, we do not intend to impose food duties, but what we intend to do is to call a conference of the Colonies to consider the whole question of preferential trade, and the question of whether or not food duties will be imposed will not arise until after those negotiations are completed.

We are told that the Colonies have made no offer ; that they do not wish such an arrangement. Well, if that is true, we shall then find out. If that is true, no food duties will be imposed under any circumstances.

We do not wish to impose them. They are not proposed by us for the sake of Protection, and there is no Protection in them. They are proposed solely for the sake of preference. If, when the conference takes place, the Colonies do not want them—I put it far stronger than that, unless the Colonies regard them as essential for preference—then also the food duties will not be imposed.

All we ask is that our countrymen should give us authority to enter into that negotiation, with power to impose certain low duties on food-stuffs within strict limits which will never be increased.

Our opponents ask us to give in detail really what we mean to do. That is impossible. The details will only be known after the negotiations have been completed.

Long before the election you will know precisely within what limits we want authority from you, and you will know that these limits will not be exceeded in the next Parliament if you return us to power. They will never be exceeded in any Parliament unless we have received the expressed sanction of the people of this country.

If the Colonies do not think these duties necessary for preference, then they will never be imposed.

I think we are right in the view we hold that the readjustment which we propose, instead of increasing, would actually diminish the cost of living in this country. But in any case, I have said many times, and I say it again now, that if I believed this change would add to the burdens of the poor in this country to any extent, however small, I should not advocate it.

I will tell you the reason why it would not do to submit these proposals to a Referendum without a completion of negotiations.

Would it be fair to the Colonies to do that ? They would come to the conference, if they came at all, in this position—that if they agree to the arrangement they would carry it out after a Session of Parliament. In other words, they would come bound, while we should come free."

The speech was a political blunder of the first magnitude. Tariff Reformers regarded it as saying both too much and too little. Free Traders looked upon it as a plan to get rid of the responsibility of imposing food-taxes on Great Britain by passing it on to a Conference of Colonial Protectionists ; and *The Times* next day frankly declared that " Unionist leaders must not expect to shift the onus of food taxation on to a Conference of Ministers from overseas. . . . If food taxes are to be passed at all, they must be justified in the first place by the domestic conditions of the British Isles."

Around that point a furious controversy raged for a month. One section of the Protectionist Press urged the dropping of the food taxes altogether; another section asked that they be dropped for a time; a third section demanded the reinstatement of the Referendum; and a fourth, led by the *Morning Post*, which declared that "the suggestion of a special referendum on the fiscal question is banished for ever,"[129] saw nothing ridiculous about Mr. Bonar Law's proposed appeal to the Empire for permission to impose the food-taxes. As the sections redivided it became clear that they all agreed with Mr. Joseph Chamberlain, the arch-originator of the hubbub, that "if you are to give a preference to the Colonies . . . you must put a tax on food"; and in the end it became possible to rearrange them into two main groups. There were those, led by Mr. Austen Chamberlain, who refused to relinquish any shred of their motley, and there were those who were willing to change their outer garments for a few years on the chance of winning the next election in disguise. If there had been leaders enough to go round, either group might have secured one, and they might now be marching side by side singing different and discordant war-songs. But the one and only "leader" who could be got to follow the crowd was Mr. Bonar Law himself. Some palanquin had to be found to carry him in, and after nearly a month of angry wrangling, the covering suggestion of the *Daily Telegraph* was adopted, and the army went forward to try to win entry by ruse.

Readers who wish to follow the story of this enlivening period in greater detail will find the material elsewhere.[130] It is necessary to refer to it here in order to show that something like the "two elections" plan which Mr. Balfour introduced in 1904, which received the conditional blessing of Mr. Chamberlain, Lord Lansdowne, Mr. Bonar Law, and the Tariff Reform League, and which was afterwards dropped, came up again, grinning, in 1913.

The *Daily Telegraph* suggestion on which the atoms regrouped themselves was " that before food duties are imposed they shall be constitutionally referred to the judgment of the people at another General Election. . . . Let there be an explicit pledge that there shall be a second General Election before any new duty can be imposed on wheat or similar food-stuffs, and the Unionist party will feel that a cloud has been lifted, and a deadly peril turned aside." [131] And the episode was closed by Mr. Bonar Law writing a letter to the chief Opposition Whip, dated January 13, 1913, in which the leader's compliance was signified in these terms: " The modification requested by those who have signed the Memorial is that if when a Unionist Government has been returned to power it proves desirable, after consultation with the Dominions, to impose new duties on any articles of food, in order to secure the most effective system of Preference, such duties should not be imposed until they have been submitted to the people of this country at a General Election. We feel that, in view of such an expression of opinion from such a quarter, it is our duty to comply with the request which has been addressed to us, and this we are prepared to do."

THE MODIFIED PREFERENCE

IT is also necessary to have a clear recollection of these recent events because they threw Mr. Bonar Law back upon a remarkable modification of the Tariff Reform Preferential proposals. It was a modification of the nature of that which Mr. Chamberlain in 1903 called "futile," and with that description of it the Tariff Reform League agrees to-day.

A few days after the publication of the above letter announcing the "change in the method of procedure," Mr. Bonar Law spoke at Edinburgh and said that "we shall give to the Dominions of the Crown in our market a preference which is possible without the imposition of new duties upon food." [132] He must have been conscious at the time he spoke of the almost invisible advantage which such a preference would be to the Dominions (from New Zealand, for example, possible preferential imports outside food and raw materials amount to about a hundred pounds a year), for he said after the lapse of a few days more that "the amount of trade to-day without a tariff is no indication of what the trade will be after the preference is given. . . . But if we find after trying that it is impossible to have a preferential system which will effect that object (the consolidation of the British Empire) without food duties, then we shall endeavour to carry food duties." [133]

Six years earlier Mr. Bonar Law had declared that he would be "perfectly satisfied" "if the Government would undertake to use even the existing taxes as a first beginning," [134] and the Tariff Reform League was then questioned on the possibility of giving a Preference to the British Dominions on such a basis. The reply of the League is noteworthy. In its official publication it observed, "on the face of these figures," which were printed in its own reply, that

" no considerable advantage can be offered to British Possessions " by such a plan ;[135] and in the next issue of the same publication was printed a statement issued by the Tariff Commission, in which it was said that " Preferences granted by the United Kingdom on the basis of existing duties would affect no part of the Empire except India and Ceylon and certain of the Crown Colonies. The duties collected in 1905 upon goods from the self-governing Colonies amounted only to £151,000, representing 79 per cent. of the value of the goods subject to duty, but only three-tenths of one per cent. of the total imports from these Colonies."[136]

To that minute fraction was the " high Imperial aim " worn down by the friction of discussion. It represents all that the Tariff Reformers have been able to save of the 1903 programme of Preference which was to prevent the Empire dissolving into its component atoms, to save British trade from destruction, to make every Colony and the Mother Country richer by preventing them from trading with others. Small wonder that the Tariff Reform League, with its hatred of tiny figures, should still insist on making a daily meal off the " full programme."

EMIGRATION

THERE is another aspect of the Empire question which the Tariff Reformers have forced to the front. Perhaps it is the most fruitful of all in contradiction and contrast.

First they have alleged that the object of the Free Traders is to get rid of the Colonies. Mr. Joseph Chamberlain invented the formula in 1903,[137] when he said that "we have gone through a time—it is a most significant fact—when the men who advocated Free Trade in this country were at the same time absolutely indifferent to all idea of Empire, and considered the Colonies as an encumbrance which we should be glad to get rid of." It has been repeated in varying degrees of distance from the truth until in 1913 it was phrased by Mr. Austen Chamberlain in these words, that "the old Cobdenite idea that the best thing we had to do with the Empire was to get rid of it, that the easiest way to settle our Imperial problem was to cut the knot that tied us to our kinsmen overseas." [138] The same accusation was made by the organizing secretary of the Duke of Westminster's Imperial Fund, who managed to state it with more accuracy. "Cobden predicted," he declared, "that Free Trade would, among its other results, 'get rid' of the British Colonial System." [139]

This is one of the most conspicuous examples—many more will follow in these pages—of wilful misrepresentation. The Tariff Reformers have gleefully fastened on it with the object of deceiving the public, leaving them to imagine that the "Colonial System" and the Colonies are one and the same thing. Cobden, of course, never said anything about getting rid of the British Colonies. The "Colonial System" to which he referred was a very different thing from the Colonies themselves. Moreover, what Cobden hoped for did indeed come true, for the "Colonial System"—a name with a definite meaning in the history of politics—no longer applies to the Dominion of Canada, the Union of South Africa, the Commonwealth of Australia, or the Dominion of New Zealand. The "Colonial System" was, in short, the old bad method of governing the Colonies exclusively from Downing Street. It was wasteful; it bred ill-feeling and caused friction; and, above all, it was utterly unsuited to the British spirit and to British folk beyond the seas. So for the "Colonial system" of government was substituted self-government. "I want to retain the Colonies," said Cobden, "by their affections."

Still, after sixty years, the distortion of Cobden was held to serve a useful purpose in heightening the effect of the Tariff Reform appeal to the Imperial sentiment. Tariff Reformers did not want to get rid of the Colonies. Quite the reverse; it was the "Cobdenites" who regarded them "as an encumbrance to be got rid of as soon as possible."[140] Why, the Tariff Reformers did not like even to see Britons being "driven" into "foreign lands," as Mr. Joseph Chamberlain said of the emigrants to the United States in 1903.[141] "Every year," he wailed in a later speech,[142] "from our surplus population we send some of our best, of our youngest, of our most energetic—we send them abroad to seek their fortunes in other climes. Where do they go? They go for the most part under a foreign flag. They, or their descendants, break the connection. Being no longer under the shelter of the Union Jack, they no longer share our Imperial sentiment. I hope that they remain friendly, but they are no longer to be counted amongst our supporters, amongst those who, with us, maintain the mighty edifice, the responsibility for which has been thrown upon us."

As far back as 1879 Mr. Farrer Ecroyd, one of the old "Fair Traders," had anticipated this desire to transfer emigration from the United States to the British overseas Dominions; and in 1904 the Tariff Reform League monthly journal[143] quoted Mr. Ecroyd as having written very boldly that if a preferential tariff were adopted, "a large field for emigration, and for the legitimate and safe investment of English savings, would thus be opened out, to the discomfiture of floaters of foreign loans, American railway bonds, and unsound limited companies." In the following year the same journal,[144] commenting sorrowfully upon the fact that in 1903 more emigrants went to the United States than to Canada, observed that "we may infer from this contrast that we are sending out of the country artisans for whom employment ought to be found at home, rather than agriculturists for whom the Canadian corn lands are waiting. Here is an immense outlying estate of the Empire the development of which promises wealth to the British nation. What it wants is first men, and secondly a secure market. A main purpose of Mr. Chamberlain's policy is to supply the second of these needs."

Nor was this all. The League was immensely impressed with what Mr. Chamberlain had said about the foreign flag. "We need not be surprised," said the League, "if we wake one of these days to find an Americanized Canada; and an Americanized Canada, it need scarcely be said, cannot be depended upon to continue giving us a preference for nothing." [145] This nightmare was provoked by the knowledge, as the Tariff Reform League put it, that "of the total immigration into Western Canada, thirty-three out of every hundred persons now come from the United States." [146] These American settlers might become good Canadian citizens, but "they have not, and there is no reason why they should have, any feeling of attachment to the mother country. On the other hand, with British settlers and their descendants the tie of sentiment is strong. But sentiment alone is not strong enough to outweigh the powerful impulse of business interest. If the farmer in Canada obtains two shillings a quarter more for his wheat than the farmer in the United States, the danger of the influx of American farmers leading to a demand for the annexation of Canada to the United States will disappear. Upon the success of the policy put forward by Mr. Chamberlain depends, therefore, not only the development of Canada's wheat resources, but the future unity of the British Empire."

A year or two later the League put the same idea in other words, when it said [147] that "the draining of our strength by emigration may be saved by diverting the outflowing stream to our own Colonies."

That last leaflet is not quoted only to show that a British wheat tax was necessary to turn an American into a Canadian and to prevent the secession of the Dominion. The argument it contained has been repeated on occasion many times since. In 1907, for instance, Mr. Austen Chamberlain spoke of the half of our emigrants going "to foreign countries, to become strangers and competitors instead of going to our own colonies to remain our kinsfolk and our customers," and of the desirability of securing "that those who leave our shores shall go to develop the sister nations beyond the seas, and shall live still under the same flag, owing all allegiance to the same Sovereign." [148] Preference, he said about the same time,[149] "will turn the stream of emigration from our shores to foreign countries to the self-governing dominions of the Empire."

But this is another example of the end, that was to be achieved by Preference only, having been won without Preference and in spite of all the eloquence of the Tariff Reformers. Gradually emigration to Canada increased and emigration to the United States decreased. Yet, as usual, the wary Tariff Reform League was quick to perceive the change and to vary its argument to suit the altered circumstances. In 1909 it said: "The great majority of our emigrants have been in the habit of going to the United States, and one useful result of Tariff Reform and Imperial Preference will certainly be to make it better worth their while than it is at present to go to Canada and other British Colonies rather than to the United States," [150] thus bearing the versatile record over the flimsy argumentative bridge to its next stage in the history of deception.

Emigrants have always been patted on the shoulders by Tariff Reformers as the saviours of the Empire. They were part of the means of building up that self-sustaining union of nations that were to subsist on taking in one another's washing. Mr. Joseph Chamberlain spoke in 1903 of the desirability of filling up the "waste land" of the overseas dominions; [151] and his earliest and chiefest Protectionist lieutenant, Mr. C. A. Vince, declared earnestly that "the development of Canadian farming" (which was to be stimulated by Preference) "means profitable employment—for whom? Not for the Canadians or their posterity only, but for the surplus agricultural population of our own country. They are emigrating to Canada at the rate of 17,000 a year. Is it not better," he asked, "that this emigration should be encouraged than that the children of our ruined agricultural industry should flock to the towns, overcrowd the slums, aggravate the cruel competition of unskilled labour, and accelerate the physical degradation of the race?"[152] Mr. Austen Chamberlain, in 1905, was even more complimentary to the pioneer instinct of the race. "We are forty millions of people in these islands, a race," he boasted, "endowed with much energy, great activity, great enterprise, a race of born colonists and explorers and leaders of men, who have played a big part in the past in the development of the world."[153] From that time down to the present there have been innumerable examples of the recognition of this truth on the part of Tariff Reformers. "Englishmen," said Mr. Hewins, the Secretary of the Tariff Commission, "had emigrated since the days of Elizabeth, and the race had not suffered from it. The only way to carry on the English tradition was to emigrate. The tradition could not be created, or extemporised, or taught in schools; it must be breathed."[154] And as for the Tariff Reform Press, printing its many pages of seductive emigration advertisements and even offering free passages to Australia by way of prizes—as the *Daily Express* did in 1913—its eloquence may be represented in the words of the *Daily Mail*,[155] which said of the great increase in the numbers of emigrants to Canada in recent years, "They have everything to gain by the change; and the Empire has everything to gain too. For the greater the man-power of the Dominion, the higher waxes our Imperial strength." Indeed, in the autumn of 1912, when Mr. Wyndham spoke of British emigrants as "exiled because of obstinacy in clinging to the fetish of Free Trade," the *Observer* (an out-and-out Protectionist paper) protested against "the habit of speaking of transfer to Canada or Australia as ' emigration ' or ' exile,' " and angrily rejected " the narrow design of keeping the best and fittest of our people at home." [156] And the *Morning Post*, most persistently Protectionist of all the London journals, actually suggested that the great towns of this country should encourage emigrants by themselves establishing colonies within colonies, so to speak, " where, say a Leeds, or a Bradford, or a Huddersfield man, would feel himself at home among friends in a special sense." [157]

There have been some attempts to put this theory to the test of practical experience. Late in 1910, Mr. J. Norton Griffiths, M.P. for Wednesbury, assisted by a few shrewd friends, began to make arrangements to acquire land in Canada (with British capital), and found thereon " a brand new little township " to be called Wednesbury. And another experiment in this direction was made on a small scale by no less prominent a Protectionist than the late Duke of Sutherland, President of the Tariff Reform League. In January 1911 the Duke of Sutherland purchased some two thousand acres of land in British Columbia, with the object of enabling a certain number of British farmers to become settlers and to acquire and cultivate their own farms. They were to be " ready made " farms to prevent " discouragement " and " heartache." This was the account his Grace gave to the *Daily Mail* when he was about to undertake a trip to Canada, the primary object of which was " to see what I can do to encourage and assist British settlers to come to Canada."[158]

Contrary to this continuous—and, let it be said, very natural—recognition of the " tradition of the race," there is to be set one example of an apparently sincere desire to prevent emigration, nay, to bring back the " exiles " to the Mother Country! It was in a letter which would have been counted unworthy of a place in this record if it had not been prominently printed in an official Tariff Reform leaflet.[159] The letter was from an English commercial traveller in Canada. " It makes me unhappy," wrote the miserable man, " to contrast the two countries ; but once get adequate Protection and England can still stand in her old place as head of the nations of the world. Her sons shall not bow their heads in shame when they hear foreigners call her stupid and hidebound, and, *given Protection, we shall see a steady flow back again to the old country of the sons who left* because foreign manufactured articles took the bread out of their mouths. That the day will not be long delayed I pray daily. If long delayed, the capital of the country must come over here, as investments yield more certain and larger interests. ENGLAND AWAKE!"

It is only fitting that the original design of capital letters should be preserved in this monument of Protectionist stupidity.

Now, all that has been written of the way in which Tariff Reformers in the first instance have been jealous of the United States taking away men who ought to go to grow wheat in Canada, and secondly have sought to encourage emigration to the Dominions, has been written because it is important to give a suitable setting to their own base use of this British tradition. For it will be hard to believe that the Tariff Reformers, all the while they have been praising the boldness of the race and bidding it go on peopling the "waste places" of their own Empire, have been holding emigration up as a lurid example of the awful kind of thing that only goes on under Free Trade! Men driven from their homes! Only very rarely have they said straight out, as the homesick commercial traveller did, that Protection would reverse the process. No; what they have done is to ask how it is that "instead of the Colonists flocking to England, Englishmen are flocking to the Colonies"; [160] or to hint that "if we want to keep the pick of our labourers and artisans in this country, we must do as Germany does, and see to it that the best and most enterprising of our working men are not deprived of work and wages in the land of their fathers by unrestricted imports of foreign goods, and the deportation to foreign countries of once flourishing British industries." [161]

Sometimes, indeed, the contrast which these quotations illustrate has been found in one and the same journal, as when the *Pall Mall Gazette*, in the same column on the same page, said first that "it is from Free Trade England, and not from Protectionist Germany, that the wage-earner takes his flight by the hundred thousand," and then went on to admonish us that "one thing is urgently required—namely, a new habit of thought at home. We must give up talking of the 'Colonies' and thinking of shifting from one shire of the Empire to another as 'emigration.'"[162]

"Emigration returns furnish a good test of employment and prosperity at home," said a Tariff Reform League editorial in 1907.[163] To that use they have been very frequently put. Publications without number have deplored the "thousands of your fellow-countrymen who have been driven from the Mother Country by cruel circumstances"[164] and Tariff Reform speakers without number have tried to bring tears to the eyes of their audiences by conjuring up a vision of a leadlong "flight from Free Trade." "Rats," said Mr. Balfour Browne, K.C., "left a sinking ship. The Blue-Books showed that in this country emigration was on the increase, while it was on the decrease in Germany, brought about by the rapid industrial expansion in Germany and the consequent demand for labour. That was what was wanted here. It was the demand for labour that raised wages, and the demand for labour in Germany kept her people within her own realm. It was this ship that was sinking, the ship of Germany was afloat. Wages in Germany were going up, and that was why the Germans did not emigrate. The wages here were going down, and there were hundreds of people unemployed and thousands of people on the verge of starvation. That was why they went away."[165] "This fiscal question," said Mr. Bonar Law, "was from top to bottom a question of employment. From a trade point of view the best system was the system which would give the best employment and the best kind of it. . . . Was there anyone out of an asylum who would deny that if employment were better here than in America, instead of our people flocking to America, the reverse process would happen, and Americans would come to the United Kingdom?"[166]

And lastly, in 1912 the Tariff Reform League published a host of new leaflets, the meaning of which, so far as they had any meaning, was that Protection will check or entirely stop emigration. This series of anti-Imperial leaflets [167] was addressed to "Men of London," "Men of Kent," "Men of Durham," and so on in turn for thirty-five parts of the country. The burden of them all was that in five years more than a million (the Tariff Reform League loves its millions!)—more than a million British subjects had "flown from Free Trade." Is it unfair to say that the implication desired by the Tariff Reform League was that Protection would keep these millions at home, and so either check the development of the Colonies or leave them to be peopled by those very foreigners who, in earlier leaflets of the League, were regarded as a distinct "danger" to the unity of the Empire?

The only remaining comment now necessary is that of Mr. Hewins himself, who said, doubtless from his heart, in the speech already quoted, that "I know the value of emigration. I also know what use is made of emigration figures!"

IV.—BRITISH TRADE

DUMPING AND DECADENCE

THE SECTIONAL APPEAL

EXHIBITIONS

"TESTS" OF VARIOUS KINDS

DUMPING AND DECADENCE

THE diminuendo of dumping is best heard in the Tariff Reform League Leaflets on the piano trade.

The first edition of Leaflet No. 166 lamented that "*For every piano we were able to sell Germany, she was able to sell us* 592 ! !" (The exclamation marks are an important notation.)

The second edition, issued a few years later, lamented that "*For every piano we were able to sell Germany, she was able to sell us* 394 ! !"

Then, after two more years, the number of the leaflet was changed to 358, and the lament was changed to : "*For every piano we were able to sell Germany, she was able to sell us* 196 ! !" (Both exclamation marks remained.)

That is an authentic summary of the Tariff Reform case ; but inasmuch as the story provides many more such examples of simulated surprise, it may be as well to put some of them in the story.

"Dumping" has been declining, but the Tariff Reformers have extended the scope of its meaning in the hope of maintaining the breadth of its significance. As early as 1906 [1a] the Secretary of the Tariff Commission thought it well to say that it was "no part of Mr. Chamberlain's policy to prove the decay of British industry." Originally dumping was the name given to the act of manufacturers who sold their goods in a foreign market at a price below the cost of production. It never was profitable to do this, and the practice declined. It declined because it was bad business, and not, as Mr. Chamberlain once flamboyantly claimed at Birmingham, because he had frightened it off by his oratory. But the meaning of the word was swelled and swelled, until it at last described all our so-called "manufactured" imports in mass. With its use was involved the pretended decadence of British industries, and in this section it is found convenient to keep the two ideas in association.

Our industries were doomed to extinction because the foreigner was said to dump his products on our shores at prices the British manufacturer could not compete with, a state of affairs that meant, according to a Protectionist authority, "cheap prices for the rich, loss of employment for the poor." [1]

"I am told," said Mr. Chamberlain in 1903,[2] "that at this moment, or within the last few months, an American salesman has come over here with 17,000 or 20,000 watches, and that he is prepared to offer them at any price he can get for them." "These watches," he added, "are sold at any price below the cost at which the British working-man could possibly make them, even if he accepted half wages. Meanwhile the Prescot Works have to take lower prices and do what they can, and have to turn off workmen, and if that goes on long enough the Prescot Works will close, the whole of their trade will be gone, and then those of you who are buying in the cheapest market and buying American watches, what do you think you will have to pay for your watches?"

The importation of foreign watches had been declining for the previous few years, but that did not matter to Mr. Chamberlain. Later on the Tariff Reform League itself announced that a New York firm was in London buying up American watches for exportation back again to the United States! "For the time being," [3] said the League, "it may be all right for the firm who are buying the dumped watches and sending them back to America, and who, even after paying a heavy import duty, are able to make a profit by selling the American watches in competition with the actual makers. But the Americans are not likely to allow their trade to be interfered with in this way for long, and are certain to make such transactions impossible either by raising the duty or prohibiting the re-importation of American goods into America. But in any case it is a very serious matter for English watchmakers, who have to face competition of watches dumped at these prices in the English market."

At Greenock, in 1903, Mr. Chamberlain predicted, on the authority of a director of the American Steel Trust, that when a falling-off came "we are not going to blow out a single furnace. . . . What we are going to do is to invade foreign markets;" and at Bristol in 1905 he asked:[4] "What is being heard in Bristol or anywhere, any port, week after week? Whole cargoes are delivered upon your quays of ready-made doors, of manufactured woodwork of one kind and another, and the carpenters and joiners who ought to make them in this country, they are walking the streets, or they are a burden upon the funds of their societies."

"We are losing both ways," he said at Greenock.[5] "We are losing our foreign markets, because wherever we begin to do a trade the door is slammed in our face with a whacking tariff. We go to another trade. We get it for a few months or a few years, and at once a tariff is imposed upon it, and that is shut out . . . and we lose our foreign trade." "We have reached our highest point. Our fate will be the fate of the empires and kingdoms of the past." "Agriculture," he cried, "agriculture as the greatest of all trades and industries of this country, has been practically destroyed; sugar has gone, silk has gone, iron is threatened, wool is threatened, cotton will come! How long are you going to stand it? At the present moment these industries, and the working men who depend upon them, are like sheep in a field. One by one they allow themselves to be led to slaughter, and there is no combination, no apparent prevision of what is in store for the rest of them."

"His persuasions and arguments—almost his very statistics," said *The Times*,[6] "were pitched in the key of emotion." In the same month[7] he wrote to a Birmingham correspondent to say that "unless we are content to fall back into the condition of a second Holland, and be a distributing and not a manufacturing nation, we must wake up and meet the new conditions." The next day, speaking at Liverpool of shipping, he asked, "What is the use of saying that the house is still standing, when you know there is rot in the foundations?" In the spring of the following year[8] his dirge continued. "We are in a state of comparative decline. We have lost the predominance that we once enjoyed, we are sinking to a lower rank among the nations. We are no longer first. We are third. We shall be fifth or sixth, if things go on as they are at present, and it is no use flaunting our increased prosperity in our faces when we are being outstripped in the race of nations."

The Times was moved again by this flight of fancy to protest that he possibly "put the thing too high when he says that from being first we have sunk to third"; but his lament was still heard loudly in the land. "You might have a nation—there are several such—where manufacturing and productive industry is at a low ebb, where the people are all either men of leisure, or hawkers, or distributors of goods, or occupying some one or other of the professions which are not productive. You may become a nation of that kind."[9] And in 1905, "It is not so many years," he said, "since Holland and Spain were amongst the greatest of great countries. Now they have fallen from their high estate because some greater countries have arisen and eclipsed them: and yet, if you look at the statistics, the positive statistics, of these two countries, you will find that never, probably in their whole history, were they richer than they are now, or was their trade greater or had they a larger population. All those things which are quoted as proofs of our prosperity they enjoy." Thus the thing to look at was not the "positive statistics," but "the test of the prosperity and the security of any nation is to be found in comparative statistics."

He had another test—indeed, he had many—to which fuller reference will be made presently. "My case," he said,[10] "is that the trade of this country, as measured—and I think it ought to be mainly measured—by the exports of this country to foreign countries and to British possessions, has during the last twenty or thirty years been practically stationary; that our export trade to all those foreign countries which have arranged tariffs against us has enormously diminished, and at the same time their exports to us have enormously increased;" and he supplemented this[11] by saying that though "our foreign trade, much of it, is gone and cannot be recovered," yet "our Colonial trade remains with us."

Emotionalism generally leads one to say too much; and the very unemotional Tariff Reform League has endeavoured, many times since, to reduce the recollection of Mr. Chamberlain's eloquence to more manageable dimensions, and to wipe out the unfortunate effect of the discovery that Mr. Chamberlain's audience at Gainsborough on February 1, 1905, was seated on 7000 chairs stamped on the bottoms, "Made in Russia." In 1905 the League declared that "Mr. Chamberlain has never said that our trade, as a whole, was declining, but that it has been practically stagnant, and would have declined but for the increase with British Possessions;[12] and further, that "the essence of Mr. Chamberlain's case is that the character of our exports has changed, and that their volume in the case of foreign, and especially protected, countries, has seriously declined, the decrease being only counteracted by enhanced exports to the Colonies. That has been Mr. Chamberlain's case from first to last, and it has been proved up to the hilt. But his opponents, it is clear, will never cease from misrepresentation of his views and speeches."[13] The difficulty which the Tariff Reform League has to face is that Mr. Chamberlain's opponents have gone to his speeches and not to the League's misrepresentations of them.

But the League itself has loved to harrow the feelings of the country by horrid tales of dumping and lurid descriptions of decadence; and in spite of the authoritative contradictions of men who knew the "going" industries from beginning to end, in spite of warnings from Protectionist sources that the cost of Protection would fall on the consumer, the wail grew shriller. In 1904, Mr. J. S. Jeans, secretary of the British Iron Trade Association, in a paper to the Tariff Commission, remarked that the agitation that was carried on against dumping was partly founded on a more or less imperfect ascertainment of essential facts. While it was in vigorous progress, he observed, a correspondent sent him a list of twenty iron works in South Wales which were alleged to have been closed by dumping. (Of some of these the Protectionist newspapers published photographs.) Yet four-fifths of the works on the list, said Mr. Jeans, "were either old finished iron works or obsolete tin-plate works, and in both cases dumping had nothing to do with their becoming derelict!" And *The Times*, in an article on German enterprise in the British electrical markets, said that the cost "falls mainly upon the German people, who enable the loss which their contractors make in obtaining entry into oversea markets to be recouped by themselves paying higher prices for articles of home consumption. The conditions of the manufacturing industry in this country are such," said the journal, "as to prevent any imitation, on the part of our manufacturers, of such a policy." [14]

In the *National Review* of May 1904, Mr. J. L. Garvin dealt a heavy blow at his leader's prestige. He attempted no less than to reconstruct Mr. Chamberlain's case on a different basis. He abjured statistics; he demolished the central assertion from which the fiscal campaign took its start. "England," he said, "is not ruined, but, for the most part, exceedingly prosperous."

Yet the cry of the Leaguers mounted higher and higher. "Nothing but ruin stares British Trade in the face." [15] In 1905, when the Aliens Act was passing through Parliament, the Tariff Reform League [16] reminded the country of "the less evident competition of the foreigner who remains in his own country, is sweated there instead of in Whitechapel, and exports his cheap products to the open market of England." There were alarming tales of Americans making bonfires of their cotton instead of selling it, in order to keep the price up; [17] of brushes made in German prisons and iron worked by American convicts, causing "honest British labour to be thrown out of employment" [18] without a word to show that a British Act of Parliament already prohibited such goods being sold in this country.[19] German plums were permitted to flood the British market; [20] German mugs and saucers for British Boy Scouts were being "dumped by the million into England"; [21] and, most shocking of all, "who would believe the British Tar employed in the British Navy was forced to keep his trousers up with buckles made in France?"

The last shriek was almost a case for the piano exclamation marks. Yet it was a question quite seriously asked by a Protectionist journal, *The Empire Illustrated*, in 1912:[22] " No one would ever dream of thinking," it said, " that the nether garments of the German naval seamen are thus supported." It even conjured up an awful vision of the British sailor, his ship in action, running about with one hand hitching up his breeches and the other signalling for a bit of string. " Think what a calamity, if in the case of war with France, these buckles were unobtainable and the British sailor, when called upon to man his gun, were found holding his trousers up, owing to the failure of the supply of French buckles ! "

When it is remembered that, two years later, so trusted a Tariff Reformer as Sir Joseph Lawrence pointed to the closing of the " Star and Garter " at Richmond, the decline of famous whitebait dinners at Greenwich, the departure of the " former glory " of the Crystal Palace, and the quietude of the old roadside hotels, as evidences of the evils wrought by Free Trade, there need be no surprise at a journal which for some years was obliged to fill several pages a month with mock evidences of those " evils " making as much as it could of Paris-made trouser-buckles.

There was the amusing " dump " of jewellery, deplored by Mr. Chamberlain in 1903, and the subject of a tearful leaflet issued from Birmingham.[23] It appeared that there was nearly twice as much jewellery imported into this country in 1902 as in the previous year. " The more jewellery we buy from foreigners, the less we sell to them," sobbed the Birmingham leaflet. " Is this Fair Trade ? Is it Free Trade ? " It turned out that a Bond Street merchant, travelling " for his health " along the coast of North Africa, made deals with local potentates whose finances were straitened, and brought home with him over a hundred thousand pounds' worth of trinkets. " Very well," observed Mr. Chamberlain. " I could not be expected to know that, and it is absolutely irrelevant to the argument ! " [24]

In like manner, it was " absolutely irrelevant to his argument " that Mr. Wyndham, nine years later,[25] should have said that " we import into this country 615 millions' worth of manufactured goods each year." He was only about 500 millions of pounds' worth wrong; yet it was upon such ground-work that the "dumping" alarm was based. "Well, Bill," said a little booklet called *Tariff Reform Truths,*[26] "it don't seem as if the likes of us 'ave much chance of doing a bit of work with all these things comin' in by the shipload ready made." That was the kind of appeal that these "irrelevant" figures about dumped jewels, prison-made goods, and plums, were used to illustrate. The Tariff Reform League called them "extreme cases," whose use was "to help us to get at principles applicable to cases where there is an observed tendency towards the extremity supposed." [27] It is as though one said that every pedestrian in these islands was bound to be drowned, because if he walked to the extremity of the land he would fall into the sea!

It would fill this book to set down all the imploring cries for help from "ruined" industries since 1903. The condition of British trade to-day is the answer to them. The sail-making industry has been "ruined by foreign competition," though the country is now making turbine engines for the steamers that have taken the place of the sailing vessels. Rural wind and water mills are stopped by the foreigner, though the huge mills at the ports are grinding more corn in a month than all the little mills in the country used to grind in a year. A deserted chemical works on the Tyne blots out the sight of its gigantic offspring in Lancashire or Cheshire. Derelict tinplate works are photographed for the Tariff Reform press, while their successors, that have followed the coal seams, are forgotten. "If the wisdom and statesmanship of the country should declare that some duties on some manufactures should be levied, cement was an article that would cry aloud to be included," said the chairman of the Associated Portland Cement Manufacturers in September 1903.

Mr. S. F. Edge in 1912 promised a thousand pounds to the Tariff Reform "Imperial Fund" in order to encourage the movement for taxing foreign-made motor cars, though he had said a few years earlier that "we have caught up our foreign competitors and passed them" ;[28] and earlier still, that "I suppose the position is to-day that in no particular type of motor-carriage is it necessary for a Briton to go abroad." "To-day," said the *Morning Post* in 1910 (April 8th), "the heart of the motoring industry has shifted wholly from France to Britain." And in 1912 the *Daily Express*,[29] after drawing attention for days "to the serious injury caused to the British motor industry by the great advance of cheap American cars," printed what is described as "an excellently devised advertisement of an excellent American car." The leading editorial article of the same issue displayed some anxiety about the morality of thus booming a thing in the paid-for columns, and wishing it elsewhere in the news columns—though the same thing had happened in the case of emigration, without comment. This time, however, the Editor wrote that "our advertisement columns are open to any sound commercial enterprise, and we see no reason in the world why the legitimate enterprise of Messrs. Studebaker [a free advertisement this time] should be checked by any foolish attempt to debar them from advertising. We would be glad indeed to see them pay a duty on their imported cars, and so in a measure make it easier for the British manufacturer to compete with them. But since they are permitted to bring in these cars free of duty, it is at least gratifying to know that they are willing and enterprising enough to spend their money on English advertisements."

So the "dumping" of American goods, over which Tariff Reformers had shown so much anger, was a "sound and legitimate commercial enterprise" when the profits from it went to swell the revenue of a Tariff Reform newspaper!

The Workington Iron Company in 1907 declared a dividend of 50 per cent. with a bonus of £1 on each £1 share, which equalled a dividend of 150 per cent.; and the Chairman of the Company was well known in West Cumberland as a Tariff Reformer who advocated Tariff Reform in the interests of the iron trade! In 1912 the *Morning Post*, writing on the cutlery trade, declared that in the United States "the door has been to all intents and purposes 'banged, bolted, and barred' to the output of the world's leading cutlery centre (Sheffield);" while its Protectionist contemporary, published in Sheffield itself, printed an article headed: "Boom Year for Plate and Cutlery: Edge Tool Revival: Scarcity of Skilled Workmen," and said that "the problem of the trade to-day is how to meet a great expansion in demand, with resources of production apparently at their limit. Occupation could have been found during the present year for 500 additional cutlers and grinders." It was the same in the tinplate trade. In his 1903 speech at Cardiff Mr. Chamberlain irrelevantly confounded tinplate with galvanized sheet mills and made out a horrible case of decadence. In 1912 the Protectionist paper published in the tinplate district [30] said: "If we could be sure that no serious labour troubles would afflict Swansea and West Wales this year, what a splendid prospect of prosperity would be offered! In this district the average wage-rate is the highest in the Kingdom, and all the staple industries are actively engaged. Bad times will come again, in conformity with the system of recurring cycles of lean and fat periods, which past experience compels us to expect, but for the immediate future the outlook is excellent, except for the one cloud represented by labour unrest. Steel, tinplate, copper and spelter works, collieries, and even the building trade, all disclose the same activity. And the ports of the district are, naturally, benefiting by it." Yet in 1913, the "serious labour troubles" having intervened, as was feared, the same journal prints columns of lamentations over a loss of trade which it argues can only be prevented by Preference.

What an outcry there was over the boot trade, too. Mr. Chamberlain, when he spoke at Bristol,[32] did not know it was a local trade there; but when he heard it was, he promptly said that "this is also a trade in which we were clearly first until, in recent times, we have not only found ourselves under-sold in our Colonies, so that all the Colonies are flooded with American boots and shoes, but we find even in our own country German uppers and German boots and shoes coming into the country." Yet again the turning of the tables on the American boot and shoe manufacturers is now part of our buoyant industrial history. In 1911 an International Shoe and Leather Fair was held in London, and the representative of the leading Tariff Reform journal closed his description of it with these words: "Great Britain, so one gathered from a tour of the stalls, was amply holding its own in the boot and shoe trade. American boots are still imported and sold here, but in nothing like the quantities that prevailed a few years ago; and coincidentally with that decline it is found that this country is beginning to export boots and shoes to America." [31]

Gloves, saddles, umbrellas, carpets, saucepans, earthenware, pianos, wall-paper, straw-plait, stone setts, barrel-hoops—the list might be prolonged into hundreds. A Scottish newspaper in 1903 referred to the kelp industry as a "conspicuous illustration of the ruinous operation of foreign competition." The kelp industry was the burning of seaweed to produce soda, potash, and iodine! Much of the same kidney was Mr. Chamberlain's ignorant wail over the decline of straw-plaiting in Bedfordshire, though the people who would have been earning a few pence plaiting straw if the "industry" had been protected, now earn shillings instead of pence making straw hats from material that cheaper labour in Protected countries has plaited for them. The example of Mr. Chamberlain was sometimes imitated by lesser Tariff Reformers with grave risk to the cherished reputations of British industries. At a Tariff Reform meeting in 1908, a League speaker said "he would take as a further instance the glove industry. He went into Dent's factory . . . and found the only work done in this country was to sew on the buttons!" [33] Thereupon Messrs. Dent, Allcroft & Co. wrote that "we need hardly say that we consider it a very grave matter, as liable to do us an immense amount of harm. As you may be aware, we are the largest glove manufacturers in the world, and our Worcester factory employs thousands of people, about fifteen hundred under the factory roof itself, and several thousands in country districts outside, both at Worcester, Sturminster, Towington, Evesham, Crowle, and Inkbarrow. At all these places we have sewing stations, where work is given out to the country people, who make up the gloves in their own homes, and who depend upon this business for their livelihood. Gloves are made entirely throughout from the staining of the leather to the finished article at this Worcester factory, and can be seen by anyone interested." [34]

The last word in contrast to the dismal decadence propaganda of the decade was uttered by the Tariff Reform *Daily Mail* in the early days of December 1912, when the paper sent its consuls to every industrial centre in the country and they reported that "on every hand are to be seen the manifestations of vast, profitable and sanguine energy." "All Britain is jingling with prosperity," the *Mail* exultingly cried. Time has taken a joyous revenge on the prophets of doom. "One by one," said Mr. Chamberlain, the industries of Great Britain "allow themselves to be led out to slaughter." One by one those vigorous beasts have turned on their slaughterers and butted them out of the pasture.

Mr. Arthur Chamberlain once said, soon after his brother had begun his campaign, that "as to decaying industries . . . there is great complaint, natural enough and in accordance with human nature; but it is not founded on fact. Men who are doing well don't advertise it. Men who are doing badly blame everything but themselves." Mr. Arthur Chamberlain is not a Protectionist; yet his shrewd words—which, indeed, have become almost a proverb in Lancashire, where they say, "If you want owt, you must have nowt!"—were echoed in 1910 by a Nottingham Protectionist journal, which remarked that "by a natural peculiarity those who are doing best in business complain most loudly of dullness, in order to conceal the truth." [35]

Was it this peculiarity that led the Chairman of the Ebbw Vale Steel, Iron and Coal Company, Limited, to cry a few days after Mr. Chamberlain's "going" speeches, that "it is only a matter of a few more months before the English steelmakers will be crushed out of existence and the English market will be at the German's mercy"? [36] Led by such a miserymonger the management of the Ebbw Vale Works has played up to the Tariff Reform League all through the ten years; and the League has made the utmost possible use of

Ebbw Vale. The Company has, indeed, become the standard mockery of the decadence cry. Scarce a quarter has passed without some reference to its varying fortunes; and on March 7, 1912, the League issued a by-election leaflet stating that "the great steel works belonging to the Ebbw Vale Steel, Iron and Coal Company are (owing to foreign competition) about to be closed, throwing out of work some 3500 men." When the leaflet came to the notice of the electioneerers on the other side, they wired to Ebbw Vale, and the Secretary of the Company replied: "Statement untrue; works are in full operation." As a matter of fact the works had been closed temporarily in 1911 for alterations and the modernizing of the plant, and just before they were re-opened the managing director declared that "they had at least confidence in the future, and he hoped that confidence was not misplaced. The works would not stop five minutes longer than he could help. They had not yet heard the last of the Ebbw Vale Steel Works. It was true they were unable to get rid of their product owing to abnormal competition. They had struggled along hoping against hope, expecting the fierce competition to come to an end. But that hope had proved vain. It was therefore necessary to try something else. (In a previous communication to a Newport journal, the managing director had spoken of running the steel works on sheet and tinplate bars.) That something else would mean an enormous outlay of capital, but he, for one, was prepared to try it." [37] In 1913 the Company issued a circular stating that the development of the operations had involved large expenditure on new works and plant, and a corresponding increase of working capital. In the ten years ending March 31, 1913, the expenditure of this character had amounted to £617,740. Of this sum £428,147 had been charged against revenue, £106,163 had been charged to property account (principally in the financial year just closed), and £83,430 remained at the debit of outlay in suspense, this amount being in respect of new plant not completed at March 31, 1913. This company, remember, was going to be "crushed out of existence" in 1903 without Protection. The Tariff Reformers have exploited it more than they have any other example in the country. Yet it has paid dividends and provided half a million sterling out of its revenue for the development of its business. Tariff Reform, it is to be supposed, would prefer to have taken that half-million out of other people's revenues.

THE SECTIONAL APPEAL

ANOTHER form in which the Tariff Reformers have put their appeal has been the shaping of their promises to fit the Protectionist desires of different localities. Indications of this method have been made plain in previous pages. Agriculture provided the most notable of them all. Mr. Chamberlain's earlier speeches dealt habitually with the industries of the localities where he happened to be speaking, and the example thus prominently set them has been followed with such humiliating results by Tariff Reformers ever since, that in October, 1912, when Mr. Douglas Newton, the candidate for West Cambs., was asked "why, as a Tariff Reformer, he purchased his seed potatoes from Scotland instead of from his own district," he felt compelled to reply, "I must change my seed." [38]

Mr. Chamberlain thoroughly systematized the sectional appeal for electioneering purposes. During the General Election of 1910 he wrote or wired messages to eagerly receptive candidates in these terms :—

> "No part of the kingdom has more to gain by Tariff Reform than Wales." [39]
>
> "Ireland has more to gain from Tariff Reform than any part of the country." [40]
>
> "I hope that the Potteries may give an unhesitating vote in favour of Tariff Reform. No trade or district has more to gain by the change." [41]
>
> "The East London constituencies stand more in need of Tariff Reform than any others." [42]
>
> "The inhabitants of the Southern Counties have as much interest as any in having fair play with the foreigner." [43]

Force of habit led Mr. Chamberlain to write to the

candidate for North Worcestershire to say that Tariff Reform was "much needed by the chain trade"; [45] though the same day that saw the publication of the letter saw also a paragraph in another Protectionist paper [46] congratulating Colonel Griffith-Boscawen on a "very fine win" at Dudley, which was "the more remarkable because Dudley is the home of the chain-making industry, in which England still stands supreme. In supporting a strong Tariff Reformer like Colonel Griffith-Boscawen," said this paper, "the Dudley chainmakers were therefore not actuated by selfish motives, for they already command almost all the trade available, but were voting for the country alone." As a matter of fact the British chain trade is not affected by foreign competition. Our imports of chain from other countries are so small—little more than dog chain—that our Board of Trade takes no separate note of them.

When Mr. Bonar Law succeeded to the leadership of this weathercock movement he showed signs of adopting the same system, for he said at Belfast, in reference to "a change in the fiscal system of this country," that "of all parts of the United Kingdom there is none which, in my opinion, will benefit more from such a change than Ireland." [44] But a mind of even Protectionist tendency cannot for ever amuse itself by pretending that Ireland needs Tariff Reform more than Wales, and that at the same time Wales needs Tariff Reform more than Ireland; and that each will profit from it more than the other. So that Mr. Bonar Law has not yet quite eaten his own tail.

Although a great deal has been written in earlier pages about agriculture, it remains to be said that the Tariff Reformers have all along regarded the agricultural labourer as the easiest victim of the "sectional appeal." Their method in his case is so perfectly characteristic of them that it is considered well to give a full description of it in the words of a Tariff Reformer who is reputed to be one of the "Confederates."

"The question of reconciling electors in rural areas to a readjustment of the existing food taxation is one still worthy of attention," wrote Mr. O. Locker Lampson, M.P., in the May (1910) *National Review.* The kind of attention given to it by Mr. Lampson was quite the most supercilious thing the Tariff Reform agitation had yet produced. The article, which was entitled "Food Duties and Country Elections," was a vainglorious avowal of the way in which the greenhorns of "All-Muggleton" were to be gulled into voting for their own undoing. "The only fair basis upon which to raise revenue," said the hon. member, "is to tax human beings upon their power of purchase, upon what is academically called their consumptive capacity. . . . We do not swallow motor-cars for breakfast . . . but daily, almost hourly, we eat and drink—all of us bread, most of us tea, not a few of us beer." "So that admittedly food must be taxed," he added, and then went on to explain the verbal trickery which he would have his fellow-Tariff Reformers use to prove to the "All-Muggletonians," "not that food taxation is necessary, but only a different form of it than at present prevails."

Mr. Locker Lampson's polite method was simplicity itself. He dubbed "Hodge" of "All - Muggleton" a "rustic," and recommended that he be talked to about his pig and his potatoes—things he could understand. "Town birds cannot easily gauge the calibre of the bucolic mind." Therefore "the idea that a tax on flour will mean cheaper feeding-stuffs for pig-breeders must have its effects so long as labourers continue to keep pigs and while offals remain as dear as the wheat of which they are a coarse by-product. And the value of the arguments which result from this tax lies in this, that here at least is a concrete instance, something tangible to the labourer, in Tariff Reform." Again, "Hodge must see and feel, before he believes. The candidate who woos his support had better leave his book-lore on the door-mat ere he enter the village hall, and make that village the theatre of interest and its green the temporary cockpit of the world. And rather than summon examples from the wheatfields round Winnipeg or the grain-growers on the Volga, let him pick out the parish allotment-holders or Hodge's own particular potato-patch. Thus alone the labourer is to be won." But all this was the greenest of generality. Mr. Locker Lampson went into details—definite details. For instance, "Tariff Reformers have a definite scheme of making a third party—the foreigner—pay. It can be illustrated to Tom Smith in his very village of All-Muggleton. He can be shown that a ton of the potatoes he grew in All-Muggleton would be charged 10s. before he could sell them in Germany, and 37s. 6d. before he could dispose of them in America; while either of these countries could come and sell their potatoes in All-Muggleton, and steal his only market from him. 'If I tax that foreigner,' he argues, 'I shall share in the spoil.' And he really hates the foreigner."

Almost as much, say, as he hates being taken for a fool! But Mr. Locker Lampson turned his back on any such possibility. The better the "rustic" the bigger the fool, he appeared to think. For, "If a constituency boasts Small Holdings the Tariff Reform case is naturally stronger, because, in a sentence, a Small Holding converts a labourer from a consumer into a producer. But even in a country constituency without Small Holders, Tariff Reform can be made a living gospel." Thereupon Mr. Lampson gave an account of how one seat was won back to Tariff Reform by means of the pig. It was in this wise. In 1906 the seat was lost on Chinese labour and rye bread. Four years later "it was found that the cry of Chinese Labour, although dead in its effect, lingered on long after that election—an unsavoury memory to all." The word "Chinese" had acquired "a dread significance, and needed only a change of venue and marriage to some local grievance in order to play as prominent a part on behalf of the Unionists as it had against them four years previously." Moreover, "it was discovered that, if one industry predominated among the electors in the division, it was undoubtedly that of pig-breeding." "The task, therefore," said Mr. Locker Lampson, "resolved itself into simply this: Could the evils of foreign dumping be demonstrated by examples in the pig trade, and could an attempt be made at the same time to evoke all the delicate associations which clustered round the name 'Chinese'?" "The foreigner was kind, and not long before the election he sent over into England some four thousand odd carcases of Chinese pork, 7 per cent. of which was found to be unfit for human food. But the Liberal Government was even kinder. For it instantly issued an order from the Board of Agriculture closing every pig-market in the division in question, owing to the death during the previous months of a few pigs from so-called swine fever. Could there be a better object-lesson of Free Trade indifference to home needs? Londoners who are independent of pork profits may not appreciate the issue, but it became vital to the pig-breeders in that constituency. So much so that men would gather on market days to denounce the latest importation of Celestial food, and raise loud voices and freckled fists to heaven in vengeance on a Government which chose to treat aliens in China better than Englishmen at home."

Thus, said Mr. Locker Lampson, "there can be no question that Tariff Reform *with the food duties* can be made plain and acceptable in country constituencies if only trouble is taken." Finally, "it no longer suffices the Unionist candidate," he assured us, "to be described in the local Press as 'neatly dressed and a perfect gentleman,' for the man they call 'a perfect gentleman' in modern politics is very often a perfect ass."

In the Tariff Reform politics the border line between the serious and the funny is often invisible. Mr. Locker Lampson may have had his tongue in his cheek, but he was very seriously bent on winning elections. So was Mr. Chamberlain when in 1904 he caused this letter to be dispatched to a teacher of music who had asked how Tariff Reform would affect him: "I am directed by Mr. Chamberlain to acknowledge the receipt of your letter of the 5th inst., and to say that he cannot see how his policy can possibly under any circumstances be of any disadvantage to the musical profession. On the other hand, as music is one of the greatest of luxuries, any improvement in the general conditions of the population would enable them to indulge in it more freely." [47]

The Tariff Reform League also was serious when it informed the Yarmouth fishermen that "it is certain that the grievance of the fishing industry will not be forgotten when the

Government of this country recovers, by the assent of the people, power to negotiate for the mitigation of hostile tariffs, and to support negotiation by the threat of retaliation." [48] And equally grave was the Member for Bootle when he promised his constituents that as soon as Tariff Reform became law he would seek to redress the grievances of the tripe industry.

This tripe story is perhaps the greatest joke of the whole wretched record of the "Sectional appeal." In 1910, one of the Bootle constituents of Colonel Sandys wrote to him politely requesting that he would ask the "President of the Local Government Board" whether he was aware that "large quantities of machinery have been imported from Germany for the purpose of taking wrinkles out of tripe, one of the staple foods of the people of Lancashire." The "wrinkles in tripe" joke was one of the oldest of its kind in Bootle; but Colonel Sandys did not know that. He answered very gravely, "I consider that you have a real grievance in the fact that large quantities of machinery are being imported from a foreign country for the purpose stated in your letter, and you and your fellow-tradesmen have my entire sympathy in this matter." But no useful result, he thought, could be obtained by putting the question now, "as no satisfactory reply is likely to be given" to it. "As soon, however, as Tariff Reform becomes law, the aspect of the matter will be entirely changed, and I should then be pleased to put a question of the nature suggested in your letter with chance of success and of getting some result." [48a]

There is no need, after this, to quote the hundreds of Tariff Reform leaflets and booklets in which this "sectional appeal" has been elaborated. They form the mainstay of Tariff Reform "literature," although Mr. Chamberlain who himself began it said as long ago as 1905,[49] that "personally I rather regret having to devote so much time to the question of what the advantage would be to a particular trade." Three years later Lord Ridley, the Chairman of the League, warned the "newer recruits of the Tariff Reform cause, who had not the four years' experience of its earlier advocates," that the policy of "promising everybody everything," was "a policy for which Mr. Chamberlain and the Tariff Reform League would never be responsible. There was," his Lordship added, "a good case for Tariff Reform, and it was a national policy worth fighting for; but those who represented that it would in a moment create a new heaven and a new earth were only spoiling a good case by over-statement."[50]

EXHIBITIONS

THE shop windows of Tariff Reform have been filled alternately with exhibitions of British decadence and exhibitions of British supremacy. "Dump shops" have been organized to show how the foreigner has forced us to buy of him. "All-British Shopping Weeks" have been organized to show how predominant the home manufacturer remains.

A toilet set shown in a window at Hanley in 1904 appears to have been the origin of the dump shops that became such a general feature of the Tariff Reform propaganda in later years. The toilet set was made in Germany. It was said to be coming into the English market at a shilling a set. As a matter of fact, the only set that had ever come in at that price was the one brought over to this exhibition. To test the matter Mr. L. L. Grimwade, of Stoke-on-Trent, offered to buy ten thousand sets at that price, "c. i. f." London; but the offer was not taken. The idea of such exhibitions, however, seems to have developed, and late in 1909 the Tariff Reformers took a shop in Nottingham and filled it with samples of what purported to be foreign-made goods placed on the English market at a lower price than they could be manufactured here. "One of the samples," said the *Nottingham Guardian*, a Protectionist paper, "is a pair of stockings bought from a Free-Trade firm of manufacturers, who can import the article at 5½d. a pair, and sell them retail at 6¾d. Similar stockings of English manufacture cannot be placed on our own market at less than 10d. a pair, so the surplus goods of the foreigner are dumped here, and our own people thrown out of employment. There are 140 articles shown, and they include toys, pottery, cloth goods, etc. A portion of lace made by Siberian exiles, and exported here to compete unfairly with our own manufactures, is also exhibited." It turned out that the exhibition was what is called a "fake." The Avenue Manufacturing Company wrote a letter [51] stating that some of the goods displayed were made in their factory in Nottingham for a firm of warehousemen in Cheapside. "The Tariff Reformers have procured a number of these articles," they said, "and are displaying them in prominent positions with a label attached, stating that they were 'made in Germany.' Their peripatetic orators are holding it out to their audiences and describing it as the sweated production of German workers. These statements we regard as injurious to ourselves, as they are absolutely devoid of truth. The goods are not made in Germany, and the labour is not sweated, as we are quite prepared to prove. It was stated by one orator that the goods could not be made on this side at a less price than 30 per cent. above what was paid in Germany. What are the facts? The article in question was sent to Germany for a quotation and the price asked was 20 per cent. above the price at which we sell the article."

While this kind of thing was going on the Tariff Reformers were endeavouring to organize a great exhibition at Earl's Court, under the motto "British Capital. British Labour. British Brains." They got out preliminary announcements, and at Earl's Court put a sign, "1910. Tariff Reform Exhibition," over one of the entrances to the grounds. An inquirer at the Earl's Court offices was referred to the offices of the Tariff Reform League, whence he was again referred to the Exhibition offices at 47 Chancery Lane. There he was told that the idea originated in a group of enthusiastic Tariff Reformers, but that when these gentlemen had progressed a good way with their plan, the Tariff Reform League stepped in and took it over. The original promoters had hoped to hold an Exhibition in some Hall, somewhere, for a few days; but the League hired Earl's Court! "We were getting on very nicely and quite a number of well-known people were helping us; but, of course, there was no use in two parties trying to run the thing, so we dropped out."

"And now the other party has dropped out as well?" asked the inquirer.

" Yes," replied the man at No. 47. " It is too big an idea altogether. Possibly if you run round to the Tariff Reform League office, they may be able to tell you something about it." [52]

This Exhibition was never held, yet during the general elections of 1910 Tariff Reform " dump-shops " were to be found in all the great towns, similar to that which the *Nottingham Guardian* described. Their main effect, it may be observed, was to illustrate the fact that free competition meant lower prices to the purchasers. But whatever effect the Tariff Reformers desired them to have on the public mind, they did their best to destroy by stimulating the organization of what were called " All-British Shopping Weeks."

These " weeks " were elaborated by the Union Jack Industries League, over whose Executive Council Viscount Hill presided ; and the first of them was held at Ealing. It was blazoned forth on the surprised view of the residents of the suburb in a garb of flags and banners, hung, as the *Morning Post* [53] carefully noted, on lamp-posts and " even on the contact poles of the tramcars." The merry week was signalized by a fancy dress ball and carnival, a pageant, a " patriotic " concert (all German bands excluded), a torch-light procession, and a military tattoo. In the procession Boy Scouts bore " samples of the produce of the various British Dominions " (*Daily Mail*), and the *Daily Express* noted what the other recorders overlooked—the presence of non-imported British Territorials in the procession. There were also illuminations. The object was to induce Ealing to forswear foreign goods and patronize those shops which displayed cards inscribed " All-British goods," or " Made in England."

The Ealing experiment was repeated in the City and West End ; and the *Daily Telegraph* [54] announced that the encouragement of home industries was " the main-spring of the movement." Preliminary booming of it was carried out by the Protectionist press with great gusto. In the *Daily Express* a well-known woman writer had a series of articles on " The All-British Woman : Who is to blame for her non-existence ? " These articles discovered a curious state of affairs. Instead of blaming the "dumper," the writer was hardy enough to blame the British Woman herself. "I discovered yesterday," she said, "that thousands of yards of beautiful and durable silk, manufactured at Bradford, are being sold in England as French silk, besides being sent over to France, Germany, Italy, and all the countries of South America for sale. In the foreign countries it sells as English-made silk, while in England it sells as foreign-made. Moreover, if it were sold here as English silk it could be disposed of at a shilling a yard retail and a profit made, but since it is sold as foreign-made silk Englishwomen are paying a greatly increased price for it." [55] As if this confession that Bradford knows its own business better than the Tariff Reformers know it were not enough, the *Daily Express* must needs bewail, as "really lamentable," the fact that "the products of the looms of Yorkshire, Lancashire, the west of England and the north of Ireland should be more sought after in France and America than they are in London." [56]

The shopping *Guide* published by the Union Jack Industries League for this "West End and City All-British Shopping Week" praised on every page the predominance of British goods. "Firm in the belief that British goods can triumph on their merits" the League asked only "that they should receive the legitimate British preference from buyers when quality and price are right." In detail, it said of woollens that "the needs of the trade are much in excess of the supply of raw material," and that "Britain's supremacy in the woollen trade is undisputed." Of cotton, that "England to-day stands first in the world in this branch of textile manufacture." Of linen, that "there is no other country whose factories can produce material that in any way approaches the universally famous Irish linen." Of silk and velvet, that "the British silk industry is not the vanishing trade that some would have us believe." Of furniture, that "if the population of Great Britain could be taken on a tour of inspection through their own country, and shown some of the wonders of the industrial life and work going on in their midst, they would not only learn the secret of Britain's position among the world-powers," etc.; and that "the number of orders received by the British firms from foreign customers speaks well for the quality and workmanship of the goods turned out by the furniture factories of the United Kingdom."

So the tale went on. The value of such just praise lay not in any novelty of the words used—for they were familiar to all who knew our country—but in the fact that they were the official utterances of an organization that was being supported heart and soul by the newspapers which had for eight or nine years sought to frighten the country with talk about the decadence of British industry. It was marvellous the way the Protectionist journals talked "All-British." They never for a moment doubted that the "quality" was right, and as to "price," the *Morning Post* reported that "beginning early in the forenoon crowds of people visited the City and West End thoroughfares, the scene of the All-British shopping experiment, and many returned home with parcels of varying bulk." Moreover, "when they looked at the windows of the big drapery establishments they found that every conceivable article that they could wish for was provided—gloves, ties, parasols, satins, brocades—everything, indeed, that the feminine heart could desire. . . . It was difficult to understand why the foreigner should come in at all. 'How is it that it has been found necessary to draw special attention to British goods?' the manager of a large establishment was asked. 'Simply because the British public are ignorant of what their own country can produce,' was the reply." [57]

Oddly enough, such an exhibition did not cause the Protectionists to think of Tariff Reform or of dumping. How could they, when their columns were filled with glowing descriptions of British-made goods that were bought in armfuls because "price and quality" were both right?

"TESTS" OF VARIOUS KINDS

RELYING rather on the creation of an "atmosphere" by the means already related and with the meagre success already realized, Tariff Reformers have never considered it part of their duty to assist the electorate to master the statistics of British trade. They have understood that there could not be much profit for them in such a duty. From the very first, the trade of the country has run away from them; and as it has run the Tariff Reformers have scurried along to try to divert public attention from it. So frequent have been these changes that it is a giddy exercise to follow them. In so far as they can only be followed by citation of figures, there have been and are so many capable guides that it is not proposed in this book to deal with statistics. But the attitude of the Tariff Reformers toward them—with which this book is concerned—does not change fundamentally: it has always been their business to explain the figures away, even though the explanation this year be in direct contradiction to the explanation last.

Thus, Mr. Chamberlain began by using a single year as a point for comparison. When the futility of that plan was shown up, "quinquennial periods" became the favourite method. At one time exports were the test of our prosperity. Exports boomed, and imports were appealed to. Exports and imports were added together, subtracted from each other. Both at times were held to be subsidiary in Tariff Reform value to the "home trade." Trade per head in comparison with other nations' trade held the field for a while. The working out of percental increases or decreases has always been a delusive pastime. Between one chosen year and another, imports would increase more than exports: we were "living on our capital"; the end of all things was at hand! During another carefully chosen period exports would increase more than imports : then we were "expatriating our capital," and our industries were "starving" for want of the raw material we could not afford to pay for! All these declamations, these Monte Carlo systems of proving that something or other was necessary to prevent decadence, being continually challenged by the evidence that there was no decadence, then the apologists fell back upon hitherto undiscovered changes in the "character" of our imports. Sometimes, with the official figures staring them out of countenance, they have called them ugly names, unreliable, incomplete, and so on. At other times they have denounced figures as altogether unnecessary to prove their case. For ten years they have kept up a jabber of confused endeavours to explain away facts that cannot be explained away! It has been more than "rash politics supported by doubtful statistics," as Lord Salisbury said of it in the first year of the controversy; for the statistics have been more rash than the politics and the politics even more doubtful than the statistics.

"My case," said Mr. Chamberlain in 1903, "is that the trade of the country, as measured—and I think it ought to be mainly measured—by the exports of this country to foreign countries and to British possessions, has during the last twenty or thirty years been practically stationary"; [58] and he often spoke as though exports were the only test necessary. In a speech of 1905,[57a] for example, after comparing the exports of various countries, he held the result to prove that "in other countries where protection is very much greater than anything I have ever suggested—trade has not decreased, but increased in a much greater proportion than yours." In his speech at Glasgow he took 1872 as the standard with which to measure the stationariness he affected to perceive. When it was pointed out to him next morning that 1872 was the year in which the prices of British goods rose enormously in consequence of the Franco-German war, and that if Mr. Chamberlain had looked, say, to 1899 or 1890 for his starting point, he would have found his case spoiled, he merely said that he did not choose 1872 "with any sinister purpose. I thought thirty years was a good long time and a fair time to go back." "In this controversy which I am commencing here I use figures as illustrations," he added, "I do not pretend they are proofs. The proofs will be found in the argument and not in the figures. But I use figures as illustrations to show what the argument is." [59]

Mr. Chamberlain was faithfully imitated in this airy regard for the ledgers of the nation's business. Mr. Vince found figures horrid, for in opening a debate in favour of the adoption of preference, he said he would confine himself to principles—"for figures, after all, only showed the amount of difference which was the result of applying them." [60] And though after a while Mr. Chamberlain himself ceased to speak of the decrease in exports but altered the phrase to "manufactured exports," [61] he still looked upon figures as negligible, and when the Board of Trade report asked for by himself was published in 1904, he contemptuously referred to it as the "library of the Free Importers." [61]

For a time this "export test" did some service on the Protectionist platform. "As a country manufacturing for export, we are actually going backward," said Mr Bonar Law in 1904.[62] Statisticians like Mr. J. Holt Schooling published misleading articles giving the rates of increase in the exports of ten countries, for example, during 1891–1900, as compared with 1881–1890; [63] and even in 1907 Mr. Wyndham looked upon our export trade as in dire need of a fiscal system, "like a jemmy to prise open the door of foreign markets to us, and not, as it now was, like a bolt to fasten that door against ourselves." [64] Indeed, the impression Mr. Chamberlain sought to make on the minds of unreflecting people has not yet entirely passed away. So late as December 1908, the Protectionist Candidate for South Northants—one among many—told a trembling meeting that "we were excluded almost entirely from sending English goods into foreign countries;" and that we had "lost the foreign markets"; [65] and echoes of the same disaster that has never happened continue to be heard in out-of-the way places.

When Mr. Chamberlain could no longer evade the obvious growth of our foreign trade he shifted the foundation of his proof, saying, " Our argument is not dependent in the slightest degree either upon an increase or a decrease of the actual exports of this country." [66] He thought it wiser to fall back on the complaint that " we are losing our comparative place in the world." His supporters certainly found this argument more agreeable; and when the huge trade figures of 1907 were published, " How did the Tariff Reformers come to lay so much stress three or four years ago upon the significance of exports ? " exclaimed the *Morning Post*.[67] The answer, " as everyone will admit," it went on, was " that in those days Germany and the United States were observed to be suffering less acutely than this country from the social complaint known as unemployment, and at the same time to be increasing their export trade more rapidly than this country. Hence there was a natural tendency on the part of Tariff Reformers to associate activity in the export trade with activity in the labour market."

This " natural tendency " was expounded in several ways. The one that was most in vogue was that adopted by the leafleteers, who set out the increases in exports over imports of manufactured goods in Germany, France, and America as being so much " gain " to those countries; and the increase in the United Kingdom of imports over exports as being so much "loss" to ourselves. Of course the gains and losses were in millions! And the tables were held to show that " British workmen are now losing every year the work and wages which belong to £52,100,000 worth of manufactured goods, being trade lost; while the workmen of the three above-named foreign countries are getting the work and wages which belong to £112,600,000 worth of the increased trade." [68]

This stage in the argument should be noted with care. An excess of exports was distinctly held to prove the prosperity of other countries, while our excess of imports was held to establish our poverty. But British exports have increased apace since then; and in 1912 the *Morning Post* [69] published an article by " Statisticus " pointing out that in 1910 and 1911 British exports of manufactured goods " increased much more considerably than our imports." It was of course just the sort of progress that the leafleteer of

1903 would have welcomed. But times had changed, and the Protectionist writer in the *Morning Post* of 1912 anxiously asked, "Is this a satisfactory feature?" Forgetting all that had gone before, he proceeded to suggest that it was not satisfactory, on the ground that we were possibly every year "giving more of British produce in payment of imports than before." That was a usefully plausible explanation that had not occurred to the earlier Tariff Reformers!

Between these two Tariff Reform opposites—that an excess of exports is bad and is also good for this country—came the convenient argument that the Board of Trade figures were inaccurate and unreliable. In 1907 the Tariff Reform League published a harrowing story of "a man employed at the London Docks who carries with him stencil plates with which he re-marks certain cases arriving from the Continent, addressing them to Australia and other of our Colonies; to which places they are then transhipped as British goods and figure in the Trade Returns as British exports. No doubt," it was said, "there are hundreds of similar cases, which go to show that 'those Trade Returns' are not a correct indication of the state of our trade." [70] When somebody complained that "the account of the famous Cullinan diamond being conveyed to this country as an ordinary registered package illustrates a serious discrepancy in our Board of Trade returns," [70a] the Tariff Reform League, remarking that the Board of Trade returns were "entirely valueless in regard to this trade," advised those who had no other source of information "to wait for the publication of the report and evidence of the Tariff Commission." [70b] And again, "the futility of relying upon the Board of Trade returns of our import and export trade has often been exposed," said the League, meaning, if it meant anything, that those who took them to prove black and those who used them to prove white, were equally engaged in a useless exercise. The rebuke would have been worth nothing in this veracious record if it had not come from the Tariff Reform League itself. It was published in 1908 [71] a few pages ahead of a report of a speech in which Mr. Austen Chamberlain himself used those same figures to draw what he called "the moral."

Mr. Chamberlain was specifically referring to the tables which the Tariff Reform League called "futile." "We have a system which, we are told," he said, "is perfect. The Germans have a system which, as we are told, is costly to their people at home, and ruinous to them in competition with us in foreign markets. And yet here are the figures in the Board of Trade returns. Instead of being handicapped by their system, the Germans are catching us up in the race for trade."

The incident is another instance of the way in which the Tariff Reform League has tried to wrap a reputation round itself. Repeatedly it has printed statements condemning the use of certain methods of argument which it had encouraged others to use. The repudiations are on record to save the face of the League; but their own people have forgotten them and remembered only the "illustrations" that impressed them so much. "If our exports exceeded our imports then he would say that all was right," is a fair Parliamentary specimen of the manner in which the "illustrations" have made their mark.[72] It is as though prosperity is only to be won by always spending more than your income.

If the Tariff Reform Member of Parliament who made that foolish but quite representative statement really believed it, he ought not to have joined the movement, for it has been declared on the authority of the League that "Under Tariff Reform more goods will be imported into this country."[73] It might almost be said that instead of exports being the test, to-day it is our imports that are held to show whether we are going forward or backward in commerce. In July 1913 an active Tariff Reform Member of Parliament, Mr. Page Croft, secured from the Board of Trade a statement of the value of our imports and of the imports of nine protected countries in 1882 compared with 1912, and on them was based a declaration that our trade was declining because the percentages of increases were greater in other countries than here. It was said to be "a complete delusion" that free imports meant the most progressive imports.[74] This was sheer "illustration," as may be seen when it is learned that the Board of Trade return showed that while British imports had increased eighty per cent. in the thirty years, Japanese imports had increased over a thousand per cent.! The absurdity of the argument may be further measured when it is pointed out that while British imports rose in the period from 413 millions to 744 millions, Japan's rose from 5 millions to 57 millions. If a country could have been found that imported nothing in 1882 and a single penny's worth in 1912, how would its percental increase have been popularized by the Tariff Reformers?

That little digression was made with the object of drawing closer attention to the emphasis laid by the Tariff Reformers upon imports when it has suited them. Already it has been seen that an excess of exports was held by Tariff Reformers to spell prosperity, yet was at the same time considered "unsatisfactory"; and that as imports increased one Tariff Reform Member became sore afraid that they would run away from the exports, while another demonstrated that Protection would make our imports increase faster than ever. These are but a few of the myriad thistles the Tariff Reform soil yields.

Nor do they complete the harvest. It used to be rather a common method of indicating the bulk of the foreign trade done by a country to add its exports and imports together. With Tariff Reformers sometimes preferring to illustrate their arguments by using the one, and sometimes by using the other, it might be supposed they would not be over-fond of losing the significance of either by blending them both in one. Yet they have done so. Nor would that be an extraordinary thing, but for the fact that they have repeatedly announced that nothing could be proved by doing it! "There is no more reason for putting these two things (exports and imports) together," said Mr. Chamberlain in 1903,[75] "than for putting together two sides of a ledger and putting debtor and creditor and adding them up and saying, 'This is the splendid result of our business during the year!'" It was "always absurd," echoed Mr. Vince, "and generally misleading";[76] while Mr. L. S. Amery, one of the most cautious advocates the Tariff Reform movement possesses, firmly laid it down that "any argument which attempts to show that one country is more prosperous than another because its export trade, or its import trade, or that fatuous jumble of the two, its 'total volume of trade' are greater, is fundamentally absurd." [77]

Vast quantities of Tariff Reform literature are swept into the wastepaper basket by that statement. It heartily condemns both the export test and the import test, but reserves its deepest scorn for the test that combines them both. Yet there have been times when the Tariff Reformers, despairing of finding comfort in either export or import figures, have not shrunk from employing this "fatuous jumble." In 1907 the Tariff Commission [78] issued a Memorandum in which the exports and imports of this country and Germany and of America were combined in order to obtain comparative percentages of the increases in "total trade." Upon that official publication was based the popular statement, made in the Protectionist press and on the platform, that whilst British trade increased in 1906 over 1905 by 10 per cent., the corresponding increases in Germany and the United States of America were 12½ and 11 per cent. Let it be remarked also that the table issued by the Commission showed that the greater percentage of increase in German and American trade was solely due to increases in imports. On the other hand, the British percentage of increase in imports was much less than in either of the other two countries, while in exports our increase was greater. It was a perfectly clear case of the Tariff Reform use, by no less a body than the Tariff Commission, of the "fatuous jumble" which Mr. Amery, Mr. Vince, and Mr. Chamberlain himself so bitterly denounced.

In 1912 the Tariff Reform League followed the example of the Commission. It sent out to the Press in December [79] a table in which the comparison described above was made between 1902 and 1912, a choice of years that gave them a more effective range, and with the table a letter drawing attention to the fact that, "adding imports and exports together," the result was as shown. More, the League declared that the figures formed "a striking vindication of the continued validity of Mr. Chamberlain's main argument."

Such an utter reversal of the argument almost defies comment. The test which in 1903 Mr. Chamberlain contemptuously described as baseless, is in 1912 spoken of by his League as his "main argument"! Borrowing the words of a stern and ceaseless exponent of these statistical contortions, it can only be said that "the test which may be fashionable at a given time, depends on the way the trade figures run. When the trend of the figures changes, the 'test' changes with it." [80]

"The popular verdict of a year ago was decisive against immediate change, and the manifest prosperity of the nation has made people unwilling for the time being to talk or think of Fiscal Reform," said a leading Tariff Reform journal in 1907; [81] and another London journal on the same side, viewing the "striking figures" of the foreign trade returns of 1906, remarked that "those members of the Unionist party who have specially devoted themselves to the advocacy of Tariff Reform would do well to consider whether it is desirable at this juncture to continue to press upon the electorate a subject which divides and therefore necessarily weakens the party. The arguments for Tariff Reform are just as sound now as ever they were, but it is certain that a majority of the electors will decline to listen to them while our trade is displaying such unexampled powers of expansion. No sane man makes a complete change in the organization of his business when that business is flourishing beyond all previous records. If, therefore, the Tariff Reformers persist in their agitation they will run the risk of meeting the fate that awaits all those who preach out of season. They will be voted bores, and nobody will listen to them when their season arrives." [82]

Those writers shockingly underestimated the versatility of the Protectionist propagandists. Did they think that because trade was good it could not be made to appear bad? The Tariff Reform League ought to have provided a training class for Tariff Reform journalists. At least two ways out of the difficulty presented themselves at once. Industry might have been active, but what about its character, its profitableness? Ah! And then, it was all very well to talk about our own prosperity, but what about other countries? Ah!

When *The Times* set itself to belittle the huge figures of our foreign trade for 1910 it said: "Another point to be considered when we gaze with complacency on rows of fat figures representing more money than the mind can grasp, is that they only stand for values, and that quantities are a different matter;" [82a] forgetting that in a year when this theory did not fit the figures the Tariff Reform League itself had explained that "the increase in the volume of trade—particularly in exports—has been *greater* than the mere declared values had made evident; but no business man is content with increased trading unless he has corresponding profits. In volume our exports have increased far more rapidly than in value." [82b] So, if values increase more than volume, ruin stares us in the face; if volume more than values, the end is at hand! Moreover, the price fluctuations, which are such a large factor in our trade statistics, must be assumed to have precisely the same effect on those of other countries, but there is no instance of the Tariff Reformers explaining that French or German trade increases "mainly in values, not in volume."

As to ourselves compared with other countries, "it did not do to look merely at our own trade," said Mr. Austen Chamberlain soon after the publication of the 1906 figures; "we must look at the trade of other nations also. If we did so, we should see that the prosperity which we had enjoyed had not been peculiar to ourselves. That prosperity was due to a world-wave of prosperity in which those benighted Protectionist countries, by whose example they were warned to profit, had benefited more than we had." [83] At once it will occur to the reader that the Tariff Reform proof lay ready to hand in Tariff Reform "percentages," of which some examples have already been given. Mr. Joseph Chamberlain had already [84] anticipated the need of some such statistical raft for derelict "tests" when he compared progress in trade with progress in warship building. To anyone who said, "Here are foreigners building every day bigger ships, employing better guns, better machinery, bringing the whole of their wealth and of their inventive faculty to bear on the creation of a fleet more powerful than ours," would it be any answer, he asked, to say that "our Fleet is much stronger than it was at Trafalgar"? And when the figures of 1906 came out he was among the first to say that while "the trade of the Germans and the United States of America" was increasing more rapidly than ours, "the trade of this country, great as it is, cannot go on successfully unless the trend is altered; unless its present course is to some extent diverted." [85]

The reply to this lay in the omission of the Tariff Reformers, first to take population into account, and secondly, to allow for the quicker growth of younger countries; and there is no doubt that the country was speedily made aware of these wilful omissions, for Mr. Bonar Law invited a Scottish audience [86] to examine the argument "that the test of percentages is unfair, that the trade of a country like Germany, with a population 50 per cent. greater than the United Kingdom, must inevitably expand more rapidly than ours." "It means, if it means anything," he said, "that in future in competition with our trade rivals we can only look for that share of the trade of the world to which our population entitles us. If that argument be sound, what is to become of us in view of the rapidly increasing population of Germany, and still more of the United States?" Then he fell back on an old method of maintaining the panic. "The Board of Trade returns after all," he declared, "are only partial. They give particulars of the foreign trade, but they leave out of account the home trade, which in every country, even the United Kingdom, is far more important than the foreign trade. The real test of expansion, therefore, would be the total production, but figures to make this test are not available."

This was very much as though one said that because two men might do more business than one man, the one was worse off than either of the two. It is an example of the way in which Tariff Reformers have always tried to frighten us by sheer size of figures. Mr. Chamberlain used a naval comparison to illustrate a commercial argument:

Mr. Bonar Law resorted to the plea that a big country might beat a little country in trade. He meant to infer, for the misguidance of people less intelligent than himself, that every man in the smaller country would have his trade taken away from him by the men in the larger countries. That is the " atmosphere " which this kind of argument was intended to create.

Percental increases here and there were worked out to serve the same end, and to cover up the growth of British trade. One example of this method has been given. One more out of hundreds must suffice. It is taken from a Tariff Reform League publication entitled *Progress under Tariff Reform and Protection: A Comparison*, published in 1910. The comparison was almost entirely made on the percentage basis, which by that time was nigh the only argument the condition of trade had left them with. Tables of figures were printed in the booklet, and every one of them, it was asserted, showed that " the record of the protected countries is better than our own." Nothing was said about populations, or natural resources, or different stages of development. Everything was directed to create the impression that if this country were protected its percental increases of trade would be at least as high as those of the protected nations. The iron and steel exports of the various countries were set down—exports was the friend this time, not imports—and though the British exports totalled nearly as much as those of France, Germany, and the United States of America put together, the percentages of increase were alarmingly printed thus : " United Kingdom 63, France 488, Germany 133, United States of America 940." The value of the last figure is shown by the information that America's total exports under this heading were only one-third of the British exports !

Another booklet in the series, of which the one already quoted formed a part, was concerned with " The Shipping Trade " ; and here, if the " percental increases " worked out in the case of America had been matched in the United Kingdom, this country would have launched nearly twice the whole world's average annual production !

Anything to make our booming trade look small! Besides this ridiculous attempt to compare what it admitted were incomparable things, the Tariff Reformers adopted another method of belittling the enormous volume of our trade. "Our trade returns deal only with one portion, and that a comparatively small one, of the whole trade of the country," said the Tariff Reform League: "and the Memorandum (of the Tariff Commission) does well to point out that while there may be great prosperity in the foreign trade, yet, owing to the fact that the home trade is four to five times as large, trade depression may still prevail throughout the country;" [87] and without giving more examples of these argumentative quicksands, there is on record a late statement of Mr. Bonar Law's that "trade statistics are very different from trade; because trade statistics cover only foreign trade, and the home trade is always far more important." [88]

The test, therefore, was now something different from anything else that had ever been tried. It was now our home trade. This was stated explicitly in December 1912 by Mr. A. D. Steel-Maitland, M.P., the present chief organizer of the Tariff Reform movement, whose words form a fitting climax to this brief review of the long series of rejected "tests." "People said look at the statistics of their foreign trade, but were they a fair test? What they lived by was trade as a whole—trade inside Great Britain, as well as foreign trade, and, as a matter of fact, the home trade was much more important than the foreign trade. Their home trade was not increasing by anything like the same rate as their foreign trade, and, therefore, to take the foreign trade as a guide was not to deal with the actual facts." [89]

Ten years of testing our trade with things that were not "actual facts" is now to be followed by using a test for which, as Mr. Bonar Law said in the speech already quoted, "figures are not available." Quite the most convenient kind of figures for Tariff Reform purposes. They can never be called in question because they are not available!

When opponents used the "exports per head" figure, "Professor" Hewins, as the Tariff Reform monthly journal then described him, declared that all "economists would agree" that it was "not a very satisfactory test to apply to the trade of any country." This declaration was useful mainly because Professor Hewins took the trouble to explain it. For "it takes no account," he said, "of variations of prices, the character of the trade, the area and population under consideration, the structure and organization of industry, and many other factors." [90] So that, though in their comparisons of the trade of one country with that of another the Tariff Reformers had used bulk and percentages and had avoided "areas and populations," it was not because they knew that those factors did not exist, but simply because they knew that were they taken into account their case would be spoiled.

With such a confused welter of arguments, proved by such contradictory tests, to guide them, it is not surprising that the Tariff Reformers should have exhibited throughout the ten years so great an ignorance of the fundamental principles of international commerce. Such profoundly important matters as the "balance of trade" still remain mysteries to their simple minds; and it ought to be said here that the publications of the Tariff Reform League have never done anything to help them. Mr. Vince once set himself to explain matters. But then he only explained the peculiar propositions he himself set up, the chief of which was that "Imports, say, from Germany, are paid for by Exports to Germany." It was a proposition that no opponent of his had ever made, yet did Mr. Vince treat it quite seriously, calling it "untrue and absurd," asking "who really believes that when he elects to buy a Swiss instead of an English watch, a telepathic impulse is conveyed to some Switzer compelling him to rush out and buy something English?" and finally announcing, as though all opposition to Tariff Reform were thereby abolished, that such a statement would not "stand the statistical test." [91] The League itself, moreover, has on occasion confessed that the balance of trade is a matter of such "great complexity" that it "can only be properly treated by considering the trade of this country with all other countries. Our imports from the United

States every year greatly exceed our exports to the States, and the fact can only be explained by trade transactions involving many other countries with which we and the States do business. It must also be remembered that a vast amount of British capital has been invested in American railways and other industrial undertakings, and that the interest on these investments reaches this country in the shape of goods. A large part of the excess of imports also represents payment for services rendered by British shipping in the carriage of American produce and manufactures." That was all right in its way; but the League went on to say that "the question as to how the difference between imports and exports is balanced has never yet been satisfactorily settled;" and to promise that the Tariff Commission, which had the whole question of the balance of trade "under consideration," should issue "a statement on the subject."[92] The promise was made in 1908. The statement has not yet been published by the Commission.

Perhaps it was the inexplicable complexity of the subject that led the Tariff Reform candidate for Newcastle to declare that the statement that "an import paid for an export or an export for an import" was "an awful rotten wheeze";[93] or a King's Counsel to lay it down at Exeter that "there was no more relation between exports and imports and unemployment than there was between the price of cheese and the height of the Himalayas;"[94] or a League speaker to relate to a West Hertfordshire audience that "a friend of his one morning went down to the docks to take a few snapshots for a book he was writing," and "first visited the import docks and soon had a dozen pictures of articles being brought into the country free of duty, among which were doors, desks, and all kinds of goods made by carpenters, a large number of tombstones, also yew trees, no doubt to be used to ornament the graves over which the tombstones were to be set. He then went to the export dock, but failed to get a single picture, as nothing was being exported that morning. Yet," said this astonished orator, "they were told that our imports were paid for by our exports!"[95]

As a matter of fact, "invisible" exports have provided

the stumbling-block to many a Tariff Reform economist. "Invisible exports," said Mr. Chamberlain, "are invisible so far as the working-man is concerned. What does he see of them?" [96] "For invisible exports there were only invisible commercial travellers," was Sir Gilbert Parker's addition; [97] and even Mr. Bonar Law has not hesitated to take advantage of the difficulty of the untrained mind to understand a complex question. In one of his earliest Edinburgh speeches [98] he gibed at the theory that "the more we bought from other countries the more they must buy from us" as a "lovely theory." If they could only believe it, he said, there was no one who would adopt it. "All that was necessary was to import; that was to buy. We had only to sit in our arm-chairs, or on our office stools, and buy freely; nature did the rest." A year or two later Mr. Bonar Law spoke on the same subject in Parliament and said that the Colonies "could not export unless they imported"; [99] and, speaking again in Scotland, he argued that one of the results of Preference would be that it would increase the exports of the Colonies, "and at the same time would increase their purchases from us exactly in proportion to the increase in exports." [100] The fact that Mr. Bonar Law could make such a statement throws some light on the failure of the Tariff Commission to publish a memorandum on that complex subject, the balance of trade. If Mr. Bonar Law were, by chance, to understand it, how many of his speeches would he be unable to repeat!

After all, there is a good deal to be said for the simplicity of the solution of the Protectionist problem offered by one of the British delegates to the Seventh Congress of the Chambers of Commerce of the Empire held at Sydney in 1910. It was Mr. Joseph Dixon, a paper-maker of Sheffield. "You do not seem to understand the conditions under which we are living in the old land," he felt impelled to say. "We are struggling to maintain our own, just as you are doing. Look at our income tax! I need not remind you that our income tax is mounting up and up. The cost of our Navy is somewhere about £1 per head of the population, including the little ragamuffins in the slums. Mind you, each man, woman, and child in England has to pay somewhere about £1 per head for the protection of these Colonies. What is that protection doing ? Do you think it is protecting British labour ? No. It is protecting the stuff from foreign lands that is coming into these colonies and into my own country. *Personally, I should like the ships that carry the stuff to sink.* In these trade relations which we are carrying on we are absolutely acting the part in our country of a demented people."

V.—WORK AND WAGES

THE STARVING MILLIONS

THE PROMISE OF PLENTY

KEEPING THEM OUT AND LETTING THEM IN

WHEN THE FOREIGNER PAYS

MORTGAGES ON THE REVENUE

THE COST OF LIVING

FEAR AND ENVY OF FOREIGN COUNTRIES

THE "ABOMINABLE" EXAMPLE OF AMERICA

THE TRIPS TO GERMANY

THE "STARVING MILLIONS"

"THE questions thus raised," said Mr. Chamberlain,[1] "although they interest every class, are more vitally important to working men than to any other, since they alone depend upon their daily employment for their daily subsistence."

And since the success of the Protectionist revival depended, in its turn, upon the daily deception of the wage-earner, this controversy has been crowded to the edges with alluring promises about more work and higher wages, cheaper food and cheaper 'baccy. First of all, the "atmospheric" effects had to be arranged. Emigration, as already shown, has been used both to create the impression that Free Trade was driving men to flight because there was no work at home, and that the Empire would be alienated without plenty of willing emigrants from the mother country. Fluctuations in industry have been magnified. When comparisons with such statistics as are obtainable from other countries have been favourable they have been spread broadcast: when unfavourable they have been described as unreliable and misleading. In November 1905 the unemployed were scraped together under Tariff Reform auspices in processions, and labelled by one Tariff Reform journal, "Victims of Free Trade"; [2] though within a few days another Tariff Reform journal [3] was saying that "industrially there is no stress of unemployment . . . the facts are the other way;" and a year after, the former journal joyously announced that "the country generally, and London in particular," had been "prosperous throughout the year"; [4] while an effort to repeat the demonstration on Christmas Day, 1911, "was highly gratifying to every one but the organizers," as the *Daily Mail* wrote next morning, "for the 'out-of-works' who 'rallied' numbered only about a score."

Dumping has been made the scapegoat. Imports of foreign goods have "robbed the wage-earner of his employment": yet "the observed law is that the rate of wages moves up and down with exports"; [5] and Mr. Chamberlain declared that "every pound of import is balanced by a pound of export." [6] A tariff was to be designed to keep these foreign goods out, but it was to be so low a tariff that the "foreigner" would pay the duties rather than lose our market; and the money thus raised by foreign goods coming in would be spent, first in providing old age pensions, and, when those pensions were provided otherwise, then it was to be devoted to making up the losses through reducing the duties on imports at present dutiable, employment being left to struggle for itself. There was to be more work, more wages, more savings. Above all, the cost of living was to be reduced. "Tariff Reform," exclaimed Mr. Chamberlain, "will tend to cheapen everything!" [7]

The first leaflet [8] of all the millions that have been thrown into the conflict, reprinted in bold, black type the questions Mr. Chamberlain put in his speech at the Constitutional Club on June 26, 1903. "Is it the fact," ran one of them, "as we are told on the authority of Sir Henry Campbell-Bannerman, that 12,000,000 of our people—more than one-fourth of the whole population—are always on the verge of starvation? Is that a proof of the blessings of Free Imports? Is it true that the workpeople employed in them have gone to join Sir Henry Campbell-Bannerman's 12,000,000, or have been forced to emigrate, where they are finding employment in competition with their comrades at home?" "Remember that, according to Sir Henry Campbell-Bannerman, the result of fifty years of Free Trade is that one-third of the British people are almost starving," ran another of the series.[9] Mr. Chamberlain himself [10] through a secretary wrote from Highbury in July to a correspondent who had said there were twelve million inhabitants of the kingdom on the verge of starvation, and had asked whether, in the event of a tax on food, these twelve millions would not be immediately starved to death: "Sir, I am directed by Mr. Chamberlain to acknowledge the receipt of your letter of the 1st inst., and to say that he will answer your question by asking two others. 1, If it be true that twelve millions of people in these Islands are on the verge of starvation, does not this prove that our present system of Free Trade or free imports is a failure? 2, If any way can be devised by which the twelve millions can find employment at fair wages, would not their position be very much improved, even though they had to pay a farthing more for a 4-lb. loaf?"

In that letter was an implied promise of employment for twelve million persons who were assumed, on the authority of a statement that was never made, to be "on the verge of starvation." A month later Sir Henry Campbell-Bannerman found it necessary to describe the Tariff Reform leaflets and speeches as "flatly erroneous."[11] "I have not said that 12,000,000 of our people are 'always on the verge of starvation.' I spoke of them in my speech at Perth on June 5th as 'underfed, and on the verge of hunger,' which is not quite the same thing; and I did not state this on my own authority, but I referred explicitly to the systematic investigations of Mr. Booth and of Mr. Rowntree, who have proved that in the two communities of East London and York 30 per cent. of the population are in that condition. If we apply that proportion to our whole population we arrive at the figure of 12,000,000. What I contended was that to tax the food of the 12,000,000 of men and women in this condition would be a crime, even if it could be expected to bring some distant and doubtful benefit to the Colonies, whose white population, as it happens, reaches about the same number. My belief is that if it had not been for Free Trade and for the general prosperity and cheap food which it has brought, these millions would really have been on the verge of starvation, if, indeed, they could have existed at all. Their present condition is bad enough, and it is not to be improved by departing from Free Trade, but by applying the same principles of freedom to other subjects, such as the tenure of land, and the laws which govern it. That is at least one way of effecting some improvement, but nothing except new misery can be caused by playing tricks with our fiscal freedom."

That flat denial did overtake the lie, but it has never killed it, for right down to the present time the Tariff Reformers talk in one part of the country of "starvation" in another part, and generally strive to preserve that atmosphere of poverty so congenial to their principles. In 1912 there was published (and sold by the Tariff Reformers) a booklet of 48 pages entitled *Free Trade Blessings and The Misery of Protection: Some Light upon the Conditions existing in the United Kingdom under Free Trade.*"[12] Its preface ought to be preserved as an example of the methods which the Tariff Reform League has always encouraged. It ran :—

> "*FOREWORD.*—In the following pages we have collected a selection of unwitting evidence of "Free Trade" speakers and writers as to industrial conditions in the United Kingdom, and some figures bearing on the subject taken from Government publications. For the most part they have already appeared in the literature of the Tariff Reform League. It is hoped, however, that in the form in which they are now presented, these admissions will prove of greater service to speakers and writers on Tariff Reform, and at the same time that the distribution of the pamphlet amongst the electors will give them a comprehensive idea of the conditions prevailing in this country, thanks to 'our fiscal wisdom,' as the *Manchester Guardian* terms it.
>
> "It is possible to attach too much importance, in debating the question of Tariff Reform *v.* 'Free Trade,' to the experience of foreign countries. A Tariff Reform Government will be called upon to deal with the evils that exist in the United Kingdom, and it is the evils that exist in the United Kingdom to which Tariff Reformers ought to direct the attention of the electorate first and foremost. We see on all sides the results obtained in large measure because of 'free imports' (again to quote the *Guardian*). Obviously it is easier by far to drive home in the minds of the electors the hard facts of their daily life than to convince them that the cities of the United

States are not full of unemployed and starving mobs, or that the Kaiser does not breakfast off potted dog. And the British electorate is quite open to be convinced that our hungry thousands cannot be fed on statistics."

The grave utterances of most of our social reformers were in this hypocritical booklet printed under the heading of "Free Trade Blessings." Cabinet Ministers, sociological writers, medical officers, poor-law administrators, Socialists, reformers of all kinds were quoted; with extracts from newspapers described as "Cobdenite" and *Labour Gazette* statistics. Two pages were devoted to extracts from "Appeals appearing in a few London Daily Papers." They were those sadly familiar mid-winter appeals of the philanthropic societies, "Please think of the forlorn and destitute little ones," "Help the poor by sending old and new garments, boots and shoes, and odds and ends"; "The Salvation Army have 2000 men on hand, while hundreds more rescued from streets and Embankment need employment." Then followed many pages of passages concerning social life in foreign countries, under the heading "Miseries of Protection." That heading was intended to be a sarcastic one, like its contrast, for the extracts selected carefully avoided all the real miseries of other countries, and presented only that side of the medal that was carefully avoided in the case of our own country. All this was done in an endeavour to "drive home in the minds of electors the hard facts of their daily life" and "to convince them that cities of the United States are not full of unemployed." And a last pitiable attempt was made to invest the comparison with the air of "millions," by printing in columns the populations of the various counties of England, Scotland, and Wales, and grouping the counties in such a manner that every group added up to a million and more, "extended," as in an account-book, to give the row of seven units greater prominence. Thus, Lancashire stood in a line to itself, 4,550,552; but Bedfordshire, Berkshire, Buckinghamshire, Hertfordshire, Rutland, and Huntingdonshire (six small and sparsely populated counties) were grouped, and their total populations "extended" in the figure 1,060,947; while, in the case of Scotland, no fewer than nineteen small populations were "extended" to reach 1,128,979. And, as if this were not enough, readers of this Protectionist booklet were asked to pay special attention to those population figures!

Such a publication deserves the rather long description here given of it in order that there may be no underestimating the persistent attempts Tariff Reformers have made to use the misery of the poor as a means of fastening upon them the "new misery" of food taxes. It must, however, be taken only as one example out of thousands that could be quoted. Did not the authors themselves say that their quotations had already appeared for the most part "in the literature of the Tariff Reform League"?

From the armoury of poisoned shafts two more examples may be directly taken. The first is Tariff Reform Leaflet No. 214, entitled "Free Trade Poverty a Cause of Shame." It related that "The Reverend Henry Pitt, Vicar of St. Mary's, Southwark, S.E., has received a unique gift of six guineas from a Bible-class in Bangkok, Siam, for the relief of the destitute unemployed in his parish. He has distributed the money among 150 men, all fathers of families, selected from the most distressing cases in the Labour Yard in Cornbury Street, Southwark. Holding up the credit note in the pulpit at Sunday's service Mr. Pitt said, 'The sad and awful necessity for heathen Siam to send this money to feed the starving poor of London, the capital of Christian England, should fill us all with shame. I fervently hope that the dreadful need so apparent to all will speedily pass away.'"[13] Thereupon this League leaflet exclaimed, "Men of Britain, arise! 'Free Trade' drives the strongest and best of your nation's unemployed to emigrate to protected countries in search of work. 'Free Trade' brings you Chinese Pork to eat. 'Free Trade' is causing Siam to make collections to feed your starving poor. Men of Britain, help yourselves! Support Tariff Reform and food without charity!"

That was not a crude example of early and now suppressed "literature" of the League. It was published in 1910. In 1908 the League published a leaflet [14] which reprinted an appeal of the Vicar of St. Barnabas, London, N., for help for his poor, "pining for the common necessaries of life"; and readers of the leaflet were asked to "compare this unfortunate state of our workers with that which exists in France and Germany, and Support Tariff Reform."

The returns of pauperism have been twisted to serve the same end. In 1906 [15] Mr. Chamberlain declared that "the pauperism of the country is rapidly increasing. There are at the present time something like one million able-bodied men, or men not, at all events, in old age, who are being maintained at the expense of the rates of the country in your workhouses and infirmaries." Thereupon Mr. John Burns, the President of the Local Government Board, replied that "the total pauperism for England and Wales on July 1st last . . . is, according to the published return, 747,662. Of these, 532,778 were in receipt of out-door relief, thus leaving 214,884 indoor paupers. . . . If we compare the sick or temporarily disabled, who numbered 13,332, with the ordinarily able-bodied men in health, we find that the latter, as stated in the Return, numbered 7615." [16] And two days later [17] Mr. Chamberlain was obliged to say that "Mr. John Burns has written to *The Times* with reference to some figures I used at Derby, and I have to admit that he has caught me out. I should have said there were at least a million paupers in this country who were in receipt of pauper relief, in-door and out-door. I withdraw altogether the statement I made in the middle of a turbulent meeting, but it does not alter the argument."

No; the "argument" went on just the same. Among the very latest leaflets of the League may be found plentiful proof of that. "Tariff Reform means more money for Social Reform;" [18] "Free Trade means no wages or low wages for the British Worker;" [19] "Free Trade gives our work to the Foreigner;" [20] and so on. "I refuse to be mesmerized," said a Tariff Reform candidate in 1909,[21] "by Board of Trade returns. How do you get over the fact that over *forty* per cent. of the workers of this country were living in 1907 on the verge of starvation?" And when, at the close of the same year, that diligent rejuvenator of defunct arguments, Mr. J. Ellis Barker, said that "according to the exhaustive researches of Booth and Rowntree, about 30 per cent. of our people, and about 45 per cent. of our workers are in poverty," a Tariff Reformer followed in the same Protectionist journal with the protest,[23] "I am amazed that this childish fiction should still survive. Mr. Charles Booth so long ago as June 1903, repudiated in the public press his responsibility for any such deduction, and as for Mr. Rowntree, his investigations have been limited to the City of York. These figures are not wholly insupportable, but they are highly dangerous." "When," he asked, will "some of our Tariff Reformers become reasonably discreet and stifle their lust for mere figures—heedless too often as to whether they are true or false?" Nevertheless, Mr. Wyndham, who always showed a "lust for mere figures," was heard in August 1912, at Cockermouth, bewailing the "millions of British unemployed," though the official rate of unemployment in that month was the lowest August figure for thirteen years!

There were other Tariff Reformers who withdrew the statement only to substitute something else in place of it. As industry increased and unemployment decreased the cry arose that though all might be well now, let us wait for bad times. In 1904 a Protectionist Member of Parliament had said, "He was not sorry trade was depressed and employment scarce, because it would assist Mr. Chamberlain and his supporters in carrying this reform." [25] "Some day," wrote the Earl of Dunraven to the Hon. Sec. of the South Wales Tariff Reform Federation, "the wage-earners and those dependent on them will awake to facts. I hope and trust that it may not take some period of terrible distress to rouse them from sleep, but they will be wise in time." [26] "As the rain was said to have rained away the Corn Laws," wrote the *Morning Post* on August 25, 1908, "so the coming winter will freeze the life out of the Free Trade fetish, and good will again have issued from misfortune." The present leader of the lugubrious movement improved on all those groans. "What happened before was going to happen again," said Mr. Bonar Law in 1907.[27] "Every one engaged in industries threatened by foreign imports believed that this country was going to be subjected soon to the dumping of foreign manufactures on a scale that had never been touched before. When that happened, then would be the opportunity of Tariff Reformers. The abolition of the Corn Laws was not carried by Cobden's speeches; it was carried by the Irish famine; and what the Irish famine had done for Cobden's cause two bad winters would do for the cause of Fiscal Reform. When British workmen went about the country seeking for work which they could not find, and when they saw the land flooded with foreign manufactures which they could make themselves, it would take something more than mere theory to convince them that a system which produced such a state of affairs could be good for them or for their country." "Bad years and lean years," the same speaker said about the same time,[28] were "visibly arriving to both Germany and America, and as their productive capacity had enormously increased, they would have to find an outlet for their manufactures. Their one possible outlet was the free British market. The consequence must be that there would be dumping in this country on a scale never equalled before, and then, when English workmen were walking the streets wishing they could have the chance of making the goods the foreigners were sending over—then would be the time when their policy was going to succeed. In that day it would take more than mere platitudes to convince the working-man that the present system was the best possible one for this country."

The slump of which Mr. Bonar Law spoke taught the country one economic lesson: even the Tariff Reform League agreed that "the truth is that neither Protection nor Free Trade is responsible for the waning of the great industrial boom — a boom in which all manufacturing nations, and especially those whose industries are protected by a tariff, have participated. It has been generally recognized," said the League,[29] " that a period of depression was bound to succeed the long spell of phenomenal commercial activity which has prevailed, and no fiscal system has been or can be invented which will prevent the recurrence of such periods."

THE PROMISE OF PLENTY

NOTWITHSTANDING all that had been said and written admitting the inadequacy of "any fiscal system" to remedy the social evils so luridly painted, the appeal to wage-earners was maintained at full pitch, since "they alone depend upon their daily employment for their daily subsistence." It is impossible to record the multitudinous promises that have been made in the name of Tariff Reform to bring to working men benefits that it was admitted "no fiscal system" could bring. A slight departure from the narrative form of this record is necessary to give the promises even a partial reflection in these pages. They have veered from positive to negative, from absolute to conditional, from the past to the dim future. To analyse them would minimize their effect. Such as they are, in all their naked casuistry, here they are. Let them stand without comment.

In January 1919, twenty one-horse political vans were touring the country in a campaign against the Free Trade Government. They were known as the "Conservative Vans," and were sent out by the National Union of Conservative and Constitutional Associations, of whose literature committee Sir Howard Vincent, an active Protectionist, was Chairman. Upon the vans were placards bearing these words: "Radicalism means dearer living. Under a Radical Government your food has cost you more. Unemployed, remember Woolwich. Fiscal Reform means work for all." [30]

When attention was drawn to these placards in the London press, they disappeared. Or, they partially disappeared, for in the summer one of them was seen in Kent,[31] still on the van, but cut so that it read "Fiscal Reform means Work."

In the General Election of January 1910, Mr. T. Ablewhite, an agent of the Central Conservative Association, published a card on which was printed, " The A.B.C. of Tariff Reform. A full cupboard containing Bread, Butter, and Beef through Constant Employment at regular wages, and Old Age Pensions absolutely guaranteed by the State."

This pick of the promises has been placed first because they indicate how the Tariff Reform propaganda affected a great party in the State, and also because they touched a depth of deceit that led many Tariff Reform members of the party to repudiate them.

Mr. Joseph Chamberlain's phraseological exercises on this point are subjoined in chronological order, beginning with 1903 and ending with the general election of January 1910.

" I am fully convinced that the prosperity of this country depends largely on our trade with the Colonies, which, under a wise system of mutual concession, will increase by leaps and bounds. We have been apt in the past to consider too much the advantage of buying cheaply and not to pay sufficient attention to the methods by which we may have the means that will enable us to pay at all. *Increased wages are even more important to the working classes than reduced cost of living.* A working-man in the Transvaal may pay two or three times as much as his comrade at home for the necessaries of life for himself and his family ; but if his wages are three or four times as much, the balance is still in his favour." [32]

" But even *if the price of food is raised, the rate of wages will certainly be raised in greater proportion.* This has been the case both in the United States and Germany. In the former country the available balance left to the working-man after he has paid for necessaries is much larger than here. These are facts which we have to bring to the notice of the working-men generally." [33]

" Ten years ago I made a speech to my constituents in which after reciting what had already been done, I pointed out to them that *the greatest of all reforms* was yet to come. The greatest boon that could be conferred upon the working people of this country, was such a reform as would ensure to every industrious man *full and constant employment at fair wages.* Do Free Imports secure this result ? Surely it is a mathematical truth that if imports of manufactured goods—which we can make as well as other nations—come into this country in constantly increasing quantities, they must displace labour. Although it may be true that these particular articles are sold a little cheaper, what is the good of that to a man who cannot afford to buy them ? " [34]

" I feel sanguine that the policy which I have hitherto only sketched out will, as soon as it is thoroughly understood, commend itself to the working-men of this country. All their interests depend upon *full employment at fair wages,* and I am confident that this can only be permanently secured by some changes in our tariff system." [35]

" Your Colonial trade as it stands at present with the prospective advantage of a preference against the foreigner means *employment and fair wages* for three quarters of a million of workmen and subsistence for nearly four millions of our population." [36]

" If the demand for labour increases, the wages of labour must rise also ; and *full work at fair prices will enable our manufacturers to pay higher wages,* without loss to themselves." [37]

" Working-men, and especially trade unionists, should support my proposals. What is the whole problem as it affects the working classes of this country ? It is all contained in one word—employment. Cheap food,—higher standard of living, higher wages ; all these things, important as they are, are contained in the word 'employment.' *If this policy will give you more employment, all the others will be added unto you.* If you lose employment, all the others put together will not compensate you for that loss." [38]

" The poor, in the case of this unauthorized programme are, as they ought to be, doubly ensured. I do not believe their expenditure will be increased ; but I take care, at any rate, that their taxation shall be decreased in an equal proportion to the greatest burden that can be placed upon them. I have made it absolutely impossible that the cost of living—and that is the point—should be increased to the poor. And I give them hope—the hope which they may well cherish—of a fuller employment—of *more continuous work, which must inevitably be followed in the course of time,* as it has been in every country in which this policy has been tried, must inevitably be followed *by higher wages.*" [39]

" You are told by the Cobden Club that your wealth is increasing. Yes, as far as the country is concerned, that is true. *You are getting richer every day. Whether the division is altogether right is another question.*" [40]

" To the labourer it (his agricultural policy) will bring benefits proportionate to those it brings to the farmer. It will give him *a better hope of regular and fairly paid employment.* I think he may rest assured that, while it is not likely in any case to raise the cost of food, it is quite certain that the general cost of living will be reduced." [41]

" Now I have tried in what I have said to you, to force you to see that this is not, as our opponents say, a rich man's question. I have never been able to see how a rich man—a man already rich—would be materially benefited by my policy. Of course if the whole country profited I suppose he would profit in a like manner ; but as he would probably have to pay more for his luxuries, I think it is possible he would lose more than he would gain. But *to the working man it is life and death.*" [42]

"I tell you I would never have—to use a well-known expression—taken off my coat in this movement unless I believed, as I do believe, that this great result will be *more remunerative employment* for those who have to gain the subsistence of themselves and their families by the work of their hands. . . . In my view the cost of living is not the most important thing for the working-man to consider. What he has to consider as most important to him is *the price which he gets for his labour.*" [42]

"From the beginning, the first object of this movement in my mind, as far as it concerned domestic conditions, was to secure *more employment at fair wages* for the working-men of this country. That is the only thing for which it is worth while to labour." [43]

"If you go back twenty or thirty years, you will find a larger proportion of the people in continuous and remunerative employment than there are to-day. That is the reason why, although it may be true that the country is getting richer, the number of unemployed is getting greater." [44]

"*The whole object of my policy is not to lessen your loaf; it is to give you more money to buy it with.*" [44]

"Charge that my policy means starvation for workmen is ridiculous. It means *more employment, higher wages,* and no increase in the cost of living." [45]

To a correspondent who wrote inquiring what benefits would accrue from his fiscal policy to the thousands of clerks earning from 16s. to 24s. per week, Mr. Chamberlain said his scheme will result in *a general increase of employment* and every class of labour would ultimately benefit.[46]

"When you have, as one gentleman said in the course of this debate, *two jobs for one man,* believe me, you will not want any strikes. The wages will undoubtedly rise." [47]

"What does the trade unionist want? What is his special reason for existence? Why do you organize and combine? You do it in order to secure fair positions for your labour, in order to secure *full employment,* and in order to maintain the standard of life common among your class. I would go further, and say not only to maintain it, but also to raise it. Very well. My proposals have exactly the same object." [47]

"Do you not think that many of the questions which they (the Socialists) are honestly trying to deal with would settle themselves if I could offer you £100,000,000 *more a year for wages* for the working men of this country?" [47]

"Give me the power to give you more employment, everything will follow. *It will be easy enough then for your employers to give you higher wages.* It will be easy enough then to promise all the legislation which is intended to raise the standard of your life." [48]

"That question of employment is at the very root of all the social reforms of our time. Do not let the working classes make any mistake. I do not think they are likely to do so. There is no dole from the State. There is no relief of taxation. There is no legislation which the wit of man can devise, no artificial combination to raise the rate of wages, which will weigh for one moment in the balance against a policy which would give to our people *some substantial increase in the demand for their labour*." (As punctuated by the Tariff Reform League 1912 Handbook.)[49]

" In the first place, my policy means *the social advantage and welfare of the masses* of the people." [50]

" The working classes have suffered long enough under our present system of Free Imports, which is really a system of protection for foreign workmen and foreign trade. We let our competitors take the bread out of the mouths of our own people, and then we are surprised at the number of the unemployed, and the millions who are on the verge of hunger. All we want is fair play in foreign trade and to treat our friends and kinsmen across the seas better than the stranger outside our gates. *Then there will be employment for all who want to work, and with full employment will come a rise in wages and in the standard of living*." [51]

" Our remedy is more employment." [52]

" Now, my policy, the policy of the Unionists, is a practical policy. We are going to put, whenever our opportunity comes, we are going to put in the hands of the working class the means of finding profitable employment for their hands. Give to every decent working-man the opportunity which his fellow has in the United States of America, give him a full market, *continuous employment, fair and even high wages*, and I will undertake to say that you will enormously increase the happiness of all, and you will help a considerable number to rise into a still higher position." [53]

" The object of my policy is to find more work in this old country of ours—*more work at reasonable and fair wages*. . . . My object is to do to foreigners as they do to us." [54]

" I have told you more than once in the course of that time that there was a greater reform than any I had yet advocated publicly before you—there was a greater reform in the future which would do more for you than all these attempts at bettering your condition, and that was a reform which would secure for the masses of the industrial population in this country *constant employment at fair wages*." [55]

" Tariff Reform gives the only prospect of *renewed prosperity and full employment* for our working classes." [56]

" I have never pretended that a reform in tariff would entirely remove all the difficulties from which we suffer, but I am more than ever convinced that it is only in this way that we can hope to recover our normal prosperity and *secure for our working people the comfort to which they have been accustomed*." [57]

" Personally I am of opinion that Tariff Reform is *necessary to remedy our present want of employment*." [58]

"We know that they (the Germans and Americans) find *full employment* for their people." [59]

"Both in America and in Germany Tariff Reform has operated to limit the unemployment which prevails in this country, and I consider that with a tariff we ought to find *ample room for employment* in our own manufactures." [60]

"I am sanguine that by such a scheme good trade and *full employment* may be secured." [61]

"Tariff Reform means *more work for all.*" [62]

No selection from the foregoing array of promises would do it justice. They are many, but not one of them ought to be missed, if only because the Tariff Reformers have tried their hardest to stifle many of them. With few exceptions, they are not to be found in the current literature of the League. The 1912 edition of the *Speakers' Handbook* devotes many pages to extracts from Mr. Chamberlain's speeches; but every utterance of his that dealt in great particularity with wages is omitted, and only the vaguest of his vague generalities are preserved. The two promises that are most full-blooded marked the eves of two general elections—in December 1905, "employment for all who want to work," and in December 1909, "more work for all." On February 26, 1908, Mr. Chamberlain declared "it had never been said that Tariff Reform would mean work for all." Strictly verbally, he did not say it himself, though he did promise "more work for all." But he also wrote in December 1909 [63] that he had "never withdrawn anything he has stated on the subject of Tariff Reform." Really, there does not appear to have been any need to withdraw one of the above promises, for the effect of the orgy on the public mind was to cancel them all.

The same eye for electioneering marked Mr. Balfour's prudently rare utterances on this question. In the House of Commons in November 1909,[64] he responded to a direct appeal to "say a word" on "what was undoubtedly a fact that the Unionist party's methods of dealing with the fiscal question in this country would have the effect of increasing employment." He said he "entirely agreed with the hon. gentleman that if anybody interpreted that as meaning that any arrangements of tariffs or anything else was going to abolish unemployment altogether he (Mr. Balfour) never had said that; he had never suggested that; he believed he had on more than one occasion done his best to warn his hearers that expectations of that sort from the Unionist party or any other party were exaggerated. It was a perfectly clear and honest opinion, but it was capable of being so stretched as to cover ground to which neither he (Mr. Balfour) nor any other responsible person thought it should be stretched." He himself would stretch it no further, it seemed, than that "The employment of the working classes will be increased by Fiscal Reform," for that was the formula he adopted in writing to a candidate a couple of months later; [65] and the Tariff Reform League was at that time so anxious to pin down Mr. Balfour whenever they could catch him that it promptly issued the statement in a leaflet.[66] Another of these eve-of-the-election diversions of Mr. Balfour was a message he delivered when passing through Stockport. "You can give this message to Stockport for me," he said, "Tariff Reform will undoubtedly do great things for the unemployed. I do not say Tariff Reform will entirely remove unemployment, but it will, beyond all question, stimulate industry, and greatly help the workers." [67] Yet he seemed to think afterwards that he had said too much, for at the end of the year, just before the election began, "Mark you," he said, "I will neither now nor on any other occasion, in private or in public, tell any of my countrymen that the whole difficulty of unemployment is going to be solved by Tariff Reform. It is not; but the greatest part of that difficulty, the unemployment of the really competent workman in the prime of life—that unemployment must be diminished by any rational system." [68] And when the election was over he safeguarded himself from ever being called upon to fulfil even that meagre promise. "I admit," he said in the House of Commons, "I admit that you will never get rid of that part of the problem of unemployment which arises out of the oscillations of trade. I agree, nothing we can do will wholly prevent these variations in the fortunes of the working classes." [69]

The present leader of the Tariff Reform movement falls between Mr. Chamberlain and Mr. Balfour as a phrase-maker on this delicate topic. In 1903 he boldly said that "the industrial classes will have to decide whether it will pay them better to pay for a slight increase in their food, if in exchange they have a larger increase of trade, which would mean more constant employment and better wages"; [70] but in later years he thrust the risk of getting those lucky tickets out of the lottery on the working-men themselves. "If the change means more business for the masters it will mean more employment," he told them; "if it means higher prices for the manufacturers, then it ought to mean, and it will be your own fault if it does not mean, higher wages." [71] Next winter he observed that the Free Traders "had been saying lately that Tariff Reformers were climbing down on the advantages of Tariff Reform as a complete cure for unemployment. Tariff Reformers never said it was a complete cure," he declared. "But he did not want to minimise what he did think. It was, he believed, a great remedy which would go a long way to cure the evil of unemployment, and was all the more necessary as periods of good trade were tending to be shorter and shorter and periods of bad trade longer and longer." [72] That was before his election to the leadership. In his first deliverance [73] after he had been invested with the giddy authority to speak the whirling minds of his party, he claimed that "such a change would do much to help what is the greatest of all our social evils—chronic unemployment"; and he added, "I believe that a change in our fiscal system will tend to raise wages; but this at least is certain, that without such a change a general rise is absolutely impossible." If there are added to these Mr. Bonar Law's subsequent declarations that "we cannot abandon Tariff Reform, because we believe that the greatest of all social reforms would be a general rise in the level of wages, and because we know, at least we believe we know, that such a rise is impossible without a change in our fiscal system"; [74] and the still more recent recital that "I believe Tariff Reform will tend to raise wages, and I am sure of this—that without it, without equality on our own market will protect our workmen at their own doors, any general rise in the level of wages is absolutely impossible" ;[75] it becomes practicable to construct a convenient omnibus to carry Mr. Bonar Law's queerly conditional opinions on wages. *At least he believes that he now knows that Tariff Reform will tend to make a general rise in wages not impossible!*

Lord Lansdowne has dwelt very little upon what he once called "the close connection of this question with that of unemployment." He did not wish to be understood as saying that "with the advent of Tariff Reform, unemployment and all the troubles of the community will vanish." Yet he "firmly believed" it would do "something to give greater solidity to the Empire; something to strengthen us in our dealings with foreign countries; something to keep markets open for us."[76]

The same prudence, in wondrous contrast to the verbal spend-thriftiness of his father, has marked Mr. Austen Chamberlain's references to the subject. In Parliament in 1908 he announced that Tariff Reformers "made no claim that fiscal reform would provide a cure for evils that were becoming year by year more serious."[77] In a later speech he went so far as to say that "Tariff Reform would find more work";[78] but when asked for whom, he could only repudiate the responsibility of details. "I was invited," he said in a speech in Cornwall, "to tell you what would be the wages of railwaymen, of quarrymen, of agricultural labourers, and I think of other classes as well, under Tariff Reform. I am not going to do anything of the kind. Is there any man here bold enough to tell me he knows what the wages of the working classes are going to be without Tariff Reform? I am not going to make statements which obviously cannot be verified, which would be the merest guess-work, and would resemble far too much the recommendations which the itinerant quack makes in favour of his goods."[79]

It would be charitable to suppose that just as the Tariff Reform League endeavours to suppress the shameless guess-work of Mr. Joseph Chamberlain, so is Mr. Austen

Chamberlain anxious to forget it also. Nevertheless, there are on record many statements out of the mouths of prominent officials connected with the Tariff Reform movement.

"This policy is propounded in the interests of the masses of the people—of the poor much more than of the rich," said Mr. Chamberlain in his Introduction to Mr. Vince's book, *Mr. Chamberlain's Proposals, What they Mean and What we shall Gain by Them.* It is unfortunate that two years later the present President of the Tariff Reform League (Viscount Ridley), who was then Chairman of its Executive Committee, should have diminished the force of the appeal by observing that "after all, this question of the definite prosperity of the working-man, important as it was, compared with the development of the Empire, was comparatively a side issue." [80] That comparison has never been forgotten. Lord Ridley's attempt to explain it away two years afterwards was rather pitiful. First he telegraphed to the Unionist agent for North Wilts that he had "never made the statement referred to, but always maintained that working-men would gain more from Tariff Reform than any other class." [81] He followed the telegram up by a letter in which he admitted the correctness of the quotation, but added: "It is sufficiently obvious that I had been arguing in favour of social measures for the prosperity of the working-man, and obvious also that the next step in the argument is to show that this prosperity is, in my opinion, entirely dependent on the development of the resources of the Empire, and opportunities for employment in England and the Colonies; and that, compared with security of employment, and of wages, which the development of the Empire will increase, all other questions must be a side issue." [82]

What did soon become obvious was that this exaltation of the Imperial sentiment over the "policy propounded in the interests of the poor" was a hook that would catch no fish. It never commended itself to the propagandist organizations. The Birmingham Tariff Committee in their *Handbook* set out to prove that "the protection of native industry by a tariff tends not only to increase employment, but to raise wages"; [83] and though the word "protection" was afterwards cut out of the argument, it still represents more or less accurately the ideas of the propagandists. True, the League itself has tried in vain to walk safely over this honeycombed ground. If it had left the direction solely to Mr. Hewins, there might have been no accident, for Mr. Hewins has been prudence itself, talking of the suggestion that Tariff Reform would gain "work for all" as an "absurd" thing that "no responsible Tariff Reformer" had ever said.[84] Yet has the League, whose "literature" he is said to edit, gone as near to the statement as it dared. In its official journal a month after Mr. Hewins had so contemptuously rejected the "work for all" idea, appeared a paragraph under the heading of "The Swiss Tariff and its Effect." "Our Consul-General reports that 'as a result of this continued activity in all branches of industry there have been practically no unemployed in this country; in some cases a difficulty has even been experienced in obtaining a sufficient supply of labour to meet the increased demand for manufacture.' If a tariff," commented the League, "can provide practically 'work for all' in Switzerland, why should it not prove to be the best solution of the unemployment problem in our own country?" [85]

The publications of the Tariff Reformers print in big type phrases on the subject almost as various as those that fell from Mr. Chamberlain's lips. "If the foreigner gets the wages you go short." [86] Tariff Reform means "more work and more wages"; [87] "The working-man's chief interests are Regular Employment and Better Wages. He will secure both by Tariff Reform," [88] and so on interminably. Speakers on Tariff Reform have given voice to statements that "Tariff Reform was coming because the working-men of the country were waking up at last. They had discovered that last year £241,000,000 of wages were paid abroad that ought to have been paid here—representing nearly 10s. a week apiece amongst ten million workers. The Free Trade Government of this country robbed the working-men last year of that amount." [89] But against all this, again, must be put the more considered views of such a responsible official of the League as the Secretary of its branch in Lancashire, who, when he was asked, " Will Tariff Reform solve the unemployed question ?" replied, "We don't say it will solve the unemployed question, but a discriminating system of tariffs will considerably lessen unemployment." [90]

Vacillation between Yea and Nay, high and low, all and none, much and little, has constantly characterized the speeches of Parliamentarians and candidates, those self-chosen prophets of the good times coming that the gods of the League could not discern from their sublimer heights. Yet the gods have never thought it necessary to check the ardour of these simple mortals. They all contributed to the desired atmosphere: let the public grope! If the candidates and members did not care to heed what they might read in the League's *Monthly Notes*, well, the League could not be responsible for that. So nobody chided Colonel Rawson, M.P., for declaring that " what they wanted was a policy which would give more work and more employment, and which would allow the rich to become richer," and that "Tariff Reform would have that effect." [92] Nobody rebuked the London candidate who, even in 1912, shamelessly flaunted a poster " Vote for Gibson and Work for all." On the contrary, the *Pall Mall Gazette* told the candidate that in sticking to Tariff Reform he had " adopted the right tactics," and chosen the subject which was of " greatest and widest urgency" ; [93] and when Sir John Rees declared that he did not despair, even, of a minimum weekly wage of 30s. for railway workers " if this country could only be blessed with a Government which would allow its industries, including the railways, decent and proper protection in its home market," [94] he was in the throes of a by-election at Kilmarnock, and, well, you know what electioneering is !

Still, that promise of 30s. may as well be contrasted with one of 25s., which was the figure mentioned in the Midlands a year or two earlier by Mr. E. M. Pollock, K.C., who asked " whether Englishmen would not gladly pay this increase of one-sixth of a farthing per loaf, if they could be assured of a wage of 25s. a week." [95] Speakers who have left the division of the spoils to the imagination of their audiences have been happier in the end. Mr. F. E. Smith, for instance, who calculated at Basingstoke that if a 10 per cent. duty kept out no more than half the imported manufactured goods, that "would mean £35,000,000 spent in wages to the men who couldn't find work to-day." [96] Nobody would think of tracing to Mr. Hewins the direct responsibility for the "solid fact" printed by a Birmingham paper, that "experts say that we could make for ourselves at least half the manufactured goods we import, and" that "if we did so there would be £5 a year extra wages for every man, woman, and child in the factories and workshops of this country, even if there were no increase in the rate of wages"; [97] though it is just about as near the truth as Mr. F. E. Smith's fluttering of the millions.

Mr. L. S. Amery, when wooing Wolverhampton East, made a much more persuasive estimate. We "could make equally well ourselves" the £100,000,000 worth of manufactured goods we import, he said, and that would mean "enough to find work for every unemployed man in this country; to give full time to all those partially employed, and largely to raise the wages of those who are already fully employed." Nevertheless, the League appears yet to have a good deal to do among the representatives of Protection; for in reply to a question as to whether it were better to have work and wages to pay for food, which perhaps might be a little dearer than it was to-day, than to have no money at all to pay for the cheapest of stuff, Mr. Henry Keswick, who was returned unopposed for the Epsom Division in 1912, met his constituents a few hours after he became their member and said that "that was a question he had very much at heart, but he had never got it straightened out in his head in such a way that he could put it to them properly that evening." [99] Perhaps if Mr. Keswick reads this chapter, it will help him.

Journalistic assistance of the kind so fervently offered by the Birmingham paper has been one of the most trying embarrassments of the Tariff Reform search for a work and wages formula. There are so many examples of it that it would be quite impossible to print even a thousandth part of them. But inasmuch as the *Morning Post* is, after all that has happened, still the most faithful of Protection's paper props, room must be found for its assurance, when commenting on statements respecting the skilled unemployed in the winter of 1908–9,[100] that " if Tariff Reform were carried out this year they might all be reinstated by next winter and assured of steadier employment than ever before." When the journal added that " the shilly-shallying of the Government is as intolerable to the country in general as it is cruel to its immediate victims, whose hopes are raised by these future promises of remedial measures," it can only be hoped that it honestly believed every one of the promises made by its own side. Much in the same manner the *Pall Mall Gazette*,[101] writing on Mr. Keir Hardie's ideal that " in the Socialist state every child should have plenty to eat; every strong man work; every aged person comfort; and all freedom," commented, " Well, we need not wait for the millennium for the realization of this programme; it is all possible under a commonsense adjustment of fiscal duties," an adjustment, say, on the lines of the promises that have been made to find " work for all." One of the London contemporaries of the *Post* and the *Pall Mall Gazette* has confirmed the very definite promise more than once; and it was an act of base ingratitude on the part of Mr. Hewins when he observed, in the speech from which a quotation has just been made, " If you will pardon me, the *Daily Express* is not one of the Tariff Reform leaders ! " No London journal has worked harder to popularize Tariff Reform than the *Express*. Was it not the *Express* which cried, during the Peckham by-election of 1908, " Tariff Reform means work for all ? It opens up vistas of happiness for the industrious and the persistent, and in such a district as that which Mr. Gooch is now contesting the meaning of this great crusade has only to be realized to bring numberless adherents into its ranks " ; [102] and did not the *Express*, at infinite trouble and expense, prosecute an " inquiry " of its own in order to ascertain how many extra hands British employers would take on and how much extra wages they would receive under Tariff Reform ?

The results of that astonishing "inquiry" were published by the *Express* in a series of several long articles between May 18 and June 21, 1909. The sum of them was that with an average duty of 10 per cent. on imports of manufactures, certain British industries would employ 534,657 "extra hands," and increase their wages bills by £765,372 a week, or £39,799,344 a year! Lord Ridley spoke of the inquiry as having discovered "a general concensus of opinion among the men who best know the circumstances." [103] But it cannot be imagined that this figure-head of the Tariff Reform League had troubled himself to investigate the methods adopted by the *Express* in making the remarkable discovery.

The journal was quite frank in showing its hand. It issued a circular to employers inquiring "(A) If the Government by an Order in Council imposed an *ad valorem* duty of 10 per cent. on imported manufactured goods and parts in your line of manufacture, do you think your trade would be increased thereby? (B) How many extra hands do you estimate you would be enabled to employ? (C) What would you estimate your weekly wage bill would be increased by?" In the industries selected by the *Express* there were, the paper said, about 26,400 employers. The *Economist* put the number at between 30,000 and 40,000. At any rate, less than 5000 received the circular. Of these only 636 gave definite answers to the questions. Of "favourable" replies (as the *Express* called them) there were 1168 altogether, and the remainder either put the "inquiry" forms into the waste-paper basket or answered "unfavourably." The scanty response was all-sufficient for the Protectionist statisticians. They revelled in ratios. In the electrical industry, for example, there were some two thousand firms. Of these 188 were circularized, and only 78 replied. The *Express* admitted that 30 of the replies were "evasive" or "unfavourable." Of the balance of 48 only 18 declared precisely what they hoped to gain by a 10 per cent. duty. They would employ 2910 extra hands and pay £4696 more every week in wages. The rule of three was applied. "The 18 firms who give figures form 23 per cent. of the total number who replied," said the *Express*. "Approximately, there are 2000 firms engaged in the manufacture of electrical apparatus, fittings, and machinery. If only 23 per cent. of these could provide increased employment and wages in the same proportion as the firms who give figures, the totals would be, estimated for whole trade : Extra hands, 74,060 ; extra weekly wages, £119,600." And this meant "£6,219,200 per annum in extra wages in the electrical industry!" Those fat millions were left to speak for themselves. It was no part of the duty of the *Express*—and certainly the statisticians of the Tariff Reform League did not consider it theirs—to work out the ultimate effect of this prolific 10 per cent. The extra wages would represent perhaps half the extra output of the industry. In place of the "imported manufactured goods and parts" which would be kept out by the duty, there would thus be produced at home electrical goods to the value of nearly twelve and a half millions. It was nothing to the *Express* that the total importation of such goods was only about one-eighth of the amount! The "vistas of happiness" which Tariff Reform would open up "for the industrious and persistent" probably included the prompt electrification of every unit of energy in the land! If the reader will consult the British trade journals of the time, immediately after the publication of these articles in the *Express*, he will be able to amuse himself further with the destructive criticisms of experts.

As a matter of fact, Protectionist employers have been exceedingly shy of underwriting this "policy propounded in the interests of the masses of the people." The records of Tariff Reform may be searched almost in vain for undertakings to pay, except, in a sense, "on demand," for did not Mr. Bonar Law advise the working-men that it would be their own fault if Tariff Reform did not mean higher wages for them ? The Tariff Reform propagandists have taken trade by trade and promised each one "increased employment and better wages" ; [104] and particular trades, iron workers and miners, for instance, have been warned that "dumping" would "take away your work." [105] But Protectionist employers in Parliament and on the platform have remained stolidly dumb on details. There was, it is true, one manufacturer in the East End of London who undertook to pay £5000 to any charity if, provided his business was protected by a "suitable" tariff, he did not increase the number of his employees by 400 per cent.; but that was a cheap promise at the price, for the tariff would obviously be unsuitable if it did not multiply both the number of his employees and the amount of his profits to the dimensions named in the conditions. In the Wolverhampton by-election of 1908 there was sent out with the poll-cards of Mr. Amery, the Tariff Reform candidate, a letter from a local firm of manufacturers, Joseph Evans & Sons (Wolverhampton) Ltd., makers of pumps and pumping machinery, declaring that "we have no hesitation in saying that if a tariff were imposed on foreign manufactured goods our firm would rapidly increase its output and employ at least a hundred more men in a very short time, and eventually in all probability employ double the men we are now employing"; [106] and the Tariff Reform League in a leaflet entitled "Facts for Papermakers," [107] informed the trade that "Messrs. P. Dixon & Son, of Sheffield, are 'quite certain' a duty would increase their trade," and that the firm had indeed said, "We estimate we could employ 200 to 400 extra hands, including women, and pay £250 to £500 more weekly in wages." If the League had printed with this the opinion of Mr. Dixon on what he would regard as a "suitable" duty the leaflet would have been more useful to the papermakers, for the head of this firm was the British delegate who told the Congress of the Chambers of Commerce of the Empire at Sydney in 1910 that "personally, I should like the ships that carry the stuff ('from foreign lands into my own country') to sink."

The hop-growers, too, have set down an alluring plea on behalf of the workers. In 1908 they called upon the Government "to take immediate action to save the industry by putting a forty-shilling duty upon all imported foreign hops, and so preserve remunerative employment and a health-giving outing to hundreds of thousands of the English working classes during the month of September every year." [108] That would seem to be more of a promise of a holiday than of a job. However it may be regarded by the "English working classes," they do not appear to choose these "outings" for recreation, for in the hop-picking season of 1912 the *Daily Express*, which on June 13, 1905, had declared that four bank holidays a year contributed "very largely to the backwardness of British industry," lamented that there were not enough pickers for Hereford and Worcestershire, because, among other reasons, "there is a great pressure of work in the Black Country." [109] Protectionists might safely promise that Tariff Reform would not leave the hop-farmer in the lurch like that.

KEEPING THEM OUT AND LETTING THEM IN

PUNCH once published a "Tariff Reform play." [110] It was a conversation between a Tariff Reform Candidate and George, who wanted to marry the Candidate's sister.

"TARIFF REFORM CANDIDATE. Yes, that all seems satisfactory. But there is one other point. Are you a Tariff Reformer ?

"GEORGE (*surprised*). What's that ?

"CANDIDATE. Have you ever studied the question ?

"GEORGE. No. Never seem to get the time, somehow.

"CANDIDATE. Then of *course* you're one. (*Warming to it.*) It's like this. All the great industries of this country are dying. Now, if we have Protection—er, that is Fiscal Reform—by which I mean a small tax on imports, we keep out the foreigner ; so that all the goods which the Germans have been selling to us will be made by Englishmen in England. That means no more unemployed.

"GEORGE (*pleased*). Quite so.

"CANDIDATE. Furthermore, this small tax, when levied upon the immense quantity of German goods which are now pouring into the country, will yield an enormous revenue, all of which will be paid by the foreigner. This will enable us to do away with the Income tax, and create Old Age Pensions.

"GEORGE (*doubtfully*). Y-yes.

"CANDIDATE (*sharply*). You see that, of course ?

"GEORGE. Er—well—I know you'll think I'm an awful ass, but just for the moment I don't quite. I mean I don't see how you get all the money by letting the bally things in, if you help the dying industries by keeping the bally things out.

"CANDIDATE (*coldly*). You don't ? Then I can only say that you are a Little Englander. No relation of mine shall marry a Little Englander."

But *Punch,* faithful mirror as it was, could not be expected to dull its surface with all the smearings of Tariff Reform finger-marks. How have they written ? Foreign manufactured goods are to be kept out by a tariff in order to provide work for the British industrial classes. This would enable the home manufacturers to raise prices. But to offset these increases the wage-earners are to have higher wages or constant employment, or both ; and if they do not get either —see how the Tariff Reformer is prepared for all emergencies —then foreign goods will not be kept out by the tariff. Only their " character " will be changed. They will come in, and the foreign exporter to these shores will pay the duties, sometimes all of them, sometimes part of them, sometimes even no more than a part of part of them, but at least enough to form a fund out of which the promised reductions in existing duties will be compensated in the national balance-sheet. Individual domestic balance-sheets must fend for themselves. The tariff will be of duties so small that they will not increase prices ; but at the same time, to meet the increase of prices that the duties will cause, existing duties are to be lowered so that the otherwise inevitable rise in the cost of living will be avoided. There have been several other suggested claims on this fund which is to be contributed by the foreigner. Old age pensions were to be paid out of it ; then the agriculturist's taxes (see Section on Agriculture) ; then the National Insurance contributions. The Navy, besides, was to be maintained out of this conjurer's hat. By way of melting the obstinacy of the electorate, which has steadily refused to see through this maze of contradictory proposals, it has at last been pointed out that even if home manufacturers do show a disposition to take advantage of the tariff, they will be smacked in the face by home competition, which the tariff will encourage, and so, triumphantly, prices will be kept down. And where that argument has failed to convince, then the Tariff Reformers have fallen back on the enormous increase which the tariff will make in home production, and everybody knows that the more a man produces, the cheaper he sells it ! The last variation completes the circle again ; for home production cannot be enlarged unless the foreign competitor is kept out, so that prices will both go up and go down, there will be "millions" taken from the pockets of the foreigner, everything will be cheaper, wages will increase, taxes will be reduced, everybody will be better off by both keeping the foreign goods out and letting them in.

This familiar contrast of the mutual destructiveness of the Tariff Reform arguments is not one whit exaggerated. The controversy has acquainted every wage-earner with the meaning of the pregnant economic term "real wages." In the face of that widespread knowledge, and in order to convince the wage-earner that there will be plenty of money coming in to enable the Protectionists to reduce existing duties on tea and sugar, and condensed milk and preserved ginger, and so on, the League itself has felt compelled to announce that "it is not the aim of Tariff Reform to 'keep out foreign goods from this country.' To do so would be merely to raise prices and produce no revenue."[111] There are many such passages as that in the official journal of the League. Tariffs "do not 'keep out the goods of a foreign country' and are not intended to."[112] "Germany has a high tariff, but its effect is not to decrease but largely to increase imports."[113] Imports of fully manufactured goods into the United States had risen. "Why should not Tariff Reform have the same effect in the United Kingdom?"[114] It is true that the plea is added that a tariff will bring about a mysterious change in the "employment-giving character" of the imports, "that will tend to increase" both exports and imports;[115] and "every genuine Tariff Reformer wishes to see increased importation of [foodstuffs, raw material, and] manufactures which for any good reason can be better produced abroad."[116]

The League, indeed, insists that foreign goods must come in. The proposed duty will be too small to keep them out! A correspondent of the League's official journal[117] referring to Mr. Austen Chamberlain's speech at Nottingham on October 12th, inquired how a "moderate" or a "small" duty, too small to keep foreign produce out, could afford "protection" to the British producer? The League replied that the "protection" of which Mr. Austen Chamberlain spoke was "not protection against any competition whatsoever, but protection against 'unfair and unequal competition.' If nothing short of 'keeping them out' altogether is worthy to be called protection there is no such thing as protection in operation under any tariff in the world. Even the American tariff, which is certainly protective, is not prohibitive; if it were, it would fail to produce revenue, whereas it is highly successful as a revenue producing tariff."

"Apparently this fallacy, though often exposed, takes a lot of killing," the League added. That is quite true. The League itself has shown no wish to kill it. Its leaflets are choked with anxiety to show the workers that the proposed protection is really to be "prohibitive." The economic disguise of the Editor of the *Monthly Notes* has been dropped when leaflets were to be prepared for circulation among the crowd. "When goods are manufactured in England they employ British labour. When similar goods come from abroad a foreigner gets a job and a British workman loses one," says one leaflet.[118] Another, "A Word to the Women," tells them that it is difficult to provide for their families "because heavy importations of foreign manufactured goods throw your husbands and sons and brothers out of work and lower their wages." [119] A score of leaflets addressed to the workers in various trades asks them to "look at the following duty-free imports of iron and steel" (or whatever it may be) and admonishes them, "If you wish to defend your trade and keep work and wages at home support Tariff Reform"; [120] and as to the pretence that the "character" of the imports will be changed, there was nothing said about that in the leaflet entitled "A Question for Workers," reminding them that we imported in 1908, "free of duty, £143,124,000 worth of foreign manufactures," and adding that "this injures not only you but also the whole country, which is heavily taxed to support the poverty and unemployment caused by these free imports." [121]

In the 1912 by-election in the Ilkeston Division the *Morning Post* said of the Tariff Reform candidate, [122] "He supported the policy of taxing the foreign teapot and tobacco pipe, articles of a class which can be and are made in this country, but are largely imported from abroad to compete with our home manufactures. To the extent that such foreign articles are excluded we shall get the trade and manufacture, and to the extent to which they are still imported we shall get the revenue. Simple expositions of this kind are well within the comprehension of the workmen."

Of course they are. That is why the workmen have rejected them. That is why the trade unions have always declared against the pretty scheme. "You must in all these cases treat the two subjects of Tariff Reform and protection of labour as being on the same level," said Mr. J. Chamberlain in 1905.[123] "I want you to bear in mind that it is absolutely impossible to reconcile Free Trade with Trade Unionism. You can have one, or you can have the other, but you cannot have both," he had said in 1903.[124] "The action of some of the trades leaders is to him entirely inexplicable and in direct contradiction to their own position in regard to trade unionism," wrote his secretary to a West Ham trade unionist in the same year. "What would Cobden have said if he had foreseen that the trade unions, whose existence he deprecated and whose influence he denounced, would be successful, with the aid of social reformers of all parties and opinions, in protecting labour in a score of ways tending to increase the rate of wages and raise the standard of living?" Mr. Chamberlain asked;[125] "would he, as a representative of the manufacturing class, have still maintained that, while the manufacturer was artificially prevented from obtaining labour at the lowest rate, he ought to rest content when the products of foreign labour, untrammelled by any of the regulations and legislation to which he has to submit, undersell him in his own market?" And Mr. Vince deplored the dreadful ignorance of trade unionists when he said,[126] "They cannot but be conscious that it is futile to call for more legislation to protect the workman against sweating at home, while foreign sweated labour is admitted to unrestrained competition with protected British labour," forgetting that trade unionists were so conscious of the existence of "foreign sweated labour" that they utterly failed to see what Protection had done to benefit the foreign sweated worker. "A man who believed in trade unionism had no more right to stand on a Free Trade platform than to demand a seat in heaven," said a popular Tariff Reform speaker in 1907.[127]

Socialism and trade unionism have been always confounded by the Tariff Reformers; yet not so badly as they have confounded their own attitude toward both. In 1905 the *Monthly Notes* of the Tariff Reform League [128] reviewed a book by Mr. Thomas Kirkup, who was described by the reviewer as "the leading historian of the Socialist movement," on *The Progress of the Fiscal Question.* "We shall not, of course, be held accountable for either acceptance or rejection of these ideals," said the reviewer, "if we point out that Mr. Kirkup's present book could not have been written had he failed to recognize the absolute incompatibility of Socialism, not with Tariff Reform, but with Free Trade, since Free Trade is deep-rooted in that principle of individualism, which is the natural antithesis of the Socialistic ideal." Yet did Mr. Chamberlain declare that "in his opinion Socialism would be worse than nothing," [129] and in the *National Review* a little later [130] that stout exponent of Tariff Reform, Mr. J. L. Garvin, claiming that "above all we are the keenest Imperialists; the Socialists are in the main the bitterest anti-Imperialists," exclaimed, "Let there at least be an end of the attempts to imply that there can be the slightest affinity of principle, the least collusion of tactics, between Mr. Chamberlain's adherents and the disciples of Karl Marx. No two parties in this country are quite so profoundly antagonistic one to the other." And, as if to emphasize this antagonism, the Women's Unionist and Tariff Reform Association issued in 1909 a pamphlet bearing the title, *The Reign of Terror —an Experiment in Free Trade Socialism.* It dealt with the French Revolution!

A "Trade Unionist Tariff Reform Association" has been formed. It still lives in hope of roping in the "millions of working men" of whom it speaks at its meetings as being "outside the trade unions." Men who are outside the trade unions and yet can join a "Trade Unionist Tariff Reform Association" would certainly make better Tariff Reformers than trade unionists, for the latter have at least a sense of logic.

WHEN THE FOREIGNER PAYS

UNASHAMED to quote Scripture to support the contention that the foreigner could be made to pay the duties on British imports, Sir Alfred Bagge, the Chairman of a Tariff Reform meeting in Norfolk in 1909, "advised his audience to look up the seventeenth chapter of the Gospel according to St. Matthew, the 24th, 25th, and 26th verses, and read them; after which he thought they would shut up their Bibles and say they were Tariff Reformers." [131] Thereat, it is recorded, the audience applauded, as though all Tariff Reformers present were so familiar with the text that it flashed at once into their minds. Presuming—perhaps unworthily—that the readers of this book have not such ready memories, the reference is here given: "And when they were come to Capernaum, they that received tribute money came to Peter, and said, Doth not your master pay tribute? He saith, Yes. And when he was come into the house, Jesus prevented him, saying, What thinkest thou, Simon? of whom do the kings of the earth take custom or tribute? of their own children or of strangers? Peter saith unto him, Of strangers. Jesus saith unto him, Then are the children free."

Mr. Chamberlain did not think it impossible to take "tribute of strangers," nor had he need to refer his audience to the Bible. He contrived to give the impression that no matter what the duty, the foreigner would pay it; and the impression has been watered, trained and pruned by the propagandists with great diligence. The Birmingham Tariff Committee entitled No. 10 of its leaflets "Taxing the Foreigner," with the sub-title "A Discredited Theory," the "theory" being the bogus one that "all import duties are paid by the consumer." "If this theory be true," said the leaflet, "it is impossible to 'tax the foreign producer,' or make him pay through an Import Duty for access to our market, as nearly all foreign nations make us pay for access to theirs." "Remember," said the Tariff Reform League, "that our present tariff taxes You. Remember that Tariff Reform proposes to tax the Foreigner." That statement appeared in Leaflet No. 104, entitled "What is Tariff Reform?" and it faithfully reproduces, in heavy type, the phrase that the League has so sedulously sought to popularize.

Mr. Chamberlain himself in his Glasgow speech of 1903 went no farther than to say that "if the tax be moderate a portion at any rate is paid by the foreigner." He did not remain long in that moderate mood. In the following year he said he wanted to raise the "great revenue" required by the country, "as far as possible from the pockets of the foreigner." At which there was "loud applause." "I think," he went on, "that it is absolutely clear and proveable that the taxes upon imports which are levied by protected countries are largely paid by ourselves and other producers. I do not object to that, but let there be a little give and take. If I have to pay for the advantage of the German Empire, I should like the German Empire to pay a little to me."[132] His moderate "portion" grew likewise. "Any tax which he proposed would be largely borne by the foreigner," he said a month later.[133] That was in the summer. In the autumn he reminded a Luton audience,[134] "I have said that the foreigner will pay;" and again in the beginning of 1905[135] he said that "in nine cases out of ten the tax is not paid wholly by the consumer, but it is paid either in part or wholly by the foreign producer of the goods. I say that that view is a view that is now held by the most able economists not only in this country, but in America and Germany; we can easily see that that is the case, otherwise when the foreign country put a duty on our goods the harm done would be inconsiderable. If it is the consumer in that foreign country who pays, how is the producer here injured? He makes his goods at the same price, and he sells them at the same price because the duty is paid by the consumer; whereas as we know from painful experience of I do not know how many trades in this country, when the foreigner puts on a duty, the first effect is to injure the British producer."

Mr. Wyndham too forgot his political economy, and swung over to the conventional and more politically comfortable Tariff Reform version. "What is the use," he asked, "of talking about social reform, if our fiscal system makes it impossible to have that mainspring of all social reform? First, tax the foreigner; then enable us to secure fairer play in foreign markets; then join with sister States of the Empire in a great party of mutual preference. This policy will cure the canker of unemployment; it will give us an ample revenue without deforming national credit; and it will enable us to embark on a policy of Social Reform." [137] So that now the foundation of the whole policy of the party was that the foreigner could be taxed to provide an "ample revenue."

The League has faced more ways than one, like its pupils. In an article dealing with agricultural machinery, the League's journal said, "Let the farmer remember that the foreigner will pay the duty, just as his own manufacturers pay the foreign duties on goods they want to sell in America or Germany." [138] In the same volume it admitted that what it told the farmer to remember in the case of machinery was still "open to debate" in the case of wheat. "Tariff Reformers believe that the tax would be entirely, or at any rate partly, paid by the foreign producer; their opponents maintained that it would be entirely borne by the consumer." [139] In 1908 the League appeared to be more doubtful still about it, for it said that the duty would "in some degree, varying in the circumstances, be paid by the foreign manufacturer." [140] One of those circumstances was, of course, the size of the duty. "No Tariff Reformer doubts that the duty on non-competitive imports (the League was talking of potatoes), especially so heavy a duty as 37s 6d. per ton, will be paid by the American importer;" [141] but there has never been any clear statement as to how heavy or how light a duty, or what proportion of either, the foreigner would pay. Mr. Chamberlain in his Glasgow speech said that "one of the highest of the official experts whom the Government consult" was of opinion that if the foreigner supplied two-ninths of the consumption, the consumer only paid two-ninths of the tax. But that piece of arithmetic did not survive. It has never been used, even by the League. The current edition of the League's *Handbook for Speakers* contents itself with a few qualified quotations from political economists, but throws no light on the size of the escapable duty. It may be observed, however, that though on one page of the "Handbook" the *Morning Post* is advertised as "a patriotic paper which can always be relied upon," the League does not even mention the *Morning Post's* declaration through the mouth of its Washington correspondent that in the United States "every one admits that the duties are paid by the consumer," and that to say otherwise was regarded in America as "not only fallacious but dishonest." [142] Perhaps the League regarded that admission as unworthy of a "patriotic paper."

Remembering Mr. Chamberlain's declaration that his was a policy more in the interests of the poor than of the rich, it may be possible to understand why the late Chief Conservative Whip (Sir Alexander A. Hood, as he was then named) should have told his Somerset constituents that "there was not the slightest reason to think that under Tariff Reform their clothes or their boots were going to cost them more," because the foreigner was bound to send his goods to this country, "and whatever duties we might charge—and they would not charge high duties but duties of quite a moderate nature—the foreigner was bound to send his surplus to this country;" [143] while in the same year Earl Percy said at Newcastle that "we want Tariff Reform; because under Tariff Reform, at any rate, you can ensure that wealthy people will pay upon their luxuries." [144]

But if these things puzzle men whose business it is to explain them to the electorate, how can it be expected that ordinary mortals should understand them? At Highworth, on October 18, 1910, Colonel Surtees, in proposing a vote of thanks to Colonel Calley, Tariff Reform Member of Parliament for North Wilts, took the meeting into his confidence and said, " I have been having a course of treatment for baldness, and lately went to Germany for a holiday. Whilst there I needed some more of the hair preparation, and although I sent home the tenpence to pay for it, I had to pay the German a 2s. tax on that bottle. Now, why can't we do the same here, and so get our own back ? "

That is what might be called going bald-headed for taxing the foreigner !

MORTGAGES ON THE REVENUE

SO unimpeachable a Tariff Reformer as the late Sir Howard Vincent clearly expressed the views of most Tariff Reformers when, faced by the dilemma that he and his friends proposed both to keep out foreign goods in the interests of the wage-earners and to let them in in the interests of the State, he said that, "2s. in the pound on wholly manufactured goods and 1s. in the pound on partially manufactured goods would not keep them out." [145] He had been arguing that this tax would provide all the money required for old age pensions. It was as easy as sneezing. "To raise the whole £15,000,000 which the Chancellor of the Exchequer said was necessary for old age pensions, 10 per cent. on wholly manufactured goods, and 5 per cent. on partly manufactured goods, would provide the whole of the money required, and the thing was done, wholly independent of the surplus, or a reduction of armaments—which would be serious to Sheffield (for which he sat), and expose it to a very great danger indeed—and wholly independent of the method of taxation or anything else. There was the £15,000,000 at once, which the Chancellor of the Exchequer could distribute in pensions of £30 or £40 a year to every aged person who required one. How very much better that would be than talking about the matter."

The sanguine estimates of this evanescent revenue have varied. They all depend alike on the assumption that the foreigner will export to us and pay the full duty on at least a half of our present imports—though it has been seen that the Tariff Reformers have never been sure that these would be the proportions obtainable. They have wanted to talk of "millions"; they have done so. The late Duke of Sutherland, President of the Tariff Reform League, put it loosely at 16 to 20 millions; [146] Mr. G. L. Courthope, M.P., at a round twenty;[147] Mr. W. A. S. Hewins, M.P. (the Secretary of the Tariff Commission), thought it would bring in "ultimately" from 24 to 30 millions;[148] *The Standard's* estimate was 17½ millions;[139] with which the Liberal Unionist Council agreed. The *Morning Post* put it at about 20,[150] which the Tariff Reform League thought an under-estimate.[151] Many times has the present Government been warned that it could get no more revenue for State needs without "taxing the foreigner." "Under our existing system the resources of taxation had reached, or almost reached, their limit if there was not to be oppression of particular classes," said Mr. Bonar Law as far back as 1906,[152] and though year has succeeded year with a balance to the credit of the national accounts, the warning has been regularly repeated.

They have thought of so many things to do with that money. There were first old age pensions, for Sir Howard Vincent was not the earliest to think of them. The idea is said to have originated with Mr. Hooley in 1896.[153] Mr. Chamberlain himself in Parliament in May 1903,[154] said that in "common justice" he would give the whole of the "very large revenue" his new taxes would produce to the working classes, first because they would pay three-fourths of them, and second because he had always promised them social reform; and a day or two later he wrote a letter to a working-man[155] saying that "as regards old age pensions, I would not myself look at the matter unless I felt able to promise that a large scheme for the provision of such pensions to all who had been thrifty and well-conducted would be assured by a revision of our system of import duties." He put in another word for what he used to call his "favourite hobby" in a speech at the Constitutional Club the same month;[156] but that did not prevent him from throwing the hobby on the scrap heap in 1906, when, having doubtless found the promise altogether too inharmoniously definite a one for Tariff Reform, he said again in Parliament[157] that "I never have, in the whole course of my life, made any promises of old age pensions." At any rate, he did try to sweep them out of the way of his successors, for in a letter to the President of the Coventry Trades Council in November

1905, he said, "I do not propose to make the question of Old Age Pensions a part of the programme of Tariff Reform."

One wonders why, after this act of renunciation, Mr. Austen Chamberlain should have taken the burden on his young shoulders. It was not much more than a year afterwards that Mr. Austen Chamberlain declared that "The greatest and most urgent of all social reforms is that of old age pensions. As time goes on it becomes more pressing." He tied it up to Tariff Reform, too. "If you wish to maintain wages at their present level," he said, "you will find it inevitable that the difficulty of old men finding employment will not be less, but greater, than it is to-day. It is from lack of the necessary financial resources more than from any other reason, that the Unionist party, which was the pioneer in this question, was unable to carry it to a successful issue. Tariff Reform is the one method open to you on which you can raise a new revenue for old age pensions and similar purposes without injustice, without hardship, without robbery and without jobbery."[158]

Perhaps it is fortunate that old age pensions have preceded Tariff Reform. It gives the other claims on the foreigners' pockets some chance. Mr. Chamberlain was very generous in dispensing that money. He earmarked it for the Navy, for the balancing of the reductions on the existing food duties, and also to lighten "some other taxes which press more hardly on different classes of the community." It was also claimed by the *Express*[159] when it cried, "Tariff Reform and No Income Tax." But "if it is to be pensions, it cannot also be no income tax," said *The Evening Standard* (April 17, 1907); "we must make a choice and stick to it." Waste words! When the revenue for Old Age Pensions at 70 was found, the *Express* said that "Tariff Reform means Old Age Pensions at 65" Looking blankly ahead, it declared that "it is impossible to find the revenue with which to finance those schemes of State insurance which have long been established in Germany";[160] and when State insurance came, the helpful suggestions of Tariff Reformers were not exhausted, for Sir George Doughty, M.P., a very popular orator on that platform, said that "if a

Radical Government wanted to bestow a great boon on the working classes, it should not tax their wages, when at times many of them had not enough to buy the necessaries of life. Would it not be better to tax the foreigner a bit?"[161] One Protectionist journal regarded this exchange of taxation as quite natural. "Who pays the insurance in Germany? *You* do," it answered, explaining that "in 1907 we exported to Germany goods to the value of £41,358,099. We paid duty on these, £10,000,000. That is how *you* pay the foreigner's insurance."[162]

Then the Navy has made its claim upon the fund at various times. "The profits of your markets," said Mr. Chamberlain in 1905, "now go to swell the profits of foreigners not always sympathetic with your aspirations, who are your competitors in peace, and may be something worse in the course of time. The profits which they make by tolling our industries enable them to create fleets and you have to pay for the increase in your own fleet to meet theirs. You pay double; you pay for the creation of their fleets and you pay for the fleet which you have to build to meet them."[163] The *Daily Mail* four years later dragged Germany into it specifically. "The gigantic German army and its vast increasing navy are largely paid for by taxes on English goods. The remark also applies to the navy of almost every country. It is we who have hitherto paid for Germany's social reform. Let Germany now pay a little for ours."[164]

Mr. Walter Long in 1907 (at Malmesbury, September 5) spoke the appropriate comment on all this mortgaging madness. He was pleading for patience toward those Unionists who had "fought loyally" with the Tariff Reformers for many years, who "shared their views on every other question," and who would, he believed, "before long realize that there was no other remedy except Tariff Reform for the difficulties with which the country was confronted. He would, however, caution those who believed in that policy not to spend the increased revenue which they believed would follow from it before they got it!"

THE COST OF LIVING

"THE repetition day by day in the Lord's Prayer of the words, 'Give us this day our daily bread,' has no doubt acted largely on the minds of many who have not found the time to enter into a serious consideration of the fiscal position."

That sentence occurred in an editorial article in the *Manchester Courier*, a Protectionist paper, on New Year's Day, 1913, in the midst of Tariff Reform's worst spasm of doubt as to whether it could better win elections by continuing to advocate food taxes or by pretending to drop them. It represents the last and lowest excuse for the failure of the Protectionist propaganda. The daily bread has been in the centre of the agitation throughout, though every man has been fully aware that more than bread was concerned. The *Morning Post*[165] once spoke of "the bread-and-butter issue," which "monopolizes the interest of a nation that finds its industrial position seriously menaced." "It is on the bread-and-butter issue that the battle must be fought."

On the other hand, those Tariff Reformers who have relied most on the Imperial sentiment have held this bread-and-butter issue in something like contempt. Lord Milner, for instance, who said "you cannot deal with a great economic national question like this in the spirit in which you would criticize your grocer's bill."[166] The first Chairman of the Tariff Reform League, Mr. C. Arthur Pearson, entertained a contempt of a different kind. He thought the bread-and butter issue one that could be eliminated altogether from the problem. Why eat bread at all? "It is a long time since I ate bread in any but microscopic quantities," he wrote to the *Daily Telegraph* in 1903,[167] "and the omission of bread from one's dietary in itself leads to eating a great deal less. It is quite the ordinary thing to eat a couple of rolls or slices of bread, or perhaps more, at lunch, and again at dinner. This is really almost entirely a matter of habit. One goes on stuffing the bread down between courses almost automatically, not because one really wants it. Bread-eating of this kind will never after a few days be missed, and to give it up will, I am sure, in almost every case tend to improve healthfulness."

The opinion of the wage-earner who could not appreciate the dyspepsia of him who only toyed with rolls " between courses " at lunch and dinner was accurately represented by the Tariff Reform Member for Mid-Essex, Sir Frederick Carne Rasch, M.P., who wrote in *The Times*[168] the same year to say that " the ardent, but unpenetrating, gaze of some of your correspondents disregards an important factor, *i.e.*, the agricultural labourer. I have found that, if the ingenious candidate suggests a tax on bread, the only question is whether he goes out of the door or window first, and it is well for him if the roads are not recently metalled. The pill may possibly be sugared," he added, " by Old Age Pensions, but his reply is, to my mind, hard to answer, ' We remember bread at 7d. and wages at 7s. under protection, and we won't have it again ; we know that bread will rise, but we don't know that wages will go up ! ' "

No amount of sugaring, no amount of contempt for bread as a toy " between courses," has served to lessen the ferocity of those who regularly eat bread as a prime necessity of life. The big loaf and the little loaf still figuratively sum up the Protectionist case and the opposition to it. It was not much use telling the man who " receives his fourteen shillings a week or so in wages," said another Tariff Reform Member of Parliament in 1904,[169] that " the Empire would be benefited by a change in fiscal policy. His reply was that he would not consent to any addition to the price of food ; he was not greatly troubled about what might happen to the Empire, but was determined to have his fourteen shillings a week." And " I don't blame him," said the hon. Member, " I rather take his view that a certain change in fiscal policy might hurt him, temporarily, at any rate." Mr. Austen Chamberlain is among the Tariff Reformers who have always regarded this matter gravely. "We have got a certain difficulty to face," he said in 1907.[170] "Let us face it. If we do not face it manfully we shall not escape the consequences. I am the first to admit that the question of food taxation, given the prejudices which exist, given the ignorance which prevails, given the latitude of expression which our opponents permit themselves in political controversy—I am the first to admit that there is a difficulty, but you never overcome a difficulty by turning your back upon it." "What is the use of pretending we are not ready to tax food?" he asked. "We have done it in the past, we are doing it now." Mr. Austen Chamberlain has frequently accused the Free Traders of being "food-taxers"; "but the difference between me and them is that, being all food-taxers, I have the courage to avow it, while they always try to conceal it. I am a food-taxer. I am in favour of a duty on corn. I think that a 2s. duty on foreign corn, with a preference to our kinsmen and with free home-grown corn is necessary to the establishment of an Imperial system of preference, and I am not afraid to tell my fellow-countrymen so. I do not believe that that will raise the price of bread to our people at home," he added, and when he was asked if he would stop at 2s., he replied, "Yes; that is enough, and I have no intention of going further. But if at any time I or others should wish to go further it would not rest with us to decide, but with you whether we should have the power to do so or not. My policy is 2s." [171]

At first Mr. Joseph Chamberlain thought it enough to intimate that the working man would be able to pay the extra food-taxes out of the extra wages Tariff Reform was to bring him. "I am prepared to go into any mechanic's house, or any labourer's house, or to address meetings of workmen or labourers," he said in one of his May 1903 speeches, "and, taking certain hypothetical calculations, for instance, that there was to be 1s. or 2s. on corn, say to them, 'Now this policy, if it is carried out, will cost you so much a week more than you are paying at present for your food.' I set aside altogether any economical question as to whether they would or would not have to pay the whole duty that might be disposed. I will assume for the sake of my argument that you pay every penny of the duty, and, having assumed that, I will tell you what the cost will be. I know how many loaves you consume, how much meat you eat, and know what you take of this, that, and the other on which it may be proposed to put a duty; and I will give you a table from which you can tell for yourself how much extra wages you must get in order to cover the extra expense of living. And that is the argument to which the hon. gentlemen opposite will have to give their serious attention. If they can show that the whole of this business will mean greater cost of living to the working men and no increase of income, well, sir, I have not the least doubt whatever that all their most optimistic prophecies will come true. But if I can show that in return for what I ask I will give more than I take, then, poorly as they may think of my judgment, I may still have a chance." [172]

In June, he worked out the sum in a different way. "If the working classes refuse to take my advice, if they prefer this immediate advantage, why it stands to reason that if, for instance, they are called upon to pay 3d. a week additional on the cost of their bread, they may be fully, entirely relieved by a reduction of a similar amount in the cost of their tea, their sugar, or even of their tobacco. In this case, what is taken out of one pocket would be put back into the other. There is no working-man in the kingdom, no man, however poor, who need fear under the system I propose that without his goodwill his cost of living will be increased by a single farthing." [173]

In October he got down more definitely to halfpennies and farthings—even half-farthings. "As regards the cost of living," he said in his Glasgow speech, "I have accepted, for the purpose of argument, the figures of the Board of Trade as to the consumption of an ordinary workman's family, both in the country districts and in the town, and I find that if he pays the whole of the new duties that I propose to impose it would cost an agricultural labourer 16½ farthings per week more than at present, and the artisan in the town 19½ farthings per week. . . . But, then, take the reduction which I have proposed. . . . In the case of the agricultural labourer 17 farthings per week, in the case of the artisan 19½ farthings per week. . . . You will see, if you follow me, that upon the assumption that you pay the whole of the new taxes yourselves, the agricultural labourer would be half a farthing per week to the better, and the artisan would be exactly the same. I have made this assumption, but I do not believe in it. I do not believe that these small taxes upon food would be paid to any large extent by the consumer in this country. I believe, on the contrary, they would be paid by the foreigner."

Later in the same month, "What does it matter," he asked, "if I want a halfpenny from you, whether I charge it on bread, which is an absolute necessity? You will not eat any less bread for that, but as you have to pay a halfpenny more you will perhaps take a halfpenny off your expenditure on tea; and, then, when you come to buy your tea, you will find it so much cheaper that you can buy as much for a penny as you could previously buy for twopence." [174] He lightly assumed that the effect of halving the duty on tea would halve the price; yet the following week he begged the country, in a phrase that inspired many a pantomime and music-hall song, to "take my pledge, and to believe in my sincerity when I give it, that if you accept my proposals as they stand I pledge that they will not add one farthing to the cost of living of any family in this country, and, in my opinion, in the case of the poorest families will somewhat reduce that cost." [175]

In his many other pledges, and what not, on this all-important point, Mr. Chamberlain assured the electorate that it would rest with them alone whether the 2s. tax should ever be increased in the future. "For my purpose 2s. is enough, and that is all that I ask. If somebody else, when I am gone, comes before you and asks for 5s. or 10s., let him argue his case, let him persuade you if he can." [176] He reckoned the increase in the price of bread at a farthing the four pound loaf, and said, "I only want you to assent to this increase of ¼d. in order that you may get a *quid pro quo*—in order that you may get millions and millions more trade, and, therefore, millions and millions more wages." [177] "Increased wages are even more important to the working classes than reduced cost of living," he wrote to Councillor Livesey; [178] and though he had said in Parliament in May that if his policy were carried out "you must put a tax on food," he found it necessary to alter the phraseology later on, saying, "This arrangement with the Colonies would necessitate not a tax on food, as you are told. That is false. But it might entail a transfer of taxation from one kind of food to another kind of food."[179]

In July 1904, Mr. Chamberlain said "the issue is so simple" that he could not believe the working-man would allow himself to be deceived.[180] It has proved by no means "so simple" as he hoped; and the working-man has not been deceived. There have had to be more "explanations" of this than of any other point in the controversy. How many times have the words of Mr. J. L. Garvin, who bluntly told Mr. Chamberlain he had blundered, been echoed by the Tariff Reformers! "Mr. Chamberlain need not have said, 'If you are to give a preference to the Colonies you must put a tax on food,'" said Mr. Garvin. "Food was already heavily taxed through tea and sugar. He might have said, 'You can give a preference to the Colonies simply by redistributing and perhaps decreasing the existing taxation upon food.' That way of putting it might have made a great difference. It is so easy for us to say these things who are wise after the event. But we have now to deal with things as they are." [181]

Mr. Bonar Law has industriously done his best to be wise after the event. In 1907 he thought it "surely very elementary" to say that "Revenue must be raised in some way, and if a certain amount of money is raised by a duty on wheat, a similar amount can be remitted from something else." [182] Mr. Law has been very fond of this phrase. Yet when he coined it in 1905, the *Yorkshire Post* [183] told him, in language quite as blunt as that which Mr. Garvin threw at Mr. Chamberlain's head, that he had done nothing to help the Tariff Reformers. "Mr. Bonar Law last evening," said this powerful North Country Unionist journal, "seemed to be discontented with the way in which that question (the Fiscal Question) had been presented. He said the Fiscal policy had not had 'a dog's chance.' This may be so; but, if so, the fault is that of Mr. Chamberlain in the first instance, who refused to have the whole subject referred to a Royal Commission for a full and free investigation, with open criticism and a sifting of every proposition advanced. Before such a tribunal it would not be possible, for instance, to suggest—as Mr. Bonar Law suggested last night—that if a tax were put on corn and the price of bread were raised by the amount of the tax, it would be practicable to give the consumer an equivalent in a remission of duty on tea and tobacco. That is a patent fallacy; for if the price of corn were raised by the amount of the duty, it would be raised alike upon the corn we import and the corn we grow here. The corn imported would yield a duty; but the rise in the price of the home-grown corn would yield nothing to the Exchequer, and, therefore, if the consumers were to be fully compensated for all they paid in the rise in price, they must get more remission from the duties on tea and tobacco than the Exchequer would get out of the corn duty. This process of finance, if extended, would certainly lead to national bankruptcy."

It is the knowledge of that fact, joined with a keen distrust of the "farthing" arithmetic, and the certainty that increased wages would not automatically accompany increased prices, that has destroyed the beautiful simplicity of Mr. Chamberlain's idea and the nursery "economics" that Mr. Bonar Law founded upon it. Already it has been shown how completely the Tariff Reformers have failed, after using every argumentative device the mind of man could conceive, to convince the electorate that Protection does not mean a rise in the cost of living and a lessening of the purchasing power of wages. It only remains to describe some of the more direct methods by which they have vainly sought to slay the monster they themselves created.

Downright assertion has been tried daily throughout the long years, beginning with the misconceived directness of Mr. Chamberlain's earliest admissions, and ending with the astounding telegram he sent to the candidate in the Hythe by-election of Midsummer 1912, "I believe that Tariff Reform will cheapen everything." Between those extremes there has been dangled every degree of assurance. Mr. Chaplin led off in 1904 by roundly stating his opinion that it "was the greatest certainty on earth" that "Mr. Chamberlain's proposals would substantially reduce the cost of living." He said that in the course of a speech in the industrial town of Dewsbury; [184] and it is fairly representative of a million utterances from Tariff Reformers of all ranks when speaking in non-agricultural districts. Mr. Balfour, in his anxiety to win the January election of 1910, joined with Mr. Joseph Chamberlain in a manifesto to the nation in these words: "Tariff Reform will not increase the cost of living of the working classes, nor the proportion of taxation paid by them. But it will enable us to reduce the present taxes upon the working classes' consumption." During the election he went a step further, "I believe that a small duty on corn with preference to the Colonies, will tend to diminish, rather than increase the price." [185] But within a week after the assembly of the new Parliament, in the debate on the fiscal amendment to the Address, Mr. Balfour considered it wise to withdraw all that he had said. "I sometimes see my opinions quoted, as if I had promised that there should be no rise in the price of food. How could I or any one else promise that?"

Mr. Balfour's wise habit of cleaning his slate has not been followed by all the Tariff Reform scholars. There was the warning example of Mr. A. D. Steel Maitland, M.P., who promised an agricultural labourer at a meeting in the Rugby Division, where he was then candidate, that if the shilling "war" duty on imported corn led to any increase in the cost of bread, he would himself pay the extra cost. Bread went up a half-penny in the village; and on March 21, 1905, Mr. Steel Maitland drew a cheque for 35s. to be forwarded through the medium of the Vicar of Tysoe to the agricultural labourer who, on January 20, 1910, made a declaration before a Commissioner of Oaths as to the truth of the statements that had been made.[186]

The League has made diligent efforts to establish the Tariff Reform contention that there is no connexion between the price of wheat and the price of the loaf. A League booklet entitled *The Food Tax Bogey*, published in 1910, declared it was " certain that fluctuations of 2s. per quarter in the price of wheat do not affect the price of bread." It may appear strange that a propagandist body that has spent so much of its breath on contending that the 2s. duty would not under any circumstances be added to the price, should find it necessary to admit, even for the sake of argument, that it might sometimes be added to the price ; but that is Tariff Reform. The booklet under notice held it to be " conclusively shown " that a rise in the price of wheat did not affect the line bread. Its demonstration consisted of placing side by side the average prices of wheat and bread for each month in 1909, and then choosing certain of the figures to illustrate a point that other figures, which it did not mention, entirely destroyed—quite a representative Tariff Reform method of " proof." " It will be seen," said the writer, " that the price of bread in September, when the price of wheat was 34s. 7d., was exactly the same as the price of bread in July, when the price of wheat was 43s. 4d." Applying that same remarkable logic to other parts of the same table it could be as easily shown—though the Tariff Reform League did not point this out—that a fall in the price of wheat had actually increased the price of bread! For in February, when wheat was 33s. 8d., bread was cheaper than in October, when wheat was 2s. lower. It can only be supposed that readers of Tariff Reform literature were expected to skip the table and read only the author's large-type conclusions therefrom.

Going back for a moment to 1903, there can be found another illustration of how the development of the world's commerce has upset the arguments of the Tariff Reformers. When Mr. Chamberlain began his campaign we were drawing upon the United States very largely for our wheat supplies. " If you depend upon a single source of supply for all that you cannot produce yourselves," he exclaimed, in mock horror, " you will create a monopoly, and a monopoly will probably end in a rise in price. And if there should be any drought in America, or any such speculation as that which took place a year or two ago and which raised the price of corn temporarily by 10s. a quarter—if that be the case, the labourer will be the first to suffer, and to him it may mean great misery and great distress."[187] That fear was worked upon in many leaflets issued by the Birmingham Committee and by the League. "Surely it were wiser to stimulate production at home and in our own great Colonies, and make the British Empire produce all our corn, as Mr. Chamberlain suggests," said one of them.[188]

Time has ruthlessly robbed the propagandists of the American monopoly bugbear, but they have found many more to frighten the children with. The League was early in the field with the statement, already referred to, that preference to Canadian wheat would so increase the supply that "the price will necessarily fall";[189]—a "large scale production" argument near akin to that which Mr. Bonar Law has so frequently used when he has said that "under modern conditions the factor which tells most on the cost of production, far more than wages or cost of raw material, is the scale on which you produce; and you cannot produce on a large scale unless you have a large market."[190] The United Kingdom is in 1913 to be preserved as the "large market" for Canadian wheat, though Mr. Chamberlain very properly warned the country against narrowing its sources of supply!

Even natural and uncontrollable variations in world prices have been used by the Tariff Reformers to adorn their arguments. When the price of corn went up in 1907 Mr. Austen Chamberlain declared it was the result of the Free Trade Government "doing nothing" to encourage the increase of the Empire's area of supply by a preferential tariff.[191] "Who taught people to believe, wrongly, that the rise in the price of food was due to Governments?" he asked. "Who but themselves? Who told the people that to put the Tariff Reformer in meant dear food, and to keep the Free Trader in meant cheap food? Let the Free Traders swallow their own medicine, and let the Tariff Reformers ram it down their throats till they were sick of it." [192] And when Mr. Goulding moved in the House of Commons "That this House is of opinion" (which it was not) "that the recent high price of bread in this country is due to natural causes and neglect of British resources," Mr. Austen Chamberlain said that "the complaint against the Government was not that they had produced this shortage by anything they had done, but that they had refused to do anything to protect the country against its recurrence." [193]

This kind of thing was useful electioneering stuff. In the Brigg by-election [194] the fact that tea had gone up in price was blamed to the Government, and the electors were asked to "Vote for Sheffield, who wants to make it cheaper"; and in the Mid-Devon contest [195] leaflets issued from the Liberal Unionist headquarters asked, "What about the big loaf now?" The "price of the quartern loaf has just been raised a halfpenny, and may rise further." "So much for the Big Loaf under Free Trade Government." Bread was dearer because of the shortage of wheat. Mr. Chamberlain "predicted this danger three years ago." "If you had then followed his advice," the leaflet went on to say, "and given preference to our Colonies, millions of acres would have come into cultivation in Canada, Australia, and other of our Dominions over the seas, and the area of the wheat supply would have been increased, in which case bread would not have risen in price." "Millions" again. "Millions of acres" in less than three years!

Against all this may be contrasted the candour of Tariff Reformers like Lord Londonderry, who said "the high price of grain was due to the bad seasons in Europe and North America; and India, which had been an exporter of grain to this country, had none to export"; [197] like Mr. Chaplin, who declared that he had "no intention of imputing to them (the Free Traders) broken pledges because the price of bread, which we can none of us control, has risen in the last few days"; [198] and even Sir George Doughty, who honestly declared that "if the Conservative Party had been in office, and the same conditions had obtained that obtained this year, the bread would have been just as dear under a Unionist Government as under a Radical Government."[199] Those three statements were actually being made while electioneerers in other parts of the country were endeavouring to convince the public that prices had gone up because the Government had " done nothing."

One of the leaflets circulated in the Mid-Devon election asked, " Do you like the price of coals under the Radicals ? " It was an appeal to a foolishly presumed ignorance almost as bad as that which the *Daily Express* made in the same winter, when it announced that the Christmas pudding would be dearer because there had been a 5d. a lb. rise in the cost of materials.[200] The arithmetic was in the purest Tariff Reform vein. Five items—raisins, sultanas, currants, suet, and sugar—were said to have risen in price a penny a pound each ; but the *Express* added the five pennies without adding the five pounds and worked out the average at " fivepence a pound " !

Carefully putting behind them all consideration of what the late Duke of Devonshire described as " the enhanced cost of all the articles which a working-man cannot dispense with in addition to his food," his house and his clothes, his boots and shoes, his household furniture, his household utensils, " every article which you find in a workman's cottage," the Tariff Reformers have sought to make the working-man so angry with existing taxes that he would be in the mood to jump out of the frying-pan into the fire.

" Would it not be better to tax (as the Americans do)," asked the League, " the ready-made foreign iron and steel, etc., instead of tea ? To tax the foreign-made tubes and machinery instead of chocolate ? To tax the foreign-manufactured glass instead of currants ? To tax the foreign-made paper instead of prunes ? To tax the foreign-made joinery instead of chicory ? To tax the foreign-made pottery instead of raisins ? To tax the foreign-made boots and shoes and leather instead of cocoa ? (Hides to be admitted free.) To tax the foreign quarried and dressed stone and marble instead of coffee ? To tax imported foreign-made steam-engines instead of sugar ? To tax foreign-manufactured cotton goods instead of figs? To tax foreign-manufactured woollen goods instead of the poor pedlar who is taxed on his licence when he tries to earn an honest living and avoid the workhouse?"[201] In July 1913 the League declared that "it is absurdly inequitable that the poor man's tea at 1s. per pound should be taxed exactly the same amount as the rich man's tea at 5s. or 6s. per pound," although in the same issue of its monthly publication the League reported a speech in Parliament by Mr. Austen Chamberlain who, weighted down by his ex-Chancellorship of the Exchequer, admonished his Tariff Reform friends that "it is not uncommon to listen to an attack on an individual tax made by speakers who ignore other taxes. We are, for instance," he said, "asked, 'How can you justify taking 5d. a pound from the poor woman's tea when you take no more from the millionaire's tea?' Of course," he added, "if that were the only tax it would not last for a day; but it is made tolerable by other taxes which the rich pay and the poor do not. If you want to consider the merits of any particular impost you must survey the whole system of taxation."[202] And it is not necessary to go back many years to find the League itself uttering a similar contradiction; for while in 1907 it sympathized with the working-man whose "chief solace is his pipe, quite as necessary as his tea and sugar," and led him to hope for relief by asking, "Is it not iniquitous that while silks, satins, motor-cars and other luxuries of the rich come into the country absolutely free of tax the working-man should have to pay twopence-halfpenny in tax for every halfpenny-worth of tobacco he uses?"[203] and that "duties on things like motor-cars, silks, satins, velvets or lace, could not possibly hurt poor people";[204] in 1909 it laid it down[205] that "Tariff Reformers will do wisely to refrain from in any way pledging themselves or their party in advance to any specific plan in regard to such reduction of duties."

So that, once again, the Reform League made it possible to quote in the hour of need a repudiation of all the promises about "readjusting taxation," given by Tariff Reformers from Mr. Joseph Chamberlain downwards.

FEAR AND ENVY OF FOREIGN COUNTRIES

MANY times in this record there have been seen signs of the manner in which the Tariff Reformers have pervaded their arguments with fear of the foreigner. Mr. Chamberlain began his campaign in 1903 with a burst of what Mr. Asquith called "anti-foreign, narrow, insular, perverted patriotism." The Germans, said Mr. Vince, writing in July 1903, [207] "had openly threatened to punish Canada by a drastic tariff for the preference Canada is giving to her metropolitan country. Why? Because to German publicists, conscious that the expansion of the German Empire is nearing its limits, and that they have but little to add to the work of Stein and Bismarck, it is a main purpose of high politics to obstruct the consolidation of the British Empire."

Within a few days of the writing of this fearsome passage *The Observer* [208] described the incident on which it was based. Canada, which enjoys fiscal independence, had chosen to give a tiny preference to the United Kingdom, and to that extent to discriminate against Germany. Thereupon the German Government pointed out that there might be a difficulty in getting the Reichstag to agree to give England the favoured-nation treatment if Crown Colonies, which were not fiscal entities, like Canada, followed her lead and discriminated in favour of England against Germany. The German authorities afterwards explained that this was not intended as a threat, but only a confidential statement of their position. "This," said *The Observer*, "is the whole story of the outrage falsely so called; and it is clear that it will tax all Mr. Balfour's ingenuity, and all Mr. Chamberlain's fiery rhetoric, to galvanize so transparent a sham into the semblance of a reality."

The Tariff Reformers found plenty of other shams,

however, with which to support their diligent contentions that the Protected nations of the earth were engaged in a conspiracy to ruin this country. Fear and envy have been the twin weapons of Tariff Reform. "Look at France!" "Look at Germany!" cry their leaflets. The "foreigners" were robbing us of our trade. Worse; they were enjoying greater prosperty than we were. The "scientific tariff" of Germany, the high money wages of the United States, the thriftiness of France, have all been held up as models that Protection would easily enable us to copy. In the early days of the movement the League was in the habit of printing long schedules of the foreign tariffs that were said to keep British goods out. But as they were at the same time avowing their intention to start with only a low tariff for this country, they found that the presence of such lists in their literature only served to remind the electorate of what Mr. Chamberlain said about these foreign countries, "they have passed tariff after tariff; they began perhaps with a low tariff"; [209] and to-day the literature of the League is devoid of all evidence showing how those low tariffs have grown.

The way in which the examples of foreign countries have been used to frighten or to hearten the British electorate cannot be properly appreciated without first of all seeing how often the Tariff Reformers have declared that nothing could be learned from them! Things declared to be non-comparable have been compared, and the lessons drawn from the comparisons have been "popularized" with all the intensity of the movement. Every reader of this book is well prepared for such a destructive contrast as that which follows.

"Comparison Impossible Here," was the heading in the League's official journal in 1905 to the following paragraph: "One of the commonest attempts to achieve the impossible which is almost daily made by fiscal controversialists is to draw comparisons between the rate of unemployment in this country and foreign protected countries. On this point the new Fiscal Blue-Book says, 'It may be said at once that no unemployed statistics exist in any foreign country which allows a comparison to be made of the actual level of employment in that country and the United Kingdom respectively at a given time.' Fiscal students will do well to take this authoritative assertion to heart, and not seek to institute comparisons in a matter where comparisons are impossible. We can hardly hope that the Cobdenites will be moved to surrender one of their favourite forms of false argument, but it cannot be too widely made known that any statements professing to show the amount of steady employment enjoyed by labour under Free Trade and Protection are not worth the paper they are printed on." [210]

Yet there appeared in the same volume a paragraph dealing with the glass trade, saying, "It is surely a wise and obvious precaution to take, before jumping from a satisfactory increase of work in a single trade to a far-reaching dogma, to compare the corresponding statistics for some protected countries." [211] And thereupon the League proceeded to select the conclusions it sought.

The warning of 1905 has of course gone utterly unheeded by the Tariff Reformers. The official journal is full of comparisons of the kind it condemned; Protectionist leaflets abound with them; even the Tariff Commission has founded ponderous arguments upon them. In its Memorandum on Unemployment [212] the Commission summed up the net result of the evidence available as follows: "(1) Materials do not at present exist for estimating the number of unemployed in any country. (2) There are no absolute or sample figures of a character to enable an exact comparison to be made of the state of employment in any one country with that in any other country! Yet (3) The available figures and information can, however, be used partially as indexes to show whether employment is increasing or diminishing in the countries to which they relate, and whether the employment in any one country is increasing or diminishing at a greater or less rate than in other countries. (4) Unemployment in all industrial countries has increased during recent months, and the evidence shows that the chief cause of this increase is the influence of the United States monetary crisis. (5) Allowing for exceptional causes at work in Germany and the

United States, unemployment in the United Kingdom is more acute than in those countries." And finally, "This conclusion from the Board of Trade returns of Trade Union unemployment is borne out by the evidence received by the Tariff Commission from manufacturers in almost every trade, where definite instances are given of the loss of certain branches of trade and the restriction of their markets at home and abroad as a direct and indirect consequence of foreign tariff systems."

The Commission, discounting official statistics, preferred to rely on the partisan complaints of Protectionist manufacturers! The League has never been able to resist the quotation of superficially favourable figures. They may not be "strictly speaking, comparable," but "they are instructive and interesting."[213] Anyhow, good enough to quote when they have suited their own ends. When they have not, toss them aside! "Accounts reach us," said the League's *Monthly Notes* in 1905, "of 10,000 men dismissed as a result of the prospective closing down of a locomotive works in Philadelphia. This, like the New York unemployment figures, may or may not be accurate and reliable. In any case, why these figures should be accepted as an argument against Protection in America or elsewhere is, to say the least of it, not very clear. No one doubts that the amazing prosperity the United States has enjoyed, under Protection, for the last seventeen years, is at present suffering a temporary set-back, but no intelligent person supposes that any fiscal system under the sun will prevent temporary fluctuations in trade."[214] Moreover, it has always been convenient and proper for Tariff Reformers to follow the example of the League in making such contrasts as this, which does not depend upon statistics that "may or may not be accurate and reliable," namely, "That the cost of living is less in France and Germany, under a protective tariff, than in England under Free Trade, is proved by the well-known fact that thousands of English men and women are now living in France and Germany simply because they find that they can live in comfort abroad on an income that would hardly support them in England."[215]

"Proved," you see, and without a single reference to statistics. Social and fiscal, national and personal considerations are all mixed up in the Tariff Reform jumble-sale. The League has not hesitated to take from the lips of others the comparisons it rejected and to put them into the mouths of its own orators. In 1906 it "recommended to the attention of our readers an article by Mr. O. Elzbacher" (who two months later became Mr. Ellis Barker), setting forth certain of these avowedly non-comparable figures, and declaring that "the foregoing figures, which are taken from the English and German Government statistics, show that unemployment was during 1904 more than three times greater in this country than it was in Germany." [216] "The land which ought, according to the Free Trade teaching, to be blessed with happiness, prosperity, and perpetual abundance, is instead cursed with a proportion of men unable to find work three times as great as that in Protectionist Germany. There seems to be something wrong with a system which produces such results and glories in them." [217] The League extracted the foregoing passage from the *Daily Mail* and printed it in its official journal so that every Tariff Reformer who did not feel himself bound by the League's own warning that such things were not "worth the paper they are printed on" might use it in his speeches.

When the official figures of the price of wheat in this country and on the Continent have been compared—always to the confusion of the Tariff Reformers—"we are on much sounder and safer ground if we refuse to enter into such comparisons," they say.[218] "Without knowing something of the manner in which these figures were compiled," said the League to one of its correspondents who had sent in some figures of French food prices, "they are, of course, of no value whatever for purposes of comparison with this country. All sorts of prices are doubtless paid for the same article in France, even in the same town, just as they are here in this country." [219] The inquiring correspondent was referred to a previous page in the same volume for "a recent statement of fact in regard to French prices." On that page appeared a comparison made on the authority of Earl Winterton between the prices of food "in the districts around Biarritz" with the prices of food "in his own constituency (Horsham, Sussex)"! Eliminating tea, because it "was not much drunk in that part of France," the comparison was well worked out in favour of France! And that is a common example of the kind of comparison which, denounced one day and relied on the next, has been delivered to the electorate as "proof" for ten years.

Similarly, when the Board of Trade Reports on the Cost of Living in France, Germany, and Belgium appeared, the Tariff Reformers denied their accuracy and minimised their usefulness except for the purpose of showing that the "percental increase" of wages, say, was greater in Germany than in Britian, where wages were always higher, both in real and money values. Yet when the series of Reports reached the United States of America, where money wages are higher, the volume was quoted with fervour, scores of new leaflets were based upon extracts from it, and it almost made the Tariff Reformers forget that such a country as Germany existed!

Savings, too, have always provided food for reflection to Tariff Reformers. One of the first of the propagandist leaflets,[220] entitled "The Savings Bank Test," quoted an eminent statistician, M. Fatio, who had worked out the amount in savings banks per head in European countries. "The one country that still clings to the system of Free Imports," said the leaflet, "is at the bottom of the list." M. Fatio's headline, indicating that he dealt only with savings banks, was speedily forgotten, and the Tariff Reformers spread it all over the country that foreigners could "save more money" than the Briton. "We see that the wages and the savings of the foreign working-man are increasing in a greater proportion than the wages and savings of the British working-men," said Mr. Chamberlain. "This is a condition of things which is almost in its infancy. In its infancy it is injurious; in its development it will be fatal."[221] He, in his turn, forgot that Mr. Austen Chamberlain, the Chancellor of the Exchequer in the British Ministry, had not many months before torn the Tariff Reform League "savings" leaflet to tatters. "The hon. member for South Islington and the hon. member for Nottingham had quoted," said Mr. Austen Chamberlain, "from a leaflet comparing the amount of the savings per head of the population in the Savings Banks in this country and in foreign countries. He thought that no simple comparison of the amount of savings per head in the Savings Banks in different countries would lead them to very definite results in regard to the position or prosperity of the people. There were a great number of other considerations which must be taken into account before any just conclusions could be drawn." [222]

Many other such shafts of destruction have been thrown at Tariff Reform by the Tariff Reformers. Mr. Samuel Roberts, one of the Members for Sheffield, once produced a razor in the House of Commons. It cost ninepence in Sheffield, he said, but the American customs charged a duty of ninepence upon it, so that the same razor cost eighteenpence in the United States.[223] The impression the awful example made on the country was, of course, exactly opposite to that which was intended. It was an admission that the consumer paid, and that the American taxes taxed the American taxpayer and not "the foreigner." So has it been with that other argument, that a tariff was necessary to keep the products of sweated labour from these shores. "It was a strange thing to him," said Mr. Jesse Collings, "that trade-unionist leaders should be against Mr. Chamberlain. They denounced blacklegs and sweating, but they were in favour of buying goods from Belgium and Germany, where blacklegs and sweaters produced them." [224] Leaflet No. 24 of the Tariff Reform League asked trade unionists of what use it was to organize for higher wages "if the consumer goes and buys articles made by sweated labour in other countries." "There is no more general ground of complaint among manufacturers than the low wages, the long hours of labour, and the lower standard of comfort prevalent in some foreign countries against which they have to compete. These conditions are not infrequently associated with a low type of industrial organization, which is practically indistinguishable from the sweating system." That is an extract from the Report of the Tariff

Commission on the Cotton industry.[225] It has always been remembered by the cotton operatives of Lancashire when they have been asked to vote for a tariff based on the German model.

It is almost forgotten that Sweden was one of the first Protectionist countries held up to the admiration of the British elector. Its "savings" had greatly increased! Denmark, too, had an early place in the picture. "The argument that Denmark only taxes imports for revenue purposes, and cannot, therefore, be styled a Protectionist country, is, of course, nonsense," said the Editor of the League's *Monthly Notes* to an inquiring correspondent in 1909. "The question of Denmark's intention has nothing to do with the point. The sole scientific test in the matter is whether or not Denmark balances every Customs duty on a competitive import by an equivalent excise duty on the home-produced article. If so, then Denmark is a Free Trade country; if not, it cannot be described as a Free Trade country. Judged by this test, Denmark is not a Free Trade country." [226] It was a rather heavy-footed attempt to prove that Protection had benefited Denmark, and it may stand here as a sample of the perishable material with which the Tariff Reformers have builded.

Late in 1912 the British Consul-General in France (Mr. Gastrell) issued his report on the trade, finance, and industry of France in 1910 and 1911. The Tariff Reform League immediately quoted passages from it in articles that were sent out from the League offices to many newspapers in the country.[227] In these articles the attempt was made to show that recent events in France provided "convincing evidence of the necessity for a change in our (British) existing tariff policy." That was the exact opposite of the real meaning of the Consul-General's report, as will be shown.

The article drew attention to figures showing that the trade of France had increased under Protection. The trade of the United Kingdom had increased still more under Free Trade, but nothing was said about that. See how the Tariff Reform League set out what it was pleased to select as the facts. It quoted the Consul-General's report as saying, "The foreign trade of France showed a development of £37,021,000 over the previous year," and there it stopped. But on page 9 of the Consul-General's Report the words quoted by the Tariff Reform League were found to be embedded in this passage, "A study of the statistics of foreign trade in 1911 reveals a further total development of £37,021,000 over the previous year, which, at first sight, may also seem to be fairly satisfactory, though it is some £20,000,000 less than that of the previous year. But an examination of the figures discloses the disquieting fact that there is an increase of £39,493,000 in imports, and a decrease of £2,472,000 in exports." The only figure out of all these that the Tariff Reform writer quoted was the first! The quotation stopped at a comma; suppressed the most important facts of all; gave the impression that the French people were well content; and was, in short, an utterly false quotation. And two lines lower down this fraudulent article impudently declared that, "Taking a general survey of the condition of France and the French people, the advantages of her tariff system are plainly to be seen." In taking "this general survey" the Tariff Reform League purposely kept both eyes shut and did not see the passage in which the Consul-General related that, "In view of the importance of the question of the rising cost of living in France, the increase in the price of bread during the present year has been an unexpected and unpleasant feature." Yet the article—whose suppressions and perversions cannot be exhausted here—concluded with the hope that "Tariff Reformers in this country will lose no opportunity of drawing public attention to these and similar interesting conclusions to be drawn from French industrial experience of 1911." The Consul-General's Report taught the very opposite lesson to that which the League attributed to it; but the Protectionist movement would not have lived a day if it had not selected its own evidence in its own manner to suit its own case.

THE "ABOMINABLE" EXAMPLE OF AMERICA

IN the first section of this book it was related that the League was at one time fond of quoting passages from the American *Protectionist,* but that the extracts ceased because the League did not wish to advertise the fact that the Tariff Reform campaign was a Protectionist campaign. That act of suppression has not prevented the League from continuing to quote the crude arguments of the United States Protectionists. Nor has any sign been given in Tariff Reform pages that the natural and social conditions of the United States are vastly different from those of this country. In September 1912 the League printed an article on the "New York Unemployment Bogey," in which New York State and New York City were employed as interchangeable terms, and the section relating to "Immigration and Unemployment" included quotations from official sources to the effect that "637,000 immigrants landed at New York last year, that the greater part settled in the Eastern States, and that over three-fifths (of the immigrants) remain in five Eastern States." This was the League's comment, "What would be the condition of the labour market in London if some hundreds of thousands of the poorest classes of aliens were to land in its port every year with no means to go further afield in search of work than the five adjacent counties?" It is not possible that the writer of the article did not know that New York State alone is as large as England, and that a proper comparison of five Eastern States would be not with five adjacent counties, but with at least two hundred counties of their size, irrespective of other incomparable conditions. A certain impression had to be made, and it was made!

The United States and Germany have commonly been held up as the great patterns of what the British Empire might become under the influence of a Protective Customs Union. "The greatest commercial prosperity of the future is for the nation with the largest Free Trade area," said Mr. Vince in the Birmingham Committee's *Handbook*.[228] "This advantage is possessed by the United States of America: hence her commercial progress." The danger of using such an illustration as that soon became apparent. Mr. Chamberlain said in his Glasgow speech in 1903, "America is the strictest of protective nations. It has a tariff which to me is an abomination. It is so immoderate, so unreasonable, so unnecessary, that, although America has profited enormously under it, yet I think it has been carried to excessive lengths." In his Limehouse speech the following year he asked, "What is the experience of the world? Take the United States of America, take our own Colonies," he said. "It is universally admitted that in those countries the general standard of living, the position of comfort and prosperity in which the working classes exist, is superior to their condition in this country. They have a tariff." Then he added, inconsequently, "I am accused of desiring to have a similar tariff in this country. I desire nothing of the sort." [229]

Very soon, however, the "abomination" became a blessing. Tariff Reform League literature abounds in statements that "the American workman under Protection" is "better off than the British workman under 'Free Trade.'" [230] When the Board of Trade published the report on the cost of living in American towns, the Tariff Reform League copied details of the wages paid in certain American industries and distributed them as leaflets bearing the words, "If you want a Tariff which will improve *your* work and wages, support Tariff Reform." [231] In its *Monthly Notes*, the League quoted the "boast" of the Hon. Joseph G. Cannon, one of the leaders of the High Protectionists of the States, that "under the policy of Protection the United States produces one-third of the manufactured and agricultural products of the civilized world; our labour receives double the compensation that labour receives in Great Britain, and three times the compensation paid to labour on the continent of Europe." On this the League observed, "There may be some rhetorical exaggeration in these rough estimates; but the statistics by which Mr. Cannon exhibits the growth of American industries under Protection are unimpeachable." [232]

Yet the "rhetorical exaggerations" which their American co-Protectionists are so fond of have been quoted again and again. Even this, extracted from a speech delivered in the House of Representatives by the Hon. A. L. Bates, of Pennsylvania: [233] "Ninety-two articles were transferred from the dutiable to the free list by the Wilson Bill, as it came from the Democratic Ways and Means Committee or as it passed the House, among them wool, sugar, coal, iron, and lumber. The farmers were stripped of the protection afforded in the M'Kinley law. Railroads went into the hands of receivers. Banks closed their doors. The smoke of industry ceased to cloud the sky. Three million labouring people were thrown out of employment. Gold left our shores with every ship. The looms and reels and spindles of Bradford and other English cities worked double forces night and day to supply our people with textile fabrics, while the working men of America languished, were being fed at soup houses, and begging for bread." That was held up as a warning of what might happen in the United Kingdom unless our fiscal system were changed!

The League and its pupils, unable to resist the temptation of borrowing the lurid language of the American Protectionist, have yet been wary enough to preserve the slender plank by which they might at any time creep back from their own odious comparisons. "Before citing Mr. Curtis's observations," said the League, "we must again premise that it is no part of the business of English Tariff Reformers to defend the American Tariff, which Mr. Chamberlain has described as 'immoderate, unreasonable, and unnecessary,' and which is enormously more stringent than the tariff proposed by the Tariff Commission. We are interested, however, in these American controversies, because our opponents are fond of representing a tariff as a sort of vice that grows on a nation that begins with moderate indulgence, as vicious habits gradually overmaster a man. It is therefore always worth while to observe that even the most shocking examples of this vice are not hopelessly ruinous." [234]

The 1913 change in the "method of procedure" obliged Mr. Bonar Law [235] to say that "it is not reasonable to suggest that we should have the same kind of tariff as exists in the United States," not because it was an "abomination," forsooth, but because it protected agriculture! And finally we have Mr. Hewins, Chairman of the committee responsible for the issue of the Tariff Reform League literature that has been described, saying that the changes being made in America by the Underwood Tariff Bill of 1913 are "designed to make the tariff more effective." This appeared in a cabled message dated London, April 8, and published in the *New York World* as the opinion of Mr. W. A. S. Hewins, M.P., Secretary to the Chamberlain Tariff Commission. "President Wilson's proposals," he said, "are not at all in the direction of Free Trade, as we understand it in England. They are designed to make the Tariff more effective. There is no feeling in the United States for abolishing it. When the United States Tariff is calculated scientifically, it will be far more dangerous to British industries than now."

In 1908, when Mr. Taft was elected President, the official monthly journal of the League emphasized what it called "the first and most obvious lesson of the election." "If a keenly intelligent people like the Americans refuse to abandon their protective policy, even at a time of great industrial depression, and decline to take even a single step towards Free Trade, it must be because they have found such a policy best suited to the needs of the nation. It may safely be said then that a tariff which safeguards the home market is one which is conducive to the development and progress of a great commercial and industrial nation." [236] In the article from which the above is quoted Free Traders were asked to "Please note . . . the remarkable industrial and commercial 'boom' in the United States immediately on the announcement of Mr. Taft's victory."

Thus in 1908 the maintenance of the American tariff was necessary to "safeguard the home-market." In 1913 its reduction is designed to make it more dangerous to British industries. In 1908 the American people were so "keenly intelligent" that they declined to take "even a single step towards Free Trade." In 1913 the big step is taken, but Mr. Hewins declares it is "not at all in the direction of Free Trade." The tariff which was "carried to excessive lengths" in 1903 was five years later "conducive to the development and progress of a great commercial nation," and again, five years later (when it was being severely cut down), it was going to be "more effective" than ever!

THE TRIPS TO GERMANY

THE sorriest, the most sordid, of the most ridiculous contrasts the Tariff Reform campaign provides are connected with its attempt to exploit Germany. At first the German was filching our trade, here, there, and everywhere. His main object was to destroy the unity of the British Empire. He was even compelling us to build his warships! The metaphor of war was regularly employed in describing the peaceful trade between the individual inhabitants of two friendly countries. The atmosphere was saturated with mystery: nobody knew what the German manufacturer would be up to next!

In October 1904, Mr. Hewins sent out a communication marked "private," asking the Press to print a letter "addressed by the president of a German chamber of commerce to a leading English manufacturer" (no names were given) and adding that there was "no need to mention my name or that of the Tariff Commission in the matter." *The Standard* [237] printed Mr. Hewins' letter. "Excuse me," wrote his mysterious German correspondent, "if I bore you with these views, which, I am sure, are not new to you. I feel compelled to add them to ease my worried mind, as I am supplying ammunition to our economic enemy, Mr. Chamberlain, and that Mr. Chamberlain is our enemy is incontestable. Our own export trade would be seriously menaced if, contrary to expectations, Mr. Chamberlain should prove victorious.—Yours truly ——."

The League also joyously quoted its "candid friend," an Australian paper, which said that "London is gradually becoming a suburb of Berlin." [238] "This is what makes the Germans so angry, you know," said a Birmingham leaflet [239] describing Mr. Chamberlain's scheme as being directed to gaining the acceptance of "the offer of the

Colonies to give us better terms in trade than they give foreigners."

A book as big as this could be filled with the Tariff Reformers' sayings about Germany. There is room for only a very few examples. Many speakers have tried to prove that the German is better off than the Briton. How many of them have had the candour of Colonel Chaloner, who wrote to a Northern paper to confess that "on Wednesday last, at a meeting in Brotton, I made a statement which I believed at the time to be true—namely, that wages in Germany were higher than in England. I now find on inquiry I was wrong, and that Mr. W. Stephens, who very courteously corrected me, was right, so will you kindly afford me space to make the correction public, which is only fair, as I made the statement in public?"[240] Even Mr. Bonar Law, so late as 1912,[241] offered as "proof" of the benefit of Protection to Germany the statement of "one of our Consuls, that in spite of a rise in the cost of living in Germany the rise in wages had been so great that it more than counter-balanced the increase in the cost of living." He did not name the Consul, but the Literary Secretary of the Tariff Reform League, defending Mr. Bonar Law, mentioned that it was Consul Ladenburg, of Baden. If Mr. Bonar Law had looked at Consul Ladenburg's report he would have seen that it concerned the trade of Baden only, and that the figures upon which the British Tariff Reform leader relied were six years old! What had become of all the warnings of the League about the unreliability of such comparisons?

Forgetting that the Germans were the "sweated" makers of the goods that robbed the British workers of their jobs, the Tariff Reformers had so often described Germany as a kind of Protectionist paradise that they determined in 1910 to send parties of working-men to that country to see what Protection had done for it. The idea was not a new one. According to *Monthly Notes*, the Bradford and District League against Protection and the Tariff Reform League decided in 1905 to send members of the local trades councils to Germany, "to find out for themselves the truth as to labour conditions on the Continent." But the plan broke down when Mr. Ogden, secretary of the League against Protection, insisted on the fulfilment of the agreed condition "that the two leagues should be satisfied as to the suitability of the persons recommended by the Trades Council." Surely it was a wise precaution; but the League declined the condition, and actually published the correspondence as "proving" that the Free Traders did not wish the truth to be found out.

A deputation of three brass-workers from Birmingham went to Berlin in 1905 to spy out the promised land of Protection, and one of them said he returned to his native land "a more convinced Free Trader than when I left it." [242] In the following year six Gainsborough working-men went out under similar auspices and with similar results, and in 1908 a Batley deputation made the trip. None of these visits made any impression; and in April 1910 the League commenced the organization of several trips, "under circumstances," as Mr. Balfour was considerate enough to suppose, "peculiarly favourable to the pursuit of truth." [243] The Berlin correspondent of the Protectionist *Morning Post* [244] warned the League that "the meaning of things in this country is learned only by long and careful study among the people themselves," and *The Times* still more emphatically declared that "unfortunately a good deal of investigation is undertaken without any consciousness of the danger, and a good deal more for the express purpose, not of seeking truth, but of gratifying prejudice. That is apt to be the case whenever a question becomes the object of strong feeling and lively controversy. The economic condition of Germany has fallen into that unfortunate category," added *The Times*. "It has become the subject of bitter political controversy of the most pronounced and nakedly partisan character, in which the aim has been, not to discover truth, but to stifle it." [245]

They were fourteen-day trips. Part of the time was spent in Belgium; and several days in travelling, drives round London, and lunches at the Hotel Metropole or the Hotel Cecil, generally with a Protectionist peer presiding.

The number of hours spent in German towns was about 130, and, deducting necessary time for sleeping and eating, it was seen that the delegates spent about fifty hours in the actual "pursuit of truth." Perhaps Mr. Balfour was quite well aware how little of it they caught. During the summer of 1910 the Tariff Reform press contained boundless descriptions of the experiences of the "Tariff trippers," as they came to be known; but inasmuch as every tripper wrote a report, and every report was printed and published by the Tariff Reform League, it is here thought better to go to that source for some account of these excursions which cost the Tariff Reformers so much money and did them so much harm.

Fortunately, Lord Ridley, the Chairman of the League's Executive Committee, promised that the reports of the deputations "would be published unaltered and unedited for all to read:" [246] and in the preface to the first volume [247] the editor wrote that "every report received, whatever opinions may be expressed, has been inserted. Only wholly irrelevant matter has been excised, and any editing has been confined to the correction of grammatical errors." Answering the objection that "residence at large hotels was not conducive to efficient investigation of working-class conditions," the editor said it would have been inconvenient to split up the party, partly for reasons of convenience and comfort, and, "Further, it would have prevented the men meeting in conference each evening to report the result of the day's investigations." The results of these conferences were apparent in the report. Over and over again the men said they did not see such and such a thing themselves, but they heard of it from a colleague. As to the objection "that their stay in Germany was too short for them to report with any real knowledge or authority on life in that country," why, that was "easily answered." "The Labour Party's deputation which has recently returned from Germany spent sixteen days in the country. In addition to studying the social conditions of the people, the Labour delegates had to secure and compile statistical information, a duty which required much time and concentration of energy. If the

Labour Party's small deputation could execute their commission in the space of sixteen days, how much easier it was for sixty men, whose duty was mainly that of careful observation, to execute theirs in eleven! That simple task they executed by going into the highways and byways of the industrial quarters and factory districts of the towns they visited. They saw the workers in the factory and workshops, at work and at play, in the café, in the Volkhaus, and at home." The old love of the rule of three again. If every member of a small band could acquaint himself with the conditions of life in Germany in sixteen days, and of a larger one in eleven, how big a party would have been necessary to do it in one? The League did not believe in its own arithmetic, for it divided its "delegates" into several parties.

No women were taken on the tour. The assistance that an observant housewife might have given had to be done without. Few of the men seem to have remembered that there was a greater thing than price—namely, quality. They regularly confused money values. Most of them were Tariff Reformers at all hazards. The index gave the names, professions, and addresses of the first party. Among them were five "ex-Socialists," one or two other malcontent "ex-" something or other, and an ex-Parliamentary candidate who dwelt at Tariff House, Worsborodale.

The volume was embellished with fifty photographs reprinted in half-tone. Of these nearly one-fourth were pictures of the model town of Essen. One was obviously "faked." Of what use was the picture of a small railway station platform, or of a mounted policeman, or of women taking their husband's dinners to the works, or of the "general view" of Stuttgart, or of a group of children eating halfpenny ice-creams in a street at Nuremburg? There was a pretty snapshot of the chimney sweep in a chimney-pot hat seen at Stuttgart. "Even the street-sweepers were in uniform," wrote one of the tourists. "A chimney sweep, too, passed by in all the glory of a silk hat, and though the circumstance appeared ludicrous to the visitors, to the natives it received no attention."

The reproduction of a view of the "old masonry" in the

city walls of Nuremburg was also given among the illustrations, and if the industrial newness of Germany astonished some of the tourists, the honourable age of the country astonished others even more. Thus, one wrote, " We spent a full day in Nuremburg, a very old-fashioned town, with many crooked streets, large quaint-looking houses, some very old, and many quite new or fresh-looking, very pretty and tastefully arranged shops; old fortresses, churches, public buildings and monuments abounded; in fact, a general air of luxury and prosperity pervaded the place. There may be such places in England, but I have never seen or heard of them, and the town was worthy of a visit. Most of us were so busy enjoying the sights, that we forgot the object of our visit."

There were several photographs of "workmen's flats," and a snapshot of a group of delegates "admiring" them. Need it be said that all the views were "front" views? The back views, with cramped court-yards, where window stares across into window; the narrow back passages that separate one flat-building from another—these were not shown. A photograph of a "Close of Sale" bill of an Essen clothier was printed to prove, presumably, what low prices prevailed throughout Germany. Several pictures of the Berlin Labour Exchange were reprinted from the last official report of "Der Central-Arbeitsnachweis in Berlin." Pictures of the various departments for the unemployed were given in that official report, and this Tariff Reform guide to Protection reproduced all of them but one. The selection was perfectly characteristic. While the youths' department was pictured, half empty, the view of the Adults' Department for Unskilled Workmen, a far bigger room with only a few seats vacant, was not printed.

The curious in these matters may amuse themselves for hours by reading the three densely-printed volumes in which the "unedited reports" were printed. An examination of the records of the first three trips revealed that the price of the four-pound wheaten loaf in Germany was anything from fivepence to a shilling; that three trippers visited the same shop in Barmen the same day and brought away different prices of bread, both wheaten and rye;

that " very large " cauliflowers were sold at Essen for 5½d.; and that eggs were anything you like (eight different prices were quoted by members of the same excursion). The Tariff Reformers had said there were no slums in Germany. One visitor to Düsseldorf obediently reported thereupon that " The poor part caused us a lot of wandering round, but it could not be found, for the simple reason that there was none existing—good for a start ; " while another member at the same time recorded, " I visited the poorest quarter of the town near the Roman Catholic Cathedral. Slums, as bad as any in the East End, were observed." There had been statements that no barefoot children were to be found in Germany; no horse-flesh shops; no empty factories. Some of the trippers saw none. Others saw plenty of all of them. Prices of all kinds of articles, wages in all places and all trades were quoted higgledy-piggledy. Most of the delegates were surprised to see no " carry-your-bag-sir ! " boys, no beggars, no match-sellers, no newsboys. Nobody explained to them that the German railways organise their own outside porter services, and that the other apparitions are forbidden by the State.

Then those cheap cigars ! " I watched seven plasterers at work upon the entrance to a new threatre, and although the ' boss ' was amongst them," said one astonished delegate, " every man-jack of them was smoking a cigar, and the ' boss ' as well." But that was as nothing to the surprise of the man who recorded that " we watched a bricklayer's labourer go up a ladder three times with bricks, and each time he came down again with—a hod full of empty lager beer bottles." Tariff Reform meant more beer, evidently! It also meant better manners. " The workers, both men and women, are excessively polite to each other," wrote another delegate. " How long should we look in England for one working-man to raise his hat to another as he passes by in the street ? He may do so when dressed up on Sundays, but I refer now to men passing each other at dinner-time ; the little courtesy is not much, but it shows the upward trend of social amenities in comparison to the state of things in our own land." And it also meant more freedom. "Talk about the freedom of the German! When the sweep, the bricklayer's labourer, the carpenter, the tram-driver, and the shop-walker can all be seen smoking their cigars while at work, it shows freedom of some sort, anyhow."

Welcoming home the ninth party of trippers at a luncheon at the Hotel Metropole, Viscount Ridley said, "They had been to inquire into the truth, the whole truth, and nothing but the truth, and he believed the official assistance they had received showed that Germany realized that they were an honest party of British working-men trying to find out the truth." [248] It so happened that the delegates of this ninth party reported at the farewell luncheon (it was at the Trocadero Restaurant) that "the language difficulty rendered it impossible for any member of the deputation to make independent investigations." [249] The "pursuit of truth" is always a hard matter.

Yet, if these ardent Tariff trippers had found what they were sent to find—it was not the truth—of what use would it be to the Tariff Reform movement to-day?

Germany is no longer the model. America's "abominable" tariff is not even to be gazed at afar off. Mr. Bonar Law, describing the latest "definite policy" of the Tariff Reformers at Edinburgh on January 24, 1913, declared that "if we are returned to power we shall impose a tariff, a moderate tariff, lower than exists now in any industrial country in the world, on foreign manufactured goods." And, looking round the world for examples, he did not look at Germany nor at America. "In Denmark," he said, "there is an industrial tariff, though a very small one, and practically no duties on agricultural produce. In Belgium, the country where the industrial situation and conditions more nearly resemble those of the United Kingdom than any other country in the world—in Belgium there is an industrial tariff higher than we mean to impose, and there is no duty on wheat and very few and very small duties on any other agricultural produce."

The great countries that have been going to crush us ever since 1903 are to keep on going to crush us. Mr. Bonar Law doesn't care! The marvellous things their tariffs have done for Germany and America are not even to be attempted here. Great Britain must in 1913 learn her tariff lesson from two busy little nations the Protectionists had scarcely ever thought of, till Mr. Bonar Law came along and discovered that the less Protection you appear to hope for, the more it appears possible to get. "The policy which I suggest to you is the policy which has been tried and has succeeded on the Continent of Europe, in the United States of America, and in our Colonies," said Mr. Chamberlain in 1904, though he also explained that those countries "began with a low tariff." The policy which Mr. Bonar Law suggests in 1913 is both low and little, less than that of two of the least-protected countries in Europe. The Tariff Reform mirage has vanished. The Protectionists are still trekking across the "illimitable veldt."

REFERENCES

I.—THE PROTECTIONIST PROPAGANDA

[1] In a letter to the *Morning Post*, July 3, 1913.

[2] At a meeting of the Tariff Reform League Executive Committee June 30, 1913. (*Morning Post* Report, July 1.)

[3] In Mitchell's *Newspaper Press Directory* for 1904.

[4] Interview in the *Morning Post*, February 18, 1908.

[5] July 1903.

[6] Birmingham, May 15, 1903.

[7] October 12, 1908.

[8] Lancaster, October 21, 1904.

[9] Epsom, February 9, 1905.

[10] *Melbourne Age*, November 7, 1904.

[11] *Outlook*, September 7, 1907.

[12] West Hartlepool, June 10, 1010.

[13] Tariff Reform League *Speakers' Handbook*, 1st ed., 1903, p. 9.

[14] Tariff Reform League *Monthly Notes*, December 1909, p. 432.

[15] September 23, 1903.

[16] Quoted in *Liberal Magazine*. August 1903, p. 436.

[17] During 1906 and the first half of 1907.

[18] Westminster Palace Hotel, February 24, 1905.

[19] See, for example, *Tariff Reform by Pen and Pencil*, published by the Tariff Reform League.

[20] Tariff Reform League *Monthly Notes*, March 1905, p. 174.

[21] Stafford House, July 21, 1904.

[22] Tariff Reform League *Monthly Notes*, May 1909, p. 351.

[23] Tariff Reform League *Monthly Notes*, August 1905, p. 103.

[24] From the *Worcester Echo*, January 28, 1908.

[25] *Daily News*, March 11, 1912.

[26] See *Southern Weekly News*, July 2, 1910.

[27] Albert Hall, July 7, 1905.

[28] *National Review*, January 1909; *Daily Mail*, February 27, 1909; *Morning Post*, January 24, 1908; *Daily Graphic*, February 2, 1909.

[29] All the Protectionist journals, June 15, 1912.

[30] Quoted in *Liberal Magazine*, 1903, p. 622.

[31] Leeds, December 16, 1903.

[32] *National Review*, February 1909.

[33] Hotel Cecil, January 15, 1904.

[34] The *Standard*, December 18, 1903.

THE PROTECTIONIST PROPAGANDA, *continued*—

35 Ipswich, March 20, 1908.

36 House of Lords, March 14, 1904.

37 See *The Times*, April 20, 1904.

38 *Yorkshire Post* report, March 23, 1904.

39 Lincoln, October 16, 1908.

40 Tariff Commission's Report on Iron and Steel.

Iron and Steel Goods

DESCRIPTION.	RANGE OF DUTIES EXPRESSED AS *AD VALOREM* RATES.
Iron Ore	Free.
Pig Iron	5 per cent.
Iron and steel, Puddled bars, ingots, blooms, billets, slabs, sheet bars, tin plate bars, or similar partly manufactured materials . .	6¼ per cent.
Rails, sleepers and fish plates, girders, joists and beams, bars—round, square, flat, and sections other than above enumerated, and slit rods	6¼ per cent.
Plates and wire rods	7½ per cent.
Sheets	10 per cent.
Nails, screws and rivets, bolts and nuts, tyres and axles, railway wheels and axles, crucible steel and manufactures of iron and steel unenumerated	Duties in no case to exceed 10 per cent.

Cotton Goods

DESCRIPTION.	RANGE OF DUTIES EXPRESSED AS *AD VALOREM* DUTIES.
Raw cotton	Free.
Yarns and twist of all descriptions . . .	Free.
Cotton tissues, grey	Free.
Other cotton tissues and manufactures . .	Duties in no case to exceed 10 per cent.

The duties are stated for convenience as *ad valorem* rates, without prejudice to the question whether the duties to be ultimately recommended by the Commission will be *ad valorem* or specific.

42 *Westminster Gazette*, September 29, 1910.

43 *Morning Post*, October 12, 1908.

44 *Birmingham Post*, December 8, 1909.

44a In his introduction to his 1903 speeches, published under the title of " Imperial Union and Tariff Reform."

45 *North Devon Journal*, April 14, 1904.

46 Preston, January 11, 1905.

47 Sleaford, March 22, 1905.

48 Albert Hall, July 7, 1905.

49 Quoted in *Free Trader*, 1905, p. 35.

50 Mr. Reginald Lucas(*Portsmouth Evening News*,November 20,1907).

51 Liverpool, December 9, 1908.

THE PROTECTIONIST PROPAGANDA, *continued*—

[52] *Salisbury Times*, March 19, 1909.
[53] Bradford, November 6, 1909.
[54] Tariff Reform League *Monthly Notes*, April 1909, p. 313.
[55] House of Commons, September 6, 1909.
[56] September 23, 1910.
[57] March 29, 1910.
[58] *Daily Chronicle*, September 26, 1910.
[59] September 27, 1910.
[60] *Manchester Guardian* report, November 9, 1910.
[61] *Morning Post*, March 3, 1911.
[62] Canterbury, February 25, 1913.
[63] Col. Boles, West Somerset (*Free Press* report, July 15, 1911).
[64] See *Stroud News*, July 21, 1911.

II.—AGRICULTURE

[1] Ipswich, December 18, 1903.
[2] October 6, 1902.
[3] York, December 17, 1903.
[4] *Carlisle Journal* report, January 17, 1904.
[5] Quoted in the Tariff Reform League *Monthly Notes*, February 1905, p. 116.
[6] Tariff Reform League leaflet No. 47.
[7] Tariff Reform League leaflets Nos. 150, 151, 173, 174, 177, 179, 186, 204, 225.
[8] January 8, 1904.
[9] " The Case against Home Rule," Chap. v., 1912.
[10] Speech at Birkenhead, January 23, 1912.
[11] Tariff Reform League leaflet No. 46.
[12] See various publications, *e.g.*, Imperial Tariff Committee leaflet No. 3 ; " Tariff Reform by Pen and Pencil," p. 25, etc.
[13] Cirencester (*Birmingham Post* report, April 22, 1904).
[14] Both quoted in Tariff Reform League *Monthly Notes*, August 1904, p. 86.
[15] November 21, 1903.
[16] December 9, 1908.
[17] August 9, 1904.
[18] See *The Times* report, November 21, 1904.
[19] March 24, 1905.
[20] Tariff Reform League leaflet No. 291.
[21] Tariff Reform League leaflet No. 105.
[22] Mr. Sebag Montefiore, October 18, 1909.
[23] Quoted in *Liberal Magazine*, 1904, p. 16.
[24] Tariff Reform League *Monthly Notes*, February 1905, p. 126.

AGRICULTURE, *continued*—

[25] Ware (*The Times* report) December 15, 1903.

[26] Edinburgh Speech, January 24, 1913.

[27] Imperial Tariff Committee leaflet No. 42.

[28] Tariff Reform League *Monthly Notes*, July 1905, p. 68.

[29] Tariff Reform League *Monthly Notes*, June 1905, p. 400.

[30] *Gainsborough News* report, quoted in the *Free Trader*, 1905, p. 93.

[31] On November 2, 1906, Tariff Reform League *Monthly Notes* Report, December 1906.

[32] Shrewsbury, January 26, 1907.

[33] *Birmingham Post*, July 13, 1904.

[34] Tariff Reform League *Monthly Notes*, February 1905, p. 135.

[35] Tariff Reform League *Monthly Notes*, February 1905, p. 135.

[36] The Tariff Commission's "Provisional Scale" of Agricultural Duties :—

	GENERAL TARIFF.	PREFERENTIAL TARIFF.
Wheat.	6d. per cwt. (or about 2s. per qr.).	3d. per cwt. (or about 1s. per qr.).
Barley, oats, rye, maize, etc.	Duties equivalent to those on wheat.	Duties equivalent to those on wheat.
Wheaten and other flour and meal.	1s. 3d. per cwt.	Subject to negotiations with the Colonies.
Animals and meat, including bacon.	General level to be 5 per cent.	
Dairy produce, including poultry and eggs. Market-garden produce, including potatoes and hops. Hay and straw.	Specific duties equivalent in general to from 5 per cent. to 10 per cent. *ad valorem*, though in particular cases some duties when calculated may be found to be lower, and in others rather higher, than these limits.	

[37] Tariff Commission Agricultural Committee's Report, section 1835.

[38] Form No. 12,113.

[39] Mr. W. A. Prout.

[40] Mr. J. Eames.

[41] Form No. 12,213.

[42] Form No. 12,447.

[43] Form No. 12,291.

[44] Mr. J. Mills White.

[45] Form No. 12,696.

[46] Mr. W. B. Blundell.

[47] Paragraph 1,628.

[48] Paragraph 1,614.

[49] Paragraph 1,598.

[50] Mr. J. Suggitt.

[51] Mr. A. Amos.

[52] Form No. 12,156.

AGRICULTURE, *continued*—

[53] Form No. 12,450.

[54] Mr. J. P. Poe.

[55] Mr. J. C. Dawson.

[56] Lord Kesteven.

[57] Mr. A. Pulling.

[58] Mr. J. Richards.

[59] Form No. 12,123.

[60] Mr. David Hume.

[61] Form No. 12,215.

[62] Mr. C. N. Humble.

[63] Mr. W. E. S. Wilson.

[64] Mr. T. S. Corpe.

[65] Mr. G. Fiske.

[66] Mr. J. Speir.

[67] Mr. E. M. Nunneley.

[68] Form No. 12,412.

[69] Mr. George A. Elliott.

[70] Tariff Commission Agricultural Committee's Report, section 541.

[71] Tariff Reform League *Monthly Notes*, February 1907, and sections therein quoted of the above report.

[72] In a letter to the *Nottingham Daily Express*, February 25, 1905.

[73] York, February 13, 1908 (reported in the *Birmingham Post*, February 14).

[74] *The Times* report, May 9, 1907.

[75] *Western Morning News* report, September 28, 1907.

[76] Mr. Bonar Law at Aberdeen, January 31, 1908 ; Mr. Chamberlain at Hackney, November 26, 1909 ; Mr. Wyndham at Liverpool, December 9, 1908 ; Mr. Amery's by-election address, 1908.

[77] Liverpool, December 9, 1908.

[78] Manchester, November 7, 1910.

[79] In the *Fortnightly Review*, August 1912.

[80] Tariff Reform League *Monthly Notes*, January 1908, p. 62.

[81] Tariff Reform League *Monthly Notes*, December 1909, p. 436.

[82] October 16, 1908 (Report published by the Lincolnshire Farmers' Union).

[83] The Fareham and Hants Farmers' Club, April 26, 1910.

[84] *Agriculture and Tariff Reform*, by J. L. Green, p. 39.

[85] Manchester, November 25, 1910.

[86] Salisbury, December 9, 1910.

[87] Putney Heath, July 16, 1910.

[88] *Wolverhampton Chronicle* Report, September 4, 1912.

[89] Tariff Reform League *Monthly Notes*, October 1912.

[90] In the House of Commons, March 18, 1909.

[90a] Leyton, December 13, 1912.

[91] *Daily Mail*, December 24, 1912.

[92] *Lincoln Leader* report, January 11, 1913.

AGRICULTURE, *continued*—

[93] *Nottingham Daily Guardian*, December 19, 1912.

[94] *Pall Mall Gazette*, December 20, 1912.

[95] *Observer*, December 22, 1912.

[96] In an article in the Fourth Annual Report of the National Farmers' Union, p. 11.

[97] February 18, 1913.

[98] Dover, January 15, 1913.

[99] *Liverpool Post*, February 10, 1913.

[100] *Morning Post*, February 13, 1913.

[101] January 22, 1913.

[102] *Daily Graphic*, January 27, 1913.

[103] *Kent Messenger*, February 8, 1913.

[104] *Kent Express*, February 1, 1913.

[105] *Morning Post*, January 23, 1913.

[106] *The Times*, January 4, 1913.

[107] *Liverpool Post*, January 24, 1913.

III.—THE EMPIRE

[1] Letter dated November 28th, 1903.

[2] Birmingham, May 15, 1903.

[3] House of Commons, June 17, 1903.

[4] Official version in Imperial Tariff Committee's leaflet No. 1*a*.

[5] *Under Five Reigns*, by Lady Dorothy Nevill, 1910, pp. 208–9.

[6] Mr. C. A. Vince in *Mr. Chamberlain's Proposals*, 1903, pp. 1 and 4.

[7] Mr. C. A. Vince in *Mr. Chamberlain's Proposals*, 1903, pp. 1 and 4.

[8] September 21, 1903 (see *Life of the Duke of Devonshire*).

[9] September 25, 1903.

[10] October 6, 1903.

[11] October 7, 1903.

[12] October 20, 1903.

[13] October 7, 1903.

[14] First Edition of the Tariff Reform League's *Speakers' Handbook*, October 1903, p. 9.

[15] First Edition of the Tariff Reform League's *Speakers' Handbook*, October 1903, p. 26.

[16] Seventh Edition of the Tariff Reform League *Speakers' Handbook* (1912), p. xvi.

[17] Leeds, December 16, 1903.

[18] January 19, 1904.

[19] Birmingham, May 12, 1904.

[20] July 8, 1904.

[21] Rochester, July 26, 1904.

[22] Gainsborough, February 1, 1905.

[23] *Outlook*, March 9, 1905.

THE EMPIRE, *continued*—

[24] Resolution at the first annual meeting of the Tariff Reform League, 1905.

[25] Handsworth, January 5, 1905.

[26] *The Times*, January 18, 1905.

[27] Kensington, April 17, 1907.

[28] November 12, 1907 (Tariff Reform League *Monthly Notes* for December).

[29] December 18, 1907.

[30] Quoted in the *Free Trader*, October 1909.

[31] January 11, 1908.

[32] *National Review*, September 1911.

[33] *Daily Express*, July 8, 1912.

[34] *Observer*, March 23, 1913.

[35] House of Commons, May 28, 1903.

[36] Constitutional Club, June 26, 1903.

[37] Letter dated June 3, 1903.

[38] October 28, 1903.

[39] November 21, 1903.

[40] July 21, 1904.

[41] February 1, 1905.

[42] June 3, 1905.

[43] Albert Hall, July 7, 1905.

[44] Albert Hall, July 14, 1904.

[45] Glasgow, December 14, 1907.

[46] October 21, 1903.

[47] Rochester, July 27, 1904.

[48] Mr. Joynson Hicks in his election address at the N.W. Manchester by-election, April 1908.

[49] Sheffield, December 5, 1907.

[50] In the *Standard of Empire*, May 22, 1908.

[51] Stirchley, December 8, 1908.

[52] October 6 and 7, 1909.

[53] Wolverhampton, February 12, 1909.

[54] June 3, 1910.

[55] February 18, 1904.

[56] January 14, 1905.

[57] Southampton, October 9, 1912.

[58] 1912 edition, p. 35.

[59] Tariff Reform League *Monthly Notes*, November 1912, p. 305.

[60] Stafford House, July 21, 1904.

[61] October 16, 1912.

[62] December 4, 1912.

[63] Tariff Reform League leaflet No. 186.

[64] Page 91, 1903 edition.

[65] Tariff Reform League *Speakers' Handbook*, 1912 edition, p. 31.

[66] Tariff Reform League *Speakers' Handbook*, pp. 4 and 110.

THE EMPIRE, *continued*—

[67] Leeds, November 16, 1911.

[68] June 27, 1905.

[69] Leaflet No. 28 (Tariff Reform League), New series.

[70] Tariff Reform League *Monthly Notes*, March 1909, p. 191.

[71] Tariff Reform League *Monthly Notes*, August 1905, p. 71.

[72] Tariff Reform League *Monthly Notes*, January 1905, p. 33.

[73] Imperial Tariff Committee leaflet No. 22.

[74] Tariff Reform League *Speakers' Handbook*, 1912 edition, p. 285.

[75] *Monthly Notes*, 1908, pp. 31 and 87.

[76] Liverpool, October 27, 1903.

[77] Imperial Tariff Committee leaflet No. 4.

[78] Tariff Reform League *Speakers' Handbook*, 1903 edition, p. 20.

[79] 1912 edition, p. 3.

[80] 1912 edition, p. 33.

[81] House of Lords, May 20, 1908.

[82] House of Commons, February 18, 1909.

[83] March 28, 1910.

[84] Manchester, March 25, 1907.

[85] *North Devon Journal*, April 14, 1904.

[86] Birmingham, November 4, 1903.

[87] Birmingham, June 5, 1906.

[88] House of Commons, October 17, 1912.

[89] Tariff Reform League *Speakers' Handbook*, 1912 edition, p. 94.

[90] Tariff Reform League leaflet No. 18.

[91] Tariff Reform League *Monthly Notes*, August 1905, p. 97.

[92] Imperial Tariff Committee leaflet No. 27.

[93] Aberdeen, January 31, 1908.

[94] Printed by R. J. Cook & Hammond, Tothill St., Westminster.

[95] Imperial Tariff Committee leaflet No. 43.

[96] Tariff Reform League *Monthly Notes*, April 1905, p. 218.

[97] *Birmingham Post*, January 26, 1905.

[98] Edinburgh, May 18, 1907.

[99] Tariff Reform League *Monthly Notes*, March 1905, p. 204.

[100] Tariff Reform League *Monthly Notes*, January 1905, p. 60.

[101] Tariff Reform League *Speakers' Handbook*, 1912 edition, p. 151 et seq.

[102] Tariff Reform League *Speakers' Handbook*, 1903 edition, p. 92.

[103] Leeds, December 16, 1903.

[104] Birmingham, December 30, 1905.

[105] Oxford, December 8, 1905.

[106] July 27, 1904.

[107] House of Lords, March 3, 1904.

[108] House of Lords, March 3, 1904.

[109] Leeds, December 18, 1905.

[110] Sydney correspondent of the *Manchester Guardian*, quoted in the *Liberal Magazine*, January 1904, p. 754.

THE EMPIRE, *continued*—

[111] At the Carlton Club Dinner to the Canadian Ministers, August 1912.

[112] Tariff Reform League *Monthly Notes*, August 1905, p. 80.

[113] *The Times*, September 28, 1912.

[114] July 17, 1906.

[115] Reuter telegram dated November 18, 1903.

[116] *The Times*, June 17, 1911.

[117] Official Report, p. 266.

[118] Newcastle, October 10, 1907.

[119] March 14, 1913.

[120] October 3, 1904.

[121] *The Times*, August 4, 1904.

[122] Luton, October 5, 1904.

[123] House of Lords, April 11, 1905.

[124] Glasgow, October 18, 1904.

[125] Warrington, March 17, 1905.

[126] *Daily Mirror*, February 11, 1905.

[127] January 16, 1908.

[128] Ashton-under-Lyne, December 16, 1912.

[129] November 15, 1912.

[130] See *The Tariff Reformers*, by the Hon. George Peel, 1913 (Methuen), and the *Free Trader*, January 16, 1913, Free Trade Union.

[131] December 30, 1912.

[132] Edinburgh, January 24, 1913.

[133] Hotel Cecil, February 7, 1913.

[134] House of Commons, February 19, 1907.

[135] Tariff Reform League *Monthly Notes*, April 1907, p. 113.

[136] Tariff Reform League *Monthly Notes*, May 1907, p. 152.

[137] Greenock, October 7, 1903.

[138] Acock's Green, January 13, 1913.

[139] Letter to the *Daily Telegraph*, September 25, 1912.

[140] Mr. Vince in *Mr. Chamberlain's Proposals*, p. 4.

[141] Constitutional Club, June 26, 1903.

[142] Birmingham, November 4, 1903.

[143] Tariff Reform League *Monthly Notes*, November 1904, p. 146.

[144] Tariff Reform League *Monthly Notes*, April 1905, p. 225.

[145] Tariff Reform League *Monthly Notes*, April 1905, p. 267.

[146] Tariff Reform League leaflet No. 33 (new series).

[147] Tariff Reform League *Monthly Notes*, May 1905, p. 295.

[148] Edinburgh, December 11, 1907.

[149] Birmingham, November 15, 1907.

[150] Tariff Reform League *Monthly Notes*, June 1909, p. 496.

[151] Birmingham, November 4, 1903.

[152] *Mr. Chamberlain's Proposals*; What they mean and what we shall gain by them, p. 36.

[153] House of Commons, February 15, 1905.

THE EMPIRE, *continued*—

[154] Quoted in the *Liberal Magazine*, April 1912, p. 197.

[155] July 3, 1912.

[156] September 1, 1912.

[157] December 27, 1911.

[158] *Daily Mail*, October 31, 1911.

[159] Imperial Tariff Committee leaflet No. 66.

[160] *Sheffield Daily Telegraph* (Protectionist), quoted in Tariff Reform League *Monthly Notes*, April 1905, p. 240.

[161] Tariff Reform League *Monthly Notes*, June 1905, p. 393.

[162] June 17, 1912.

[163] Tariff Reform League *Monthly Notes*, November 1907, p. 320.

[164] *A Self-Sustaining Empire* (see ref. 94, supra).

[165] Mouswald, September 14, 1905.

[166] Glasgow, February 17, 1909.

[167] Tariff Reform League leaflets Nos. 383 to 418.

IV.—BRITISH TRADE

[1a] Putney, October 8, 1906.

[1] Imperial Tariff Committee leaflet No. 19.

[2] Liverpool, October 27, 1903.

[3] Tariff Reform League *Monthly Notes*, February 1906, p. 66.

[4] November 21, 1905.

[5] October 7, 1903.

[6] October 8, 1903.

[7] October 26, 1903.

[8] Birmingham, May 12, 1904.

[9] Luton, June 5, 1904.

[10] Liverpool, October 27, 1903.

[11] October 20, 1903.

[12] Tariff Reform League *Monthly Notes*, February 1905, p. 132.

[13] Tariff Reform League *Monthly Notes*, December 1905, p. 402.

[14] Engineering Supplement, November 14, 1906.

[15] Imperial Tariff Committee leaflet No. 25.

[16] Tariff Reform League *Monthly Notes*, May 1905, p. 293.

[17] Tariff Reform League *Monthly Notes*, January 1905, p. 57.

[18] Tariff Reform League leaflet No. 15, and Imperial Tariff Committee leaflet No. 62.

[19] 60 and 61 Vict., c. 63.

[20] *Free Trader*, 1903, p. 52.

[21] *Daily Express*, quoted in *Free Trader* for July 1910, p. 179.

[22] The *Empire Illustrated*, June 1912.

[23] Imperial Tariff Committee leaflet No. 23.

[24] Birmingham, January 11, 1904.

BRITISH TRADE, *continued*—

[25] Cockermouth Castle, August 31, 1912.

[26] Printed and Published (in 1903 or 1904) by E. Willoughby, 3 Johnson's Court, Fleet Street.

[27] Tariff Reform League *Monthly Notes*, January 1907, p. 32.

[28] In the *Weekly Dispatch*, November 17, 1907.

[29] August 28, 1912.

[30] *Sheffield Daily Telegraph*, December 28, 1912.

[30a] *South Wales Daily Post*, January 9, 1912.

[31] *Morning Post*, October 31, 1911.

[32] November 21, 1905.

[33] *Surrey Mirror*, March 13, 1908.

[34] Letter dated March 12, 1908, published in the *Liberal Magazine* for April 1908, p. 195.

[35] *Nottingham Evening Post*, July 8, 1910.

[36] Mr. Joseph Brailsford in a letter to *The Times*, November 30, 1903.

[37] *South Wales Daily News*, September 25, 1911.

[38] *Cambridge Daily News* Report.

[39] To the Candidate for Pembroke Boroughs.

[40] To the Candidate for South Londonderry.

[41] To the Candidate for Stoke-on-Trent.

[42] To the Candidate for Stepney.

[43] To the Candidate for E. Wiltshire.

[44] April 9, 1912.

[45] *The Times*, December 8, 1910.

[46] *The Globe*, December 8, 1910.

[47] September 5, 1904 (quoted by Lord Rosebery in a speech at Lincoln, September 20, 1904).

[48] Tariff Reform League *Monthly Notes*, January 1904, p. 7.

[48a] *Bootle Times*, April 1, 1910.

[49] Preston, January 11, 1905.

[50] *Morning Post*, June 5, 1908.

[51] Dated November 1, and published in the *Daily News* (*Free Trader*, November 1909, p. 312).

[52] *Free Trader*, May 1910, p. 126.

[53] November 8, 1910.

[54] January 6, 1912.

[55] *Daily Express*, December 29, 1910.

[56] *Daily Express*, January 7, 1911.

[57] *Morning Post*, March 28, 1911.

[57a] Preston, January 11, 1905.

[58] October 27, 1903.

[59] Greenock, October 7, 1903.

[60] Edgbaston, November 11, 1903.

[61] City of London, January 18, 1904.

[62] United Club, February 26, 1904.

BRITISH TRADE, *continued*—

[63] *Windsor Magazine*, September 1903.

[64] Dover, November 20, 1907.

[65] Kings Sutton, December 17, and Cosgrove, December 18.

[66] Birmingham, November 3, 1905.

[67] February 28, 1908.

[68] Imperial Tariff Committee leaflet No. 32.

[69] January 8, 1912.

[70] Tariff Reform League *Monthly Notes*, October 1907, p. 277 (quoting from the *Referee*).

[70a] Tariff Reform League *Monthly Notes*, December 1907, p. 410.

[70b] Tariff Reform League *Monthly Notes*, November 1907, p. 356.

[71] Tariff Reform League *Monthly Notes*, January 1908, pp. 49 and 88.

[72] Sir A. S. Haslam in the House of Commons, February 15, 1904.

[73] Tariff Reform League leaflet No. 100.

[74] *Pall Mall Gazette*, July 24, 1913.

[75] Newcastle, October 20, 1903.

[76] *Mr. Chamberlain's Proposals*, p. 44.

[77] In *Fundamental Fallacies of Free Trade*, p. 40.

[78] Memorandum 29, p. 2.

[79] Tariff Reform League *Monthly Notes*, January 1913, p. 14.

[80] E. G. Brunker in *Notes on the Fiscal Controversy*, 1912 edition, p. 13.

[81] *Daily Telegraph*, February 4, 1907.

[82] *Daily Graphic*, January 8, 1907.

[82a] January 9, 1911.

[82b] Tariff Reform League *Monthly Notes*, May 1906, p. 151.

[83] Walsall, January 31, 1907.

[84] Birmingham, November 3, 1905.

[85] Liberal Union Club, May 11, 1905.

[86] Dundee, January 29, 1907.

[87] Tariff Reform League *Monthly Notes*, February 1907, reviewing Memorandum 29 of the Tariff Commission.

[88] Glasgow, May 21, 1912.

[89] *North-Eastern Daily Gazette*, December 4, 1912.

[90] Tariff Reform League *Monthly Notes*, April 1906, p. 101.

[91] *Mr. Chamberlain's Proposals*, p. 24.

[92] Tariff Reform League *Monthly Notes*, February 1908, p. 147.

[93] Capt. Grogan, February 23, 1909.

[94] Mr. H. E. Duke, K.C., *Western Daily Mercury*, November 23, 1907.

[95] Mr. Hewson (see *Free Trader*, May 1909, p. 148).

[96] Birmingham, May 12, 1904.

[97] Bristol, February 20, 1904.

[98] November 8, 1904.

[99] House of Commons, May 13, 1907.

[100] Aberdeen, January 31, 1908.

V.—WORK AND WAGES

[1] In his introduction to *Imperial Union and Tariff Reform*, a reprint of his 1903 speeches, p. ix.

[2] *Daily Mail*, November 6, 1905.

[3] *The Times*, November 22, 1905.

[4] *Daily Mail*, December 10, 1906.

[5] Mr. C. A. Vince in his *Handbook for Speakers*, 1903, p. 25.

[6] Preston, January 11, 1905.

[7] Message to Hythe at the by-election of June 1912.

[8] Imperial Tariff Committee leaflet No. 1.

[9] Imperial Tariff Committee leaflet No. 15.

[10] Letter dated July 4, 1903 (published in *The Clarion*).

[11] Letter dated August 31, 1903.

[12] By C. F. and W. B., printed and published by Jas. Truscott & Son Ltd., Suffolk Lane, E.C.

[13] Paragraph quoted from *The People*, January 2, 1910.

[14] No. 168.

[15] Derby, January 4, 1906.

[16] Letter to *The Times*, January 8, 1906.

[17] Birmingham, January 10, 1906.

[18] Tariff Reform League leaflet No. 321.

[19] Tariff Reform League leaflet No. 322.

[20] Tariff Reform League leaflet No. 337.

[21] Mr. Arthur Colefax, South-West Manchester, reported in the *Manchester Courier*, March 13, 1909.

[23] *Pall Mall Gazette*, December 28, 1909.

[24] *Pall Mall Gazette*, December 30, 1909.

[25] Sir P. A. Muntz, M.P. (*Rugby Advertiser* report, December 3, 1904).

[26] Tariff Reform League *Monthly Notes*, March 1907, p. 87.

[27] At the Hotel Cecil, November 26, 1907 (*The Times* report).

[28] Birmingham, November 15, 1907.

[29] Tariff Reform League *Monthly Notes*, January 1907, p. 1.

[30] Various London papers, and *Liberal Magazine*, January 1909, p. 721.

[31] *Free Trader*, June 1909, p. 177.

[32] Letter to Councillor Lovesey, of Birmingham, May 20, 1903.

[33] Letter to a Working Man, June 3, 1903.

[34] Speech at the Constitutional Club, June 26, 1903.

[35] Letter to the Candidate for the Crewe Division, August 26, 1903.

[36] Speech at Glasgow, October 6, 1903.

[37] In his preface to a reprint of *Daily Telegraph* articles on Fiscal Reform.

[38] Speech at Liverpool, October 27, 1903.

WORK AND WAGES, *continued*—

[39] Speech at Birmingham, May 12, 1904.

[40] Speech at Birmingham, May 12, 1904.

[41] Speech at Welbeck, August 4, 1904.

[42] Speech at Limehouse, December 15, 1904.

[43] Speech at Preston, January 11, 1905.

[44] Speech at Gainsborough, February 1, 1905.

[45] Telegram to the Candidate in the Everton by-election, February 1905.

[46] Letter published April 24, 1905.

[47] Speech at the Annual Conference of the Organised Labour Branch of the Tariff Reform League, May 17, 1905.

[48] Speech at St. Helens, June 3, 1905.

[49] Speech at the Albert Hall, July 7, 1905.

[50] Speech at Bristol, November 21, 1905.

[51] Letter to Capt. Newman, Candidate for S.-E. Essex (*The Times*, December 30, 1905).

[52] Speech at Derby, January 4, 1906.

[53] Speech at Wellington, January 20, 1906.

[54] Speech at Sandon Heath, June 30, 1906.

[55] Speech at Birmingham, July 9, 1906.

[56] Letter to the *Pembrokeshire Herald*, January 1909 (quoted in *Free Trader*, May 1909, p. 141).

[57] Letter to the fifth Annual Conference of the Tariff Reform League, April 2, 1909.

[58] Letter to the Chairman of a Birmingham Meeting (quoted in the Tariff Reform League *Monthly Notes*, October 1909, p. 218).

[59] Letter to Sir Joseph Lawrence, December 1909.

[60] Letter to Mr. J. Parker Smith, December 1909.

[61] Letter to Mr. Paget, January 1910.

[62] Letter to Mr. Foster, January 1910.

[63] Letter to a Clergyman, December 21, 1909.

[64] November 5, 1909 (*Morning Post* report, November 6).

[65] Letter to the Candidate for N. Suffolk, December 31, 1909.

[66] Tariff Reform League leaflet No. 209.

[67] November 18, 1909.

[68] Haddington, December 30, 1909.

[69] February 24, 1910.

[70] Chester, May 23, 1903.

[71] Newcastle, October 10, 1907.

[72] Sheffield, November 5, 1908.

[73] Leeds, November 16, 1911.

[74] London, January 26, 1912.

[75] Ashton-under-Lyne, December 16, 1912.

[76] Manchester, November 2, 1908.

[77] Debate on the Address, January 30, 1908.

[78] Hackney, November 26, 1909.

WORK AND WAGES, *continued*—

[79] Truro, October 28, 1910.

[80] Edinburgh, November 7, 1905 (*Scotsman* report, November 8).

[81] Telegram to Capt. Powell, November 26, 1907.

[82] Quoted in *Liberal Magazine*, January 1908, p. 729.

[83] The Birmingham Tariff Committee's *Handbook for Speakers*, 1903, p. 25.

[84] *Eastbourne Chronicle*, April 11, 1908.

[85] Tariff Reform League *Monthly Notes*, May 1908, p. 356.

[86] Tariff Reform League leaflet No. 202.

[87] *Tariff Reform by Pen and Pencil.*

[88] Tariff Reform League leaflet No. 334, p. 6.

[89] Mrs. Fletcher speaking on behalf of the Unionist Candidate, who was present, at Woking (*Surrey Times* report, July 25, 1908).

[90] *Northern Daily Telegraph*, May 13, 1909.

[92] Dorking, July 20, 1910.

[93] May 20, 1912.

[94] *The Times*, September 25, 1911.

[95] *Birmingham Post*, October 7, 1908.

[96] Basingstoke, July 8, 1909.

[97] *Birmingham Gazette*, October 20, 1908 (the *Gazette* is now again, happily, a Free Trade paper).

[99] *Surrey Times*, March 23, 1912.

[100] December 18, 1908.

[101] October 19, 1909.

[102] March 20, 1908.

[103] Quoted in the *Economist*, July 27, 1909.

[104] See, for instance, Tariff Reform League leaflets Nos. 188, 190, 199.

[105] Tariff Reform League Leaflets.

[106] Letter dated April 28, 1908.

[107] Tariff Reform League leaflet No. 161.

[108] Tariff Reform League *Monthly Notes*, April 1908, p. 272.

[109] September 21, 1912.

[110] *Punch*, February 26, 1908.

[111] Tariff Reform League *Monthly Notes*, August 1911, p. 94.

[112] Tariff Reform League *Monthly Notes*, August 1911, p. 95.

[113] Tariff Reform League *Monthly Notes*, October 1911, p. 215.

[114] Tariff Reform League *Monthly Notes*, September 1910, p. 181.

[115] Tariff Reform League *Monthly Notes*, January 1908, p. 62.

[116] Tariff Reform League *Monthly Notes*, September 1911, p. 144.

[117] Tariff Reform League *Monthly Notes*, February 1907, p. 47.

[118] Tariff Reform League leaflet No. 215.

[119] Tariff Reform League leaflet No. 74.

[120] Tariff Reform League leaflets Nos. 154 to 167.

[121] Tariff Reform League leaflet No. 193.

[122] June 26, 1912.

[123] Westminster Palace Hotel, May 17, 1905.

WORK AND WAGES, *continued*—

[124] Liverpool, October 27, 1903.

[125] In his Introduction to *Mr. Chamberlain's Proposals* (Vince).

[126] *Mr. Chamberlain's Proposals*, p. 83.

[127] Will Dyson (*Sheffield Telegraph* report, January 29, 1907).

[128] Tariff Reform League *Monthly Notes*, March 1905, p. 198.

[129] Smethwick, January 18, 1906.

[130] December 1907.

[131] *Eastern Daily Press*, March 5, 1909.

[132] Birmingham, May 12, 1904.

[133] At a dinner given in his honour by the Welsh Unionists, June 9, 1904.

[134] October 5, 1904.

[135] Preston, January 11, 1905.

[136] Tunbridge Wells, April 17, 1907.

[137] Hexham, October 25, 1907.

[138] Tariff Reform League *Monthly Notes*, February 1905, p. 127.

[139] Tariff Reform League *Monthly Notes*, February 1905, p. 86.

[140] Tariff Reform League *Monthly Notes*, April 1908, p. 280.

[141] Tariff Reform League *Monthly Notes*, June 1909, p. 496.

[142] *Morning Post*, December 25, 1912.

[143] *West Somerset Free Press*, April 24, 1909.

[144] September 3, 1909.

[145] House of Commons, February 13, 1907.

[146] In his Christmas Greeting to his employees and pensioners, 1909.

[147] Little Common, September 20, 1908.

[148] Lincoln, October 16, 1908.

[149] November 12, 1908.

[150] July 5, 1909.

[151] Tariff Reform League *Monthly Notes*, November 1909, p. 293.

[152] *Standard* report, December 13, 1906.

[153] *Westminster Gazette*, June 15, 1903.

[154] House of Commons, May 28, 1903.

[155] June 3, 1903.

[156] June 26, 1903.

[157] May 1, 1906.

[158] Walsall, January 31, 1907.

[159] April 19, 1907.

[160] July 18, 1910.

[161] *Morning Post*, June 6, 1911.

[162] *Empire Illustrated*, June 1911.

[163] Bristol, November 21, 1905.

[164] August 6, 1909.

[165] May 6, 1910.

[166] Ealing, October 19, 1909.

[167] November 20, 1903.

[168] June 26, 1903.

WORK AND WAGES, *continued*—

[169] Mr. E. Beckett Faber (*Yorkshire Post*, September 12, 1904).
[170] Constitutional Club, April 11, 1907.
[171] Hackney, November 26, 1909.
[172] House of Commons, May 28, 1903.
[173] Constitutional Club, June 26, 1903.
[174] Newcastle, October 20, 1903.
[175] Liverpool, October 27, 1903.
[176] Bristol, November 21, 1905.
[177] Westminster Palace Hotel, May 17, 1905.
[178] May 20, 1903.
[179] St. Helens, June 3, 1905.
[180] Letter to N.-E. Lanark, July 1904.
[181] In the *Daily Mail Year Book*, 1908.
[182] Newcastle, October 10, 1907.
[183] October 25, 1905.
[184] Dewsbury, April 27, 1904.
[185] York, January 12, 1910.
[186] *Free Trader*, June 1911.
[187] Welbeck, August 4, 1904.
[188] Imperial Tariff Committee leaflet No. 27.
[189] Tariff Reform League leaflet No. 18.
[190] Manchester, March 25, 1907.
[191] Edinburgh, December 11, 1907.
[192] Horticultural Hall, February 7, 1908.
[193] House of Commons, March 4, 1905.
[194] February 1907.
[195] January 1908.
[197] Darlington, December 23, 1907.
[198] Letter to *Westminster Gazette*, May 31, 1907.
[199] Bridgwater, January 8, 1908.
[200] September 30, 1907.
[201] Tariff Reform League *Monthly Notes*, November 1905, p. 322.
[202] Tariff Reform League *Monthly Notes*, July 1913, pp. 7 and 56.
[203] Tariff Reform League *Monthly Notes*, September 1907, p. 191.
[204] Tariff Reform League leaflet No. 104.
[205] Tariff Reform League *Monthly Notes*, April 1909, p. 313.
[206] *Evening Times*, Glasgow, December 15, 1912.
[207] *Mr. Chamberlain's Proposals*, p. 64.
[208] July 26, 1903.
[209] Greenock, October 7, 1903.
[210] Tariff Reform League *Monthly Notes*, January 1905, p. 56.
[211] Tariff Reform League *Monthly Notes*, April 1905, p. 225.
[212] No. 37, issued in 1908.
[213] Tariff Reform League *Monthly Notes*, November 1907, p. 351.
[214] Tariff Reform League *Monthly Notes*, March 1908, p. 209.
[215] Tariff Reform League *Monthly Notes*, 1st number, 1904, p. 17.

WORK AND WAGES, *continued—*

216 *Nineteenth Century*, December 1905 (quoted in the Tariff Reform League *Monthly Notes*, January 1906, p. 20).

217 Tariff Reform League *Monthly Notes*, June 1905, p. 346 (quoting the *Daily Mail*).

218 Tariff Reform League *Monthly Notes*, September 1909, p. 196.

219 Tariff Reform League *Monthly Notes*, June 1908, p. 472.

220 Tariff Reform League leaflet (new series) No. 14.

221 Mr. J. Chamberlain at the Second Annual Meeting of the Tariff Reform League, July 7, 1905.

222 House of Commons, March 18, 1904.

223 February 23, 1910.

224 Birmingham, November 24, 1903.

225 Paragraph 74.

226 Tariff Reform League *Monthly Notes*, April 1909, p. 313.

227 See *Grimsby Daily Telegraph*, October 21, 1912. (The article was printed also in the Tariff Reform League *Monthly Notes*, November 1912, p. 311).

228 Page 6 (1903 edition).

229 Limehouse, December 15, 1904.

230 Tariff Reform League leaflet No. 328.

231 Tariff Reform League leaflets Nos. 300 to 309.

232 Tariff Reform League *Monthly Notes*, October 1906, p. 108.

233 Tariff Reform League *Monthly Notes*, July 1906, p. 19.

234 Tariff Reform League *Monthly Notes*, September 1906, p. 90.

235 House of Commons, April 2, 1913.

236 Tariff Reform League *Monthly Notes*, December 1908, p. 387.

237 October 19, 1904.

238 Tariff Reform League *Monthly Notes*, April 1905, p. 266.

239 Imperial Tariff Committee leaflet No. 22.

240 *North-Eastern Daily Gazette*, May 2, 1908.

241 Glasgow, May 21, 1912.

242 Mr. W. J. Davis, letter dated August 24, 1905, to the *Birmingham Daily Mail*.

243 April 25, 1910.

244 June 15, 1910.

245 May 10, 1910.

246 *The Times*, June 6, 1910.

247 Reports on Labour and Social Conditions in Germany, vol. i., *Working Men's Tours*, Nos. 1, 2, and 3, published by the Tariff Reform League.

248 September 26, 1910.

249 *The Times*, November 7, 1910.

INDEX

INDEX

For Product Safety Concerns and Information please contact our EU representative GPSR@taylorandfrancis.com
Taylor & Francis Verlag GmbH, Kaufingerstraße 24, 80331 München, Germany

www.ingramcontent.com/pod-product-compliance
Lightning Source LLC
Chambersburg PA
CBHW070546270326
41926CB00013B/2220

* 9 7 8 1 1 3 8 2 9 8 0 7 1 *